Xanthé Mallett is a forensic anthropologist and criminologist, author and TV presenter. Xanthé's first book, *Mothers Who Murder* (Penguin Random House, 2014), aimed to re-evaluate the evidence in a number of potential miscarriages of justice, as well as improve our understanding of how, when and why women can be driven to intentionally hurt their own children.

Xanthé is also a forensic practitioner, and works with police forces across Australia assisting with the identification of persons of interest in criminal cases, as well as providing advanced DNA technologies that assist with the identification of long-term deceased persons and suspects.

In addition to her academic and professional work, Xanthé has contributed to various true crime television series, most recently *Murder, Lies & Alibis* on Channel 9, and is a regular contributor to crime news stories for television, radio and print media.

COLD CASE
INVESTIGATIONS

Dr XANTHÉ MALLETT

MACMILLAN
Pan Macmillan Australia

First published 2019 in Macmillan by Pan Macmillan Australia Pty Ltd
1 Market Street, Sydney, New South Wales, Australia, 2000

Cataloguing-in-Publication entry is available
from the National Library of Australia
http://catalogue.nla.gov.au

Maps on pages 125, 149 and 162 by KI229 design
Typeset in 12/16pt Adobe Garamond by Midland Typesetters, Australia
Printed by McPherson's Printing Group

For Mum

For Mary

CONTENTS

OUR OBSESSION
WITH COLD CASES

'The one question I want you to answer for me is
a simple one – why?'
Bruce Pearce, father and grandfather of murder victims
Karlie Pearce-Stevenson and her daughter Khandalyce Pearce

On any other day the scene would be a picture of normality. A kitchen – washing-up in the sink, the sound of a chat show coming from the TV in the lounge, a magazine on the kitchen table left open on a story about the latest diet craze.

Not today. Today a young woman died here.

The bright police lights blind you as you enter the kitchen from the relative darkness of the hall. Investigators haven't switched the lights on in here as they are a potential source of evidence – fingerprints need to be collected from the switches before they are contaminated. The kitchen is a mess, blood spatter everywhere, a glass smashed on the floor, and what remains of the victim's last meal sitting on a plate by the sink. There's a metallic smell of blood in the air.

There are bare footprints in the blood on the tiled floor, leading down the hall towards the front door. Two sets, one belongs to the female victim who staggered outside before she lost consciousness due to blood loss. The other set is yet to be identified, but from what you can see, they are fairly small, so they either belong to a woman or a small man.

From the pattern, it appears the victim left first, staggering unsteadily on her feet – there are bloodied handprints smeared down the wall where she has leaned to steady herself. The other person followed them, walking not running, their footprints overlaying the victim's in places. This second person has to be considered the main person of interest in this murder as no one from the house called this in – a neighbour did that when they found the victim unconscious in the street just 50 metres from her front door. Footprints are as individual as fingerprints, so if the prints from the scene can be matched to a suspect, this would place them at this scene around the time of death.

Looking around, there's little of value on display. Nothing was taken from the house, so this does not look like a robbery gone wrong.

The female victim has 27 stab wounds, all to her upper torso and neck. Blood loss was massive and death would have been rapid. A number of the victim's injuries would have been fatal. In fact the offender stabbed her many more times than was necessary to kill her; overkill. The murder weapon was a kitchen knife taken from a block on the counter. It was dropped in the hallway, suggesting this was a spur of the moment attack and was unplanned, and the weapon of choice opportunistic.

This was personal and spontaneous.

Now it's up to you to figure out what happened and why.

It's almost like rewinding a scene in a film – you have your conclusion, a still taken when the police arrive, but to unravel what happened you need to step backwards, moment by moment. To understand how the evidence presents the way it does, you need to know who was here and how the players interacted with each other and the environment to create the scene in front of you.

You're also aware that the family will soon be getting the horrific news that a loved one has died in violent circumstances. Someone's world is about to fall apart. And it is your job to help make sure that whoever is responsible for that is brought to justice.

In a case like this one, the first 48 hours are critical. Evidence has to be collected before it is lost or contaminated, the scene has to be meticulously searched and recorded, witnesses have to be identified and interviewed, and any significant persons of interest need to be found before they have a chance to flee. The forensic and contextual evidence collected now may make or break the investigation.

A person of interest has been identified – a rival in a love triangle – but she vanished after the murder, and has not been seen in the area since. Her footprints may or may not match those left in blood at the scene, but unless she can be located, she can't be ruled in or out as a suspect. And no one is talking. It's a small town, close-knit, remote. No one wants to talk to the police.

The case goes cold.

Now imagine this same crime happened 30 years ago. You've been tasked with reinvestigating the murder of this young woman. You have the crime scene photographs, reports, witness statements, but where to start re-evaluating that evidence? How can you find a suspect and sufficient evidence to lead to an arrest and conviction so many years later?

Time has been your enemy in so many ways.

But it has also been your friend. Two unidentified blood samples were collected that night – one we believe to be from the victim's assailant, who left traces of blood on the handle of the knife, presumably because they cut themselves during the attack.

Small traces, and 30 years ago not enough to lead to the generation of a profile, but today, with advanced DNA techniques, we may be able to repair the small and degraded sample. It may be possible, decades later, to identify the murderer at last.

The reality of cold case investigation is that it's hard. Information provided to investigators is often incomplete, evidence degrades, memories fade, witnesses move on and can't be located or die.

That does not mean the investigators give up though. And neither do the public.

There is something about an enduring mystery that captures people's attention, and none more so than cold cases. Jack the Ripper is a case in point – a serial killer who stalked the streets of London in 1888 and brutally murdered five women, potentially more. Why has this story endured and become so embedded in our social consciousness? There are a number of reasons, I think, the most important being that the murderer remains unidentified. This allows continued speculation as to who it could have been. Then there's the violence with which he killed the women, and the heady links to celebrity or royalty in suspects put forward over the years. Mix in the idea that the murderer had medical knowledge (or at least anatomical understanding, as the offender could as easily have been a butcher as a doctor), as evidenced by the injuries to the bodies, with the fact that the perpetrator hunted in one of the poorest areas of London, Whitechapel, and you can see why the story can still generate headlines today.

Not all cold cases have such fascination for us as Jack the Ripper, but there is always something disquieting about an unsolved murder. And it's not only the fact that the murderer goes unpunished. I believe it's because as children we learn to fear the bogeyman, the mythical monster that hides in the shadows as we try to sleep. As adults we know the bogeyman is make believe, but we learn that monsters do exist in the real world. Their crimes haunt us and stain our collective consciousness, because if the real monsters like Jack the Ripper are never caught – if they are still hiding in the shadows – how can we sleep safely in our beds?

At the heart of every cold case, regardless of the time and place in which the crime was committed, are the victims. One thing I've noticed throughout my own career is that the victims are often forgotten by the public. For example, everyone knows the nickname Jack the Ripper, and just the mention of it conjures up images of unspeakable horror and violence. But how many know his five victims by name – Mary Ann Nichols, Annie Chapman, Elizabeth Stride, Catherine Eddowes, and Mary Jane Kelly?

My point is that although I have spent a good proportion of the last 10 years of my life looking at and reinvestigating cold cases, I try to never forget the victims, even when we are focusing on identifying the offender.

So here in this book that will cover seven cases, the victims will play a primary role. You will get to know them. Not only because, criminologically speaking, the more you can learn about your victim the more you can extrapolate about the person who killed or abducted them, but also because they deserve their stories to be told. They deserve for people to know their names. They shouldn't be someone's nameless victim.

But be warned, the cases we will cover are not for the faint-hearted. Sadly, some of Australia's most criminologically compelling cases include very violent acts, including against children. In these chapters you will read some disturbing facts about what the offenders did to their victims, but I have done my best to provide only the details necessary to help you to understand the crime, whilst showing the victims respect. We need to take a very close look at the offender's modus operandi (or MO, from the Latin phrase meaning 'mode of operation') to try to understand what they did and why. Only when we look through their eyes can we hope to recognise the signs of similar behaviour in the future and prevent such terrible crimes happening again.

Some of the cases will be familiar to you but I will include new elements. For example, the chapter on Ivan Milat looks at whether there are likely to be more Milat victims as yet undiscovered. Other stories you won't have heard, such as the horrendous story of Christopher Wilder, an equally violent and sadistic serial killer and sex offender, who murdered at least ten young women before being shot by police after a murderous spree across the US.

We rarely know the whole story, even in the most infamous of cases. Each case included in this book has been chosen because there is a question mark hanging over it: either the perpetrator is unknown, or there are likely more victims or other crimes yet to be attributed to an offender.

We also need to remember that for some cold cases, even stretching back several decades, the victims and immediate family may still be alive, and there may also be offenders to prosecute. So when you think cold cases, don't think over and done with. They are still very much alive. There is also a chance that surviving victims or their families will read these chapters, and that it will take them over painful ground. Respect for them has to be at the centre of a book like this – these are not stories; these are people's lives. I have spoken to many victims' families, and in each and every case the sentiment is the same – if they lost a loved one, or something awful happened, they need answers. They need to know why. Therefore, this book is hoping to ask some new questions, suggest new scientific or investigative techniques, that may be able to progress some of these cases.

A JOURNEY

I am a forensic scientist and criminologist. I have worked murder cases with police in Australia and in the UK, as well as cases of child sexual abuse. My world is dark and I see the worst of humanity every day.

People often ask me why I do this work, why I choose to immerse myself in such horror. Usually I say it is because I am a scientist at heart; I am logical, I look for facts and only believe what can be proven. I'm also incredibly curious; I want to know how things work, or why they don't. That's all true, but it's only half the story.

Since I was a child I have abhorred bullies and cannot abide cruelty in any form. My sister, who's four years older than me, was bullied at school. She was quiet and gentle and therefore a target. As a five-year-old I used to go into her playground, which was next to mine, every break time to look after her. The bullies were twice my size but that didn't faze me – no one was going to hurt my sister.

In truth I think this is at the heart of what I do now. I'm evidence driven, yes, but when I see vulnerability in others I feel protective of them and that pushes me to find and call out those who target others' weaknesses. I want to stop them hurting anyone else.

Many of the cases we'll look at involve bullies of the worst kind. Predators who seek out vulnerability.

Some of the cases included here have a personal attachment for me as I've worked on them myself. For example, in 2013 I was contracted as an expert forensic contributor to a true crime series on Channel Ten called *Wanted*, and the first case I looked at was of an unidentified young woman's remains found in Belanglo State Forest, NSW, in 2010. She had been dubbed 'Angel' by the media, because of a motif on a T-shirt found with her remains. Angel's case stayed with me, and although she was identified in 2015, I have included her story here as it is an example of how luck, police determination, solid forensic science, and the public's help all combined to get a young woman identified and her body returned to her family.

Throughout my career as a forensic criminologist, university lecturer, forensic practitioner and television presenter, I've learned that my audience – be that students, television viewers or readers – don't want to be told what to think. You are intelligent, thoughtful people who want to be given facts and information and then be left to make up your own mind as to what happened.

So that is my intention with this book. I will take you through some of the most intriguing, baffling, interesting and ultimately sad cases in Australian history. I will show you data and talk to experts who will provide technical information where it will assist us to understand what happened and why. I will also introduce you to new forensic techniques or scientific methods that could – or did – help move the case forward.

It's true that my work investigates the darkness in human beings, but I have also seen the light and the hope in ordinary people. Investigators who never give up looking for answers, families who fight for justice, the public who engage to help solve cases. So I know that whilst there is certainly dark, there is also light. I am also thankful for the fact that although I need to step into the dark to understand these crimes, I can step back out into the light again when I'm done.

ONE

THE WANDA BEACH MURDERS AND THE BEAUTY QUEEN KILLER

'Their lives had been callously taken,
and our childhood innocence destroyed.'
Hans Schmidt in a piece for *That's Life* in November 2017

Windswept sand dunes, kilometres of gently sweeping beaches bordering pristine blue water. Located at Cronulla in Sydney's southeastern suburbs, Wanda Beach is a jewel in the city's landscape.

There aren't any families or couples here today; it's late May and summer is well and truly over. So I have the beach to myself, except for a dog walker far off in the distance. But it's still 22 °C and sunny, with light clouds drifting across the sky, casting shadows on the sea.

I've been to this beach before, as I was part of a team that reviewed the Wanda Beach case for Channel 7's *Sunday Night* program in 2018, and where possible I like to visit the scene of the crimes I'm investigating – to try to see through the eyes of the victims and offender.

Wanda Beach is picturesque, idyllic. Deserted.

And the setting for one of Australia's most enduring cold case mysteries – the sexual assault and violent murder of teenagers Marianne Schmidt and Christine Sharrock, on 11 January 1965.

Sitting among the shifting sand dunes to escape the autumn breeze coming in off the sea, I can see why this place was so appealing – especially for a group of children coming to the end of their summer holiday.

But it wasn't a perfect summer's day when the girls took Marianne's four younger siblings – Peter (ten), Trixie (nine), Wolfgang (eight), and Norbert (six) – to Wanda Beach for the day; the sunny weather had turned squally in the afternoon, and the beach was closed due to the windy conditions. But the kids decided to go anyway.

The reason the older girls were so keen to go to the beach has always been a big question in this case. Something drew them there that day, aside from the sea and sand.

This chapter will explore why Marianne and Christine went to the beach on such an inclement day, what happened to them there, and will investigate the links between this case and one of Australia's little known but most prolific sex offenders and serial killers – Christopher Wilder, also known as the Beauty Queen Killer.

THE CASE

Things were different in 1965. It really was a more innocent time, when kids could go off for the day in safety, and no one worried about the bogeyman.

But on 11 January there was a monster in the making hunting at Wanda Beach.

Marianne Schmidt and Christine Sharrock were just 15 years old, best friends and neighbours. The two girls had decided to take Marianne's siblings to the beach, even though it was quite a hike – over two hours by train – from their home in West Ryde, in Sydney's west. They'd left early, arriving at the beach by 11 am, hoping to get some decent sunshine before the weather turned nasty. The girls were familiar with the journey, as they'd done it a few times over the summer break.

But when they got to the beach the wind had already picked up, so they hid their bags among some rocks to lighten the load and headed to the southern end, to explore in the shelter of the rocks and eat the picnic they'd brought with them. At some point Christine went off by herself, and didn't tell the younger children where she was going.

After Christine came back to the group, they decided to go for a walk together, but it had gotten cold and very windy and the younger Schmidt children had begun to complain. So Marianne and Christine said that the two of them would go back to where they'd stashed their bags in the rocks, then return to the younger kids and take them home.

But the girls walked off in the opposite direction from where they'd hidden their things. The younger kids called after them, telling them they were headed the wrong way, but the girls kept walking, laughing as they went.

This was out of character; it was unusual for the girls to ignore the younger children. Something had changed, and the younger Schmidt children were left thinking that something strange was going on.

When I reviewed the evidence from Marianne's brothers and sister, I was left with one very strong impression – Christine and Marianne were meeting a boy. Nothing else better explains why two 15-year-olds known for being sensible, caring and mature would be happy to leave their four young charges and head off into the sand dunes, giddy and laughing with excitement.

The girls didn't come back.

But they were seen again, by eight-year-old Wolfgang. He'd gotten bored waiting for the older girls to return, so he'd gone off to do some exploring. A little before 1 pm, he saw his sister and her friend, but they weren't alone. They were with a boy Wolfgang estimated to be about 16 or 17 years old – a boy he'd noticed earlier that day spear fishing with a home-made spear and/or a fishing knife. Wolfgang described the boy as being a tanned, surfie type, with white cream on his nose and long, blond hair. He was wearing grey trousers and carrying a towel.

When Wolfgang saw them they were walking together, the boy in the centre with Marianne and Christine on either side of him, and he had his arms around them. It looked friendly, intimate even. The group were still walking away from where the girls had left their bags, so they had lied to the younger children – they weren't collecting their belongings in preparation for heading home.

Surely this boy was the reason for the girls' strange and uncharacteristic behaviour?

Wolfgang lost sight of Christine, Marianne and the boy, so he returned to his other siblings who were sheltering next to a sand dune out of the wind, to wait.

There were other confirmed sightings of the girls. Dennis Dostine, a local, spotted them walking through the sand dunes. He later told the police it looked like the girls were in a hurry, and one of them kept looking behind her like she thought she might be being followed. But Dostine didn't see anyone else with them.

A while later Wolfgang saw the same boy for a third time, and on this occasion he was alone. Wolfgang asked him where the girls were, but the boy was walking away and didn't answer.

By 5 pm – after four hours of waiting in the cold – the four younger Schmidt siblings were worried and decided they shouldn't stay any longer, so they went back to collect the bags themselves, including the older girls' purses, and caught the last train home without Christine and Marianne, arriving about 8 pm.

THE SCENE

The girls were found the next afternoon around 2.30 pm by Peter Smith, who had taken his three young nephews for a beach walk.

Initially, he thought he'd found a shop mannequin half-buried among the dunes. But when he brushed back some of the loose sand from the head, he realised it was the body of a young woman.

He raced to the local surf club to report what he had found and the police were called.

Upon arrival the police thought they were dealing with one murder, but they soon discovered that the dunes were hiding the remains of two girls – Christine was lying face down and Marianne was on her right side, with her head against her friend's foot.

A drag mark at the scene suggested that Christine had tried to flee across the dunes, possibly as the girls' assailant was attacking Marianne, but that the killer had caught her and dragged her back to the body of her friend. There was blood spattered along this drag mark, and in three distinct places the blood was more highly concentrated, indicating that the person dragging Christine had paused for a moment before again pulling her back towards the dunes and Marianne's body.

The scene was thoroughly examined, and tonnes of sand was sifted in the search for evidence. A knife blade was found about 5 metres from the girls' bodies, but with the technology available in 1965 the police were unable to link it to the murders.

Today, it is highly likely that fingerprint or DNA evidence would have remained on the partial knife blade that could have led to the identity of the killer. In fact, it's still possible that, if that blade piece were available for analysis with modern techniques, it may yet yield clues as to the killer's identity.

Fingerprint techniques have advanced so significantly since 1965 that it is also possible that the offender's prints could have been lifted from Christine and Marianne's skin – something the scientists would never have dreamt possible at the time of the murders.

EXPERT INSERT: FRICTION RIDGES

Everyone is familiar with the capture of fingerprints for forensic purposes – commonly collected at a crime scene for comparison with an offender's prints, or taken from a person to confirm their identity. Fingerprints are one of the four primary methods of forensic human identification, the others being DNA comparison, dental analysis, and unique medical conditions (for example, joint replacements such as hips are each stamped with a unique number, which if found in association with a body can be matched to those in medical records to confirm an identity). Friction prints are the impressions left by the friction ridges (also known as dermal ridges or dermal papillae), the function of which is to increase the surface area on those parts of the human body that require increased grip.

These types of prints can be taken not only from the fingers but from the palm of the hand, as well as the toes and soles of the feet (known as the 'plantar' surface). In fact, palm prints are routinely collected from suspects or persons of interest, in addition to prints of the ten fingers, as they are regularly left at crime scenes – when people lean against or touch surfaces, they often do so with the entire hand, not just the fingers. Footprints are interesting too, as these can be left at scenes when people walk in blood. And footprints can be matched back to an individual in the same way as a fingerprint.

The process of comparing friction ridge prints is complex, due to the flexible nature of friction ridge skin, which means that no two prints are ever technically identical, even two prints taken of the same finger only minutes apart. To determine if prints match (i.e., they were made by the same part of the same person's body), a forensic examiner will assess the points of similarity and difference. The more points in common, the more likely that the two belong to the same person, unless there are differences that cannot be explained by distortion, angle, smudging and any number of other factors that can affect a print.

We say that fingerprints are unique, but this is a problematic word in a forensic context, as we cannot prove that no two people have ever had a fingerprint that was identical. The best we can say is that no two people have ever been found to share a fingerprint. But unless we could test every single person's prints and compare them to everyone else's, we can't truly say fingerprints are unique to an individual.

The reason prints are so variable between people is because of the influences on their formation. Friction ridges on the hands and feet develop when the foetus is still forming in the mother's uterus, beginning to form at ten weeks' gestation and taking on their adult patterning (but not scale) by the time the foetus is six months old. The print is formed in the deep tissue; therefore superficial and transient injuries to the fingers will not destroy the print, and even if someone wears their print away through repetitive use of an abrasive, the print will return as the activity ceases and the skin tissue is

7

replenished. However, if the deep generating layer of the skin is damaged, as a result of trauma such as a burn or cut, the fingerprint may be permanently changed.

There is a genetic component to the ridge patterns, so if you were to look at your siblings' fingerprints you may find they look more like yours than those of someone not as closely related to you. However, there is also an environmental influence, in that the intra-uterine fluid also affects the shapes formed. This means that because each of your ten fingers is in a slightly different place in utero, the fluid will have a different effect on each finger and the final pattern will also be slightly different. A fingerprint expert could differentiate between each of your fingers and determine which one of the ten made the impression. That's why identical twins, who share a genetic code, can be distinguished from each other by their fingerprints.

Tim Doran, Assistant Chief of Police in Colorado
and a retired Federal Bureau of Investigation Special Agent

The autopsy revealed a number of key facts. Firstly, Christine was found to have eaten items that were not included in the picnic they'd taken with them that day, meaning she got the food elsewhere – and the only time she could have eaten other food was when she wandered off by herself earlier in the day.

The murders were violent. Christine had been hit from behind with a blunt instrument, hard enough to fracture her skull. This is the blow that most likely incapacitated her as she tried to run for her life. She had then been stabbed seven times, largely in her back and the rear of her neck, indicating that her attacker was behind her, and there were also six parallel cuts on the front of her neck, indicating he had also tried to slit her throat.

Marianne was also stabbed, six times, and her throat had been cut very deeply. She suffered stab wounds to her arms and chest (one of which was so deep it penetrated her heart, and was the likely cause of death), as well as others to her back.

The pathologist determined that the same knife had been used to kill both girls.

The motive appeared to be sexual, as the girls' underwear had been cut and their genitalia exposed – and while no sperm was found on Christine, a semen sample was recovered from Marianne and stored as a vital piece of evidence should a suspect in the murders be identified. However, the attacker hadn't been able to rape the girls, as both girls' hymens were intact.

Time of death was difficult to determine with any accuracy, and would have been based on the victims' body temperature compared with the ambient temperature at the time the pathologist undertook their analysis. However, given that the pathologist would not have had the benefit of contemporary data and information regarding the variables that can affect body heat loss after death, all that could be said was that the girls were killed within thirty minutes of each other and before midnight on 11 January. As they were last seen around 1 pm, that leaves an eleven-hour window.

HEARTBREAK FOR THE FAMILIES

Hans (13) and Helmut Jnr (17), the two oldest Schmidt boys, had stayed home that day to clean the house while Marianne took the young ones to the beach, as their mother, Elisabeth, was in hospital.

They were the men of the house since their father, Helmut, had sadly died of Hodgkin's disease in mid-1964, leaving their mum to look after seven children.

When the four younger Schmidt siblings got home that evening without Marianne and Christine, Hans and Helmut were naturally alarmed, and went next door to Christine's house. Her grandmother reported both girls missing to the police. This was at about 8.30 pm.

Hans Schmidt has spoken about the case publicly in recent years, and described the devastation the family still feels, over fifty years later. He had the unenviable task of visiting his mum in hospital to tell her the girls hadn't come home. He said, 'Mum looked at me sadly and said she didn't think the girls would ever be back – she knew they were dead'.

Sadly, Elisabeth Schmidt died of stomach cancer in 2009 without knowing who killed her daughter or why. But during her life she never gave up hope that one day her daughter's murderer would be named.

The girls' funerals were held on 20 January 1965, and a reward of 10,000 Australian pounds (equivalent to over $270,000 today) was offered for information, but the case went cold.

In April 1996 a coronial inquiry was held into the double murder. Marianne's younger brother Peter was one of the witnesses, and again told the story of the girls wandering off in the wrong direction, giggling, when they'd said they were going to collect their bags. Marianne's older brother, Helmut, also gave evidence, and told the court how he had visited Cronulla a week before the murders with Marianne and Christine, and on that occasion his sister had gone off by herself for over an hour. When she got back she said she'd been to North Wanda, but had refused to tell him why.

Was this evidence of an earlier pre-arranged meeting with the same boy that Marianne and Christine met on 11 January?

WHAT WE LEARN ABOUT OUR OFFENDER

The situation and scene, the injuries to the victims, and the offender's inability to rape the girls tell us a lot about the offender.

Firstly, the situation: It appears clear that Marianne and Christine planned to meet someone at the beach that day – this seems the best explanation for why they would have insisted on the trip on a day when the weather was going to be cold and windy. Also, as the time of their liaison approached, the girls became giddy and excited, the predictable reaction of teenage girls to the prospect of meeting a boy. The fact that Christine had already gone off by herself and eaten food they had not brought with them indicates that she had already had one illicit rendezvous that day, before both girls hurried off to keep their date. This suggests this was not the first time the girls had met this boy. They had gone willingly to meet their murderer.

Secondly, the scene: Attacking two victims at once is a bold and confident move, especially if it is one enacted by such a young assailant as the teenage boy Wolfgang describes seeing with Marianne and Christine. It speaks of self-assurance; the offender clearly thought he could handle and subdue the two girls. He did come prepared, though, with at least one weapon (the knife used to stab the victims), as well as sourcing the item he used to hit Christine over the head and cause her blunt force injury (possibly a rock or other heavy object found at the beach). He took the blunt weapon away with him or hid it elsewhere, as it was not recovered, and the knife blade found at the scene could not be linked to the murders. The killer would have been covered in blood, yet he managed to avoid being seen. This made me wonder if the choice of meeting venue was his, as the crime was clearly premeditated. So did the offender select a very secluded spot to reduce his risk of being caught? If so, we are talking about an organised offender.

Thirdly, the injuries and attempted rape of the victims: There is evidence that the offender was young. People start to have sexual fantasies in their teens, when they become sexually mature.

Those with violent or sadistic tendencies may begin to have violent sexual fantasies from the age of 12 or 13, but it may be several years (if ever) before they develop the confidence to act on them. If the surfie boy Wolfgang saw was the offender, at around 16 or 17 years of age he may have been fantasising about violently assaulting and murdering girls for some time. Which means by the time he acted on those fantasies, he could have been so overwhelmed, leading to premature ejaculation and his subsequent inability to rape the girls. If this is true, the level of violence enacted on Marianne and Christine indicates a very dangerous offender, especially if he is capable of this level of ferocity at such an early age.

And he got away with it, which would have further fuelled his confidence.

This may have been his first serious crime, but I doubt it. He may have sexually assaulted girls before, as he knew he could control and dominate Christine and Marianne. He brought the knife with him to make sure. Perhaps he intended to stop at sexual assault, but it went wrong and he ended up killing the girls. However, if that is the case, the level of violence was overkill (literally where more injuries are caused than are necessary to cause death), and the premature ejaculation speaks to his excitement. So intentional or not, the killer enjoyed the experience. So much so that this would not be his last violent, sexually motivated offence.

And if he got a kick out of attacking two victims simultaneously, then this may have become a signature for him.

SUSPECTS

Clearly the teenage boy Wolfgang described seeing with Christine and Marianne has to be the prime suspect, but he has never been formally identified. We'll come back to him, as there is a strong candidate for who this may have been.

There were also other people who were seen at the beach that afternoon, some of whom have been identified and cleared of involvement, while others have not been found and have never come forward.

In addition to people seen there that day, a total of six identikit images were produced of four men the police wanted to talk to because they were known to hang around the beach, and they each had records of having behaved 'offensively to women' (as one news report from the time puts it). One of these men indecently exposed himself to a woman, and another attacked a girl at Caringbah, a 10-minute drive from Wanda Beach, in August 1965.

These identikits received significant public attention, and were widely publicised on television and in newspapers across the country, but yielded nothing.

The police search for Christine and Marianne's murderer was extensive – they interviewed over 14,000 people (a record in Australia), identified around 5000 persons of interest, and travelled thousands of kilometres across the country, and still the killer evaded them.

In 2007, then Police Commissioner Andrew Scipione established the (now disbanded) NSW Police Cold Case Justice Project. Inspector Ian Waterson (now retired) was appointed as head, and one of the specific directives for the unit was to review the Wanda Beach murders. Police investigators reviewed over 50 boxes of case files, reading them all, as well as speaking to detectives who had previously worked on the case, and sought modern technologies that could help progress the investigation.

All to no avail.

However, as is inevitable in cases of this nature, a number of persons of interest have been named over the years.

Alan Bassett came to the attention of well-respected detective Cec Johnson who was assigned the double murder case at Wanda, after Bassett sent Johnson a painting he'd done called *A Bloody Awful Thing*. Bassett was a violent offender, and was already in prison for the assault, rape and murder of 19-year-old Carolyn Orphin near Wollongong, an hour's drive south of Wanda Beach. This crime took place in June 1966, just 19 months after Christine and Marianne were brutally murdered at Wanda.

Johnson was retired by the time Bassett sent him the painting, but he became convinced that Bassett had murdered Christine and Marianne, largely because he thought the painting depicted an abstract version of the murder scene, together with the body of one of the girls, a broken knife, and blood trails. Most importantly, Johnson felt the perspective was one that only the offender or someone who had personally witnessed the scene could have created – making Bassett his prime suspect in the killings. Bassett was never charged with the double murder, however, and was released in 1995 after serving 29 years in prison.

Johnson's former colleagues, while retaining the utmost respect for the former detective, believe he was wrong in his conviction that Bassett was responsible for Marianne and Christine's murders. It seems highly unlikely that Bassett was the killer; he committed his crime in Wollongong and his modus operandi was very different to the Wanda Beach killings, and there is no evidence putting him anywhere near Wanda at the time of the murders. Bassett has always denied any involvement. When he was released from prison, Bassett volunteered a DNA sample so that he could be formally excluded from any further police inquiries.

Derek Percy was another strong suspect in the Wanda Beach murders. Percy was sent to prison for the murder of 12-year-old Yvonne Tuohy at a beach on Western Port, a large tidal bay in Victoria, in July 1969, and was a person of interest in the deaths of nine children in the 1960s. Percy started his criminal career in 1964, when as a boy, he began stealing and wearing women's underwear. Percy was a good fit for the Wanda Beach killer as he abducted Yvonne at knifepoint and had simultaneously attempted to kidnap her friend, Shane Spiller (11), who managed to escape. Spiller was able to describe the abductor and his car, and Percy was located and arrested – he was washing blood off himself at the time. Percy denied any involvement in Yvonne's killing, but did eventually lead the police to her body. In 1970 he was prosecuted for murder, but found not guilty by reason of insanity.

Percy was remanded indefinitely, and died from lung cancer in 2013 at age 64 without admitting his involvement in any further crimes. But he did volunteer a DNA sample five months before his death, which the Victorian police collected and made available to NSW police, the purpose being to see if Percy could be forensically linked to any other crimes.

As when any violent killer who has been linked to other crimes dies, families of other possible Percy victims were devastated that he had potentially taken the answers they desperately seek to his grave. And it is not just the murders at Wanda Beach that Percy has been linked to. There was also six-year-old Allen Redston who was killed in Curtin, Canberra, in 1966, and three-year-old Simon Brook, murdered in Sydney in 1968.

Percy was also questioned over the disappearance of the three Beaumont siblings who vanished from Glenelg Beach in January 1966 (covered in chapter two). His name came up after thousands of documents were discovered in a self-storage unit in Melbourne rented by Percy for over twenty years. The documents comprised newspaper cuttings on sex crimes, pictures of children, a video with a rape theme, and stories about abduction and torture. Diaries written by Percy detailed his violent sexual fantasies, which he'd been having since he was a teenager. Most worryingly, Percy had written about his plans to abduct and torture children, which ultimately he acted upon.

But in 2014, one family did get answers, as Derek Percy was formally named as the killer of seven-year-old Linda Stilwell, who was abducted from the St Kilda foreshore in 1968. Although Linda's remains have never been found, and Percy denied any involvement in her disappearance at an emergency death-bed hearing in 2013, the deputy state coroner of Victoria, Iain West, found that Percy did murder Linda. Hopefully it brought closure to the family, who had waited for years to know what happened.

Percy has been recognised as a serial, violent offender who preyed on children. There is little doubt there are more victims as yet not formally connected to Percy.

At least with his DNA sample on file, the potential exists that one day, if he was involved with other crimes not yet attributed to him, the families of those victims can get the answers they seek.

THE PRIME SUSPECT: CHRISTOPHER WILDER

You have probably not heard the name Christopher Wilder, even though he is one of Australia's most prolific sex offenders and serial killers. But Wilder is a strong suspect in the killings of Christine and Marianne.

Wilder, like so many other violent and sadistic psychopaths, had good looks and charm on his side. He was a chameleon; he could fit in and blend, and had the gift of the gab – in his case, this was a lethal combination. Wilder was also financially successful, which afforded him the playboy lifestyle that he loved to flaunt – cars, houses, women. Here was a man with it all. This included an appetite for abducting, torturing, raping, and in at least ten cases, murdering, young women. He often targeted pairs of victims.

Christopher was born in Sydney in 1945 to an Australian mother and American father. The family moved around a lot because Wilder's father, Coley, was in the US navy. Consequently, Wilder spent the first few years of his life in the US, Asia and the Pacific, returning to Sydney in 1958 when Wilder was 13, at which time Coley retired from the military. The Wilders bought a house in Ryde, in Sydney's inner west.

At age 17 Wilder was arrested for raping a girl. He wasn't working alone. Wilder persuaded two younger boys at Freshwater Beach (near Manly) to help him get a young girl into his car to go for a drive. Unfortunately, the drive was to a quarry in Beacon Hill about five kilometres away. Wilder sent the two boys away, raped the girl, then drove them all back to the beach. Wilder eventually pled guilty to 'carnal knowledge' for this offence, which was a lesser charge.

In 1967 the then 22-year-old Wilder began to court the Read family – daughters Sarah and Emma, and parents Claire and Brian (the family's names have been changed to protect their identities) – after the Reads had gone to Palm Beach, north of Sydney, for a day out. Claire later gave a statement to police, saying that she had noticed a man (who later turned out to be Wilder) driving a red sports car. He parked and sat on the sand near his car watching the girls on the beach all day. As they were leaving, Wilder struck up a conversation with Sarah and Emma.

With a strong American accent and a sports car, Wilder seemed exotic and exciting to the young Read daughters.

Wilder quickly became acquainted with the family, and arranged to come and pick up Sarah and Emma the next day to take them to the beach for the day. His first interest was in 16-year-old Sarah, but her parents disapproved, with Brian telling him, 'Sarah is too young to go out with a boy of your age'.

So Wilder moved his attention to the older sister, Emma, who was 20. The pair started dating, and after about two months Wilder offered to take Emma on another trip to Palm Beach.

But instead of heading to the popular beach, Wilder pulled over in a secluded spot and told Emma he wanted to take photos of her. Emma refused, which angered Wilder; he pulled at her clothes, ripping her bra, and pushed her down onto a blanket. He took his photos, ignoring her continued protests.

Despite this assault, the pair continued dating, and initiated a sexual relationship after about six months.

By this time Emma's mother, Claire, had noticed Wilder's violent temper. He had also behaved inappropriately with her, turning up at the family home one day when she was alone and letting himself in uninvited through the back door. Wilder asked Claire if he could take her to the beach to photograph her in a bikini, and when she refused he forced her onto the bed. She told him to get off her or she'd call the police, so he left.

Not put off by this, Wilder rang the Read family home a few days after the assault on Claire, saying he wanted to take photographs of Sarah, who was still at school. Needless to say, this was not allowed to happen.

Notwithstanding all the warning signs, Emma married Wilder in 1968.

Unsurprisingly, the marriage was not a happy one. The sex soon turned kinky, with Wilder wanting to be hurt by Emma, as well as wanting to cause her pain. He also had a voracious sexual appetite, wanting intercourse several times a day. When Emma refused to have sex because she was on her period, Wilder would get angry and hit her.

Emma left Wilder on two occasions, returning to her family home, but each time went back to him after 10 days.

Things took an even worse turn when, after only three months of marriage, Emma found pictures of naked women hidden in a drawer under Wilder's clothes. She also discovered photographic equipment, negatives and photos in the car boot of women draped in towels, or wearing bikinis or dresses. Emma was shocked to see that the clothes the women were wearing were all items Emma had noticed had gone missing from her own wardrobe.

She also thought Wilder tried to kill her on a number of occasions – once using her car as a weapon when her brakes failed and another time when her steering failed. This was only around four months after they were married. Wilder knew about mechanics and regularly checked Emma's car. Approximately eight months into their doomed marriage, she believes he made a third attempt on her life when the gas stove in their home was left on full. All the windows in the house had been closed, and Wilder had been waiting outside.

By 1969 Wilder had come to the attention of the police again, and was taken to Manly Police Station for questioning about the sexual assault of a young nursing student. It had taken the young woman a few days to report the incident, and she was very clear that she did not want to press charges – she simply wanted to tell the police what had happened to try to stop it happening to any other women. The police tracked Wilder down, who admitted having sex with the young woman, and that he used fear to coerce her. However, the police were given legal advice that without a formal complaint, in addition to the delay in the crime being committed and therefore the lack of physical evidence to substantiate the assault, charges against Wilder would not succeed and Wilder was released. There was nothing else the detectives could do.

The police suggested that Emma move back in with her parents, and never go back to Wilder.

By February 1969 Emma had again left Wilder and returned to her parents' house, and the family's concerns over Wilder's behaviour had become so serious that on 19 February all three women went to Hornsby Police Station and gave detailed statements – which included their suspicions that Wilder may have been involved in the 1965 murders at Wanda Beach.

Emma never went back to him. The disastrous union had lasted almost exactly one year. She went on to divorce Wilder, and may have had a very lucky escape, as his criminal trajectory will show.

The police were unable to substantiate any link between Wilder and the Wanda Beach murders, and couldn't actually find Wilder to question him. When they eventually did track him down at his parents' house in Ryde, they were told by his mother, June, that he had gone to the US in May 1969. Wilder had started working in the US, made possible because he had dual nationality as his father was a US citizen. June also told the NSW police that Wilder had settled in the US, and had no intention of returning to Australia.

The police did manage to ascertain from his mother that he had been living in Sydney at the time of the brutal Wanda Beach murders. However, because he had left the country and there was no concrete evidence linking him to the murders, further inquiries were suspended.

CHRISTOPHER WILDER'S CRIMINAL HISTORY

Wilder only went for the lookers, and he'd developed a routine to reel them in. He adopted the guise of a photographer for a well-known (and genuine) modelling agency, and approached young girls with the story that he wanted to help them become models. He even had business cards made up, and had all the photographic equipment he would own as part of his trade.

He sold the romantic ideal of success and fortune, and he did it fast. He could groom girls and young women within a few minutes of meeting them, and many would quickly do anything he said.

Now in the US, he used his charm and patter to continue his violent sexual activities. In 1976 Wilder was charged with the sexual battery of the 16-year-old daughter of the owners of a house he was hired to work on as a labourer. The charges were later dropped.

In 1980 he struck again, his target a 17-year-old girl who Wilder coerced with his photographer chat, asking her to pose for a poster advert. He got her to try on high heels and shorts, which he said would help him assess her as a model. He also gave her a slice of pizza to pose with, which he had laced with a sedative. After she'd eaten it, he had sex with her. He was convicted of attempted sexual battery with physical force, and put on a five-year bond.

Wilder returned to Sydney on 6 December 1982 to visit his parents. On 7 December – one day after landing – he went to Manly Beach and picked up Phionna Parsons. He was again playing the part of a photographer, and persuaded Phionna to dress up in high heels and pose for him. He also managed to get her to become complicit in his game, using her to lure other girls on the beach away from their friends so he could try to convince them to pose for him as well.

Late in December he was back at Manly, and this time he targeted two 15-year-old girls (who can't be named for legal reasons), who were at the beach with friends. Wilder approached the girls when they left their friends to get some lunch with the line, 'Would you like to be in advertising commercials?' Both girls said they would, and he started to groom them, telling them they'd have to work hard if they wanted to be successful models . . . and do everything he said. This was clearly a well-rehearsed routine. Wilder knew how to choose potential targets, and just what to say to get them totally under his control very quickly.

He showed them his business card, and persuaded the girls to go with him in his car. He drove them towards Dee Why, about a 15-minute car ride from Manly Beach, where he produced a bag from the front footwell containing high heels and stockings for the girls to wear. He then drove them to the Sydney Harbour National Park, where he got the girls to pose on a rock while he took photos. He wasn't finished. He then blindfolded them both and took them to Kings Cross, another 15–20 minute trip. He took the girls to the Imperial Hotel where he hired a room. Here he took images of the girls naked and sexually assaulted them. They would later describe Wilder as 'commanding' throughout: he was definitely in charge.

Wilder then let the girls go, dropping them at Central Station. He was still playing the part of a modelling scout, and took their contact details, saying he would get in touch with them later in the week. The girls described their attacker as between 35–40 years old, of medium height, suntanned, with light blondish hair and a dark beard and moustache. Wilder was 37 at this time.

When the girls told their parents what had happened, they took them straight to the police station where the girls gave detailed statements of the abuse. They knew Wilder's car registration, as well as the model. The car had been hired from Avis, who were quickly able to provide the name of the man who had rented it; Christopher Wilder. The description matched the one given by the girls.

But when they checked, the police records listed only one juvenile conviction for Wilder, and made no mention of possible links to the Wanda Beach murders and they did not have his US convictions or charges on file. Wilder was charged with 'enticing the girls away for your own advantage and indecently assaulting them'. He was held overnight, and eventually bailed, on the strict condition that he would return for the next hearing of the case against him.

He left court. And then left the country, returning immediately to the US.

You might think that having the case hanging over him in Australia might curb his criminal activities. But not Wilder.

In 1983 he began to hunt again.

He met and fell for Elizabeth (Beth) Kenyon, a beautiful young teacher. She had aspirations to make it big as a model and had some success, appearing in various advertising campaigns, and she was a finalist in the Miss Florida USA pageant in 1983.

That's where Wilder spotted her, in his familiar guise as a fashion photographer and scout. She was a perfect target – young, beautiful, but also vulnerable and innocent. Just his type. They started dating, and things soon escalated to the point where Wilder proposed marriage. During their courtship he had remained the perfect gentleman, never pushy or overly forward. He charmed both Beth and her family, who were all taken in by his superficial appeal.

However, Beth declined his proposal, even though she liked Wilder. Wilder seemed to take this in his stride, but it may have dented his ego enough to act as a catalyst for the devastation that was to come.

In July 1983 Wilder approached two young girls, aged twelve and nine, at Boynton Beach, Florida. He did his normal photographer routine, and offered to take them to the modelling agency he worked at for a shoot. They both agreed and got into his car.

But instead he pulled out a gun, threatened them, and found a secluded spot where he sexually assaulted them. He also brutally beat the girls. After the attack, he reverted to the charming man he had been before, and asked for the girls' contact details. In their terrified state they gave him their address and phone number.

Perhaps because of bravado, and his knack for getting away with his crimes, Wilder was not afraid of being identified by his young victims, because after the assault he drove them back to Boynton Beach.

And the girls were able to describe their abductor to the police. It wasn't until a year later, however, when Wilder was on the front page of the newspapers in relation to a separate incident, that an officer thought to show Wilder's image to the girls. They picked him out straightaway. Wilder was the man who had attacked and assaulted them.

Wilder interrupted his US crimes with a short trip back to Sydney in July 1983, to attend the next stage of the case against him for the attacks on the teens he'd lured into his car in December 1982.

In August he appeared in court and vigorously defended the charges against him. The case against him was complex, and it was decided it would take longer than the three days that had been put aside for it. The case was adjourned until April 1984, and Wilder was again given bail. The delay was because of other cases already listed to be heard, after which came the extended Christmas holiday, and then Wilder's lawyer was already booked for other trials.

So in August 1983 Wilder went back to Florida.

By this point, things weren't looking good for Wilder. He would have known that when the case resumed there was a good chance he would go to prison – and that was without the Australian courts knowing anything about the crimes he had committed in the US.

Back on American soil, Wilder resumed his contact with the Kenyon family, as well as his attendance at high-profile events as a photographer.

At this time, Wilder was also heavily into fast cars. He loved to race. He was mysterious, an exotic man of danger, and a consummate show-off, all of which made him attractive to the women he targeted. At one such racing event in 1984, the Miami Grand Prix, Wilder made his debut as a solo driver.

Promotions girls were part of the show, dressed in scanty outfits and handing out freebies to attendees. One of the girls working the race was Rosario Gonzalez, a gorgeous 20-year-old woman. Rosario was working on 26 February. She was missing from work in the afternoon, having left for lunch but not returning, and although her co-workers were worried, the police weren't informed as it just didn't seem that serious. She had told her parents, who she lived with, that she would be home at about 5 pm. When she wasn't back by 6.30 pm her parents got worried, and by 7 pm they had started calling around looking for her. Her parents reported her missing at 9 pm that night.

Rosario's car was found where she'd parked for work that morning, but there was no sign of Rosario. She was never seen alive again, and her body has not been located, although she is assumed deceased.

Wilder is linked to her disappearance and probable murder, as it later transpired that the pair had met in 1982, probably at a local fashion show that Rosario had worked at and Wilder attended. She had fallen for Wilder's lies, and had posed for him.

Beth Kenyon, the girl who turned down his proposal, was still on Wilder's mind. And she too disappeared, never to be seen again.

Beth was last seen at a service station in Coral Gables, Miami, on Sunday, 5 March 1984. Beth was due home to catch up with visiting relatives, but she didn't show up. When the family began to ring around, they discovered that she hadn't turned up to her job as a teacher on the Monday, which was totally out of character for her.

They called everyone they could think of with any links to Beth, which included Wilder. Beth's mother spoke to him, and later said that she knew something was wrong. He couldn't wait to get off the phone, and didn't act like a man who had loved Beth enough to propose to her. Alarm bells began ringing for the family.

The Kenyons weren't happy with the response to the missing persons report they filed, as it was clear that the police believed Beth had run away. So they hired private investigators who soon started chasing Wilder down. And there was good reason. The investigators had visited the petrol station where Beth was last seen alive, and an attendant there told them she'd been with a man. He'd overheard the conversation, and it appeared they were on their way to the airport and were running late. When shown a photo of Wilder, the attendant confirmed that he was the man at the service station that day.

Beth's car was found at Miami International Airport.

The investigators tracked down Wilder's phone number and called him. He denied knowing anything about Beth's disappearance, but was clearly shaken by the call.

The family gave what information they had to the police, but yet again the authorities were slow to act. So instead, the investigators went to interview Wilder themselves, but he wasn't home and they couldn't find him.

Although they were looking for Wilder in relation to Beth's disappearance, the PIs soon heard about Rosario's case and immediately saw the similarities. As a result, they called the detectives heading up Rosario's case, who agreed to accompany them to Boynton Beach, where Wilder was living. But that wasn't going to happen immediately, so the investigators again went themselves.

They couldn't locate Wilder at home, but after patiently waiting covertly at his workplace, he showed up and they pounced. The PIs took him into the office of the construction company he worked for, to the surprise of the secretary. The secretary asked what it was in relation to and when they told her, she answered, 'Oh, the girl whose car was found at the airport'. She said that was what Wilder had told her – this was a major slip on his part, as at the time this fact had not been publicly released. So the only person who could know about the car being at the airport was the person who had parked it there. Christopher Wilder.

Although Wilder was clearly in the frame, the private investigators did not have the authority to arrest him.

Again Wilder evaded his hunters: a fact that would prove fatal for at least eight other women.

WILDER'S CROSS-COUNTRY KILLING SPREE

Wilder's next victim was 15-year-old Colleen Orsborn, who was abducted from Daytona Beach on 15 March 1984. Colleen had skipped school and headed to the beach. When she didn't return home that afternoon her mother began to worry, but Colleen was a bit of a wild child, and this wasn't the first time she'd gone off for a little while. However, she'd always come back in two or three days. When she wasn't back by 19 March, her mother reported her missing. When police began to investigate, they were told by one of her friends that Colleen had been offered $100 to pose for some photos. The description of the would-be photographer matched Wilder, and he was staying close to Daytona Beach at the time. Wilder quickly became a suspect in Colleen's disappearance, but without a body there was little police could do.

Colleen's body was found several weeks later, but was not formally identified until 2010 when advances in DNA facilitated a match to two of Colleen's sisters. Identification was delayed in part due to the fact that Colleen's body was badly decomposed, added to the fact Colleen was known to have suffered a fracture to her right arm that was not noted when the body was X-rayed – therefore, whilst the physical description was obviously very similar to Colleen's missing persons report, the missed evidence of the fracture on the unidentified body led to Colleen being dismissed as a possible match.

Wilder was now in a downward spiral, and the abductions and murders were coming closer together.

On Sunday, 18 March – just three days after Colleen vanished – Theresa (Terry) Wait Ferguson disappeared from a shopping centre 220 kilometres north of Boynton Beach, at Indian Harbour. Like so many young girls, Terry dreamt of becoming a model. She'd gone shopping alone, and simply hadn't come back. Her family found her car still parked at the shopping centre around 10 pm that night.

The police investigation into her whereabouts soon turned up a witness who had seen Terry talking to a man with a camera around his neck. The witness identified Wilder from a set of photographs, but this was a few weeks later, and by then more women would be dead.

Terry's body was found on 21 March 120 kilometres from where she was taken. Her hands and feet had been bound, and a rope had been tied around her neck. She had also been beaten, but there were no signs of sexual assault.

Linda Grober was the next to fall victim to Wilder. A 19-year-old student at Florida State University, Linda was an attractive young woman with a passion for photography. On Tuesday, 20 March, she was out shopping when a man – Wilder – came up to her and asked if she wanted to be a model, as he was a photographer looking for a model for a job. She passed on the offer, but he was persistent. He came up to her again in the car park, when she was getting into her car. He was parked next to her, which suggests he had spotted her earlier and specifically targeted her. Again she refused his offer to go with him to his studio to take some photos, so Wilder went to plan B – he punched her in the stomach and threw her into the back of his car. When she regained consciousness, they'd parked somewhere secluded. Wilder pulled Linda out of the car and tied her up, gagged her and forced her into the boot of his car.

They drove for hours, with Linda still bound and gagged in the boot, thinking she was going to die.

Although they were on the road for a long time, it seems they were driving in circles, as eventually Wilder pulled into a motel only 60 kilometres from where he'd abducted Linda. On the way he had stopped to buy various implements which he would later use to torture her. He took Linda into a motel room, and over the course of the next few hours either ignored her or acted out his perverse pleasures, which included electrocution and supergluing her eyes closed. He also sexually assaulted her.

With unbelievable fortitude under those circumstances, Linda decided her only chance to survive was to fight. When Wilder was distracted, she attacked him, and tried to make it out of the motel door. He stopped her, but she managed to reach the relative safety of the bathroom and locked the door.

But locks and the doors themselves in roadside motels are not made to keep out monsters, and Linda fully expected Wilder to break straight through the door and kill her.

But there was only silence. He didn't come.

Linda hid in the bath and waited and waited. Eventually, she built up enough courage to open the door, thinking her torturer was lying in wait on the other side.

He wasn't. When Linda opened the door she was alone in the bedroom. Wilder had fled, taking all of their personal belongings with him.

Linda was able to describe Wilder, but Wilder was on the run. However, by taking Linda across state lines, Wilder had elevated the investigation to federal level, and the FBI took over the hunt. Law enforcement agencies across the US were put on alert.

Maybe Wilder knew the end was nearing, and he was desperate to evade capture. The pressure sent him into a frenzy. Over the next few days he abducted at least eight more women.

On 23 March he kidnapped Terry Walden from Beaumont, Texas, a very attractive nursing student whose body was found three days later. She had been stabbed and beaten to death, and she had been bound at the hands and feet. A few days before she vanished, she had told her husband that a man had approached her, asking if she wanted to be a model. She had declined. Wilder was still in control at this point, though he must have known the FBI was on his trail. He took his time, selected his prey, and waited for an opportunity to pounce.

Just two days later, on 25 March, 20-year-old Suzanne Logan was abducted from a shopping centre – one of Wilder's favourite hunting grounds – in Oklahoma. He held her for one day before murdering her and disposing of her body. There was evidence she had been sexually assaulted, and she had been stabbed and beaten. Small stab wounds to her lower back appear to be the result of Wilder torturing his victim, before he inflicted the final, fatal stab wound to Suzanne's mid-back. There were also bite marks on her breasts; not uncommon in violent, sexually motivated crimes. The pathologist determined that the victim had only been dead for around an hour before her body was discovered, yet Wilder slipped through the police net again.

On 29 March, 18-year-old Sheryl Bonaventura became Wilder's next victim. An aspiring model, she was taken from a Colorado shopping centre. Wilder stabbed and shot Sheryl, and her body was discovered on 3 May. This was a change of MO for Wilder, as it was the first time he'd shot any of his victims. It would not be the last.

Seventeen-year-old Michelle Korfman was kidnapped from Nevada on 1 April. A beautiful girl, if a little taller than Wilder's normal targets at 175 centimetres, Michelle was already a model, and the day she vanished she'd been modelling in a fashion show at a shopping centre in Las Vegas, hoping it would be her big break.

Wilder was actually photographed at the show, so he certainly wasn't in hiding, even though the FBI hunt for the predator was really heating up. Witnesses later identified him as a man they had seen talking to Michelle after the show. Michelle's body was found on 11 May, but due to decomposition, she was not formally identified until late June. She had died of asphyxia.

On 4 April Wilder abducted 16-year-old Tina Risico in California. He approached her with his photographer spiel, and Tina was taken in immediately. He told her he wanted to take some photos in a more secluded spot a short drive away. Tina willingly went with him. They stopped to take the shots and all seemed fine until Wilder pulled a gun on her. He then put the gun into the terrified girl's mouth, and told her he had killed before and wouldn't hesitate to kill her. She believed him. He then pulled out a knife and ran it across her face and body, making sure she knew he was serious. He sexually assaulted her, but didn't kill her. He tied her up, blindfolded her, and put her on the back seat of the car. They would travel together for a few days, sometimes stopping at motels where he would torture her with electricity, as he had done with Linda Grober, and sexually assault her. But he also schooled Tina in how to survive her ordeal, as he planned to use her for bait to lure other girls to their deaths. Although at times exceptionally cruel, Wilder was occasionally chatty and friendly with Tina. She played along with whatever he wanted in a bid to stay alive. Her compliance seemed to satisfy him, and because she was too afraid to try to flee, he began to trust her.

Six days into her ordeal, Wilder took Tina to a shopping centre in Indiana where he selected his next victim, 16-year-old Dawnette Wilt. It was now 10 April. He coerced Dawnette outside, with Tina's reluctant help, then forced her into his car at gunpoint. Wilder took the two girls on another long drive, occasionally stopping at motels where he tortured and raped Dawnette in front of Tina. On Thursday, 12 April, Wilder drugged Dawnette with sleeping tablets, bound and blindfolded her, before they left the motel and continued their seemingly never-ending road trip. After a while, in a very secluded spot, they pulled over and Wilder took Dawnette out of the car and into the forest. They were gone about half an hour before Wilder returned alone. He and Tina drove off, but within 15 minutes Wilder decided he wanted to go back to check if Dawnette was dead. They parked where they had before, and Wilder again went into the forest, in the direction he'd taken Dawnette just 45 minutes previously. When he returned he was still alone, but he looked shaken – perhaps because for the first time he was not in charge of what was going on. He confessed to Tina that Dawnette was not where he had left her. Wilder thought he had killed her, having suffocated and stabbed her. But somehow she had survived and her luck had held, as she'd managed to get the attention of one of the very few passing motorists. This had all happened in the 15 minutes before Wilder had returned to make sure he had completed his murderous task. Dawnette's rescuer took her straight to the local hospital, and her injuries and story led to a fast police response. For the first time, the police had knowledge of Wilder's very recent location.

Wilder knew the police were after him. He had made the FBI's top 10 most wanted list, and his face was all over the news. But in his mind he could still escape arrest. He needed to change vehicles. After finding that Dawnette had escaped, he drove to a local shopping centre and carjacked 33-year-old Beth Dodge at gunpoint. He shot Beth and dumped her body in the woods.

By this time, Dawnette's survival was all over the media, as was the fact that Wilder was travelling with a young woman.

The biggest manhunt in US history was on.

Wilder decided he needed to leave Tina, and inexplicably, instead of killing her, he released her at Logan Airport in Boston.

By this stage Wilder had travelled over 13,000 kilometres in what appears to be a haphazard trek from one side of the US to the other. He was now pushing for the Canadian border – even with the police and FBI on his heels, this walking ego thought he could outmanoeuvre them. But in the end it was luck on the part of the police that led to Christopher Wilder's downfall.

On 13 April Wilder was buying petrol in the small town of Colebrook, New Hampshire, where he asked for directions to Canada.

As Wilder was leaving, two troopers in an unmarked car happened to pull into the station parking lot. Wilder seemed to be paying them a lot of attention, which in turn made them notice him. They decided to check out the car – and although Wilder had swapped Beth's plates, the description of the car matched hers and the officers recognised Wilder as the man everyone was looking for.

The officers locked eyes with Wilder, and each knew that it was on – Wilder had correctly identified the men as law enforcement.

True to form, Wilder chose to go out in a blaze of bullets and mayhem. And on his terms, as you'd expect from the narcissistic psychopath that he was.

No way was this one going to prison.

The state troopers approached his car, where Wilder was searching for a weapon he'd stashed under the seat. One of the officers jumped on Wilder, trying to subdue him before he could reach his gun. The officer was unsuccessful, and Wilder managed to get off a shot – through his own chest but also wounding the trooper. Wilder then shot himself again, committing suicide.

One of Australia's most prolific serial killers in history was dead, his rampage finally over.

WILDER AND THE WANDA BEACH MURDERS

By 1984, FBI records indicate that NSW law enforcement were not looking at Wilder in relation to the murders of Christine Sharrock and Marianne Schmidt in 1965, and were favouring the notion that the Wanda Beach killer was a currently 'institutionalised psychotic'. Furthermore, a report dated 17 April 1984 states that Wilder was not a suspect in any other NSW investigations.

This is particularly unfortunate, as at the same time – 1984 – Wilder was on his rampage across the US that would lead to the deaths or disappearances of ten women, and possibly many more. If the NSW police had looked more carefully into his background he may never have made it back to the US, and those women might still be alive.

As it stands, Wilder's murderous downward spiral across the US offers some of the strongest evidence we have that he could also be responsible for Christine and Marianne's murders in 1965.

The Wanda Beach killer had targeted girls who were of a similar type to the ones Wilder would go on to assault and kill, had picked a pair of girls, and had charmed and coerced them to go somewhere he could be alone with them. Wilder was also the right height, build and colouring at the time to have been the surfie type seen by Marianne's brother Wolfgang.

I worked with Duncan McNab, ex-NSW detective, author and TV producer on the story for a news special for Channel 7 in 2018, and Duncan proceeded to write a book about the murders at Wanda Beach and Wilder's potential involvement, entitled *The Snapshot Killer*. He is the guru of all things Christopher Wilder.

Duncan and I have had many conversations about Wilder and whether he is a good fit for the Wanda Beach killings. As an ex-police officer, Duncan is good at detailing and reading an offender, and for him, Wilder is the prime suspect.

'The man who killed Christine and Marianne in 1965 in Sydney was a hunter. Perhaps young, inexperienced, but already with the gift of the gab and the looks to charm unsuspecting girls. That fits Wilder to a tee. He was a predator and they were his ideal prey,' Duncan says.

And Duncan is not alone in thinking Wilder and the Wanda Beach killer are one and the same.

Wilder has been named as an official suspect by retired NSW Detective Ian Waterson, who was put in charge of the Wanda Beach cold case in 2007 as part of the NSW Police Cold Case Justice Project.

Ian gave an interview for a Channel 7 news special, during which he recounted his memories of the case. Ian remembers that – as with any high-profile murder – there were lots of potential suspects. But he was able to bring fresh eyes to one of NSW's most notorious cold cases; and for him, there were only a couple of suspects that stood out.

Alan Bassett and Derek Percy were obvious candidates, but Ian said his team ruled both out as having any involvement in the Wanda Beach murders; Bassett volunteered DNA and Percy wasn't around Sydney at the time of the murders.

One suspect did stand up to Ian's intense investigative scrutiny, and that was Christopher Wilder. Ian says, 'Yeah, I think it's him. He's my number one suspect'.

Ian gave his reasons as 'his [Wilder's] propensity for violence, his sexual appetite, and history of attacking girls and murder . . . and he was around Sydney at the time, he liked to hang around beaches . . . there's a lot of evidence in my mind that points towards him'.

I must say, I agree.

WHERE WE ARE NOW

In 2012 a possible breakthrough came when it was announced that a bloody mark found on an item of the girls' clothing, possibly smeared from the knife used to kill them, had been tested for DNA. A weak profile had been detected, but using the techniques at the time, it was not possible to obtain a full genotypic profile.

However, DNA advances are occurring all the time, and it is feasible that with today's advanced DNA technologies (including methods of repairing damaged DNA) it may be possible to obtain a full profile.

If it transpires that the DNA sample belongs to an unknown male (that is, none of the Schmidt boys are a match, which would simply indicate one of them had inadvertently bled onto the material that day), the sample could belong to the murderer.

The other DNA sample obtained from the Wanda Beach murder scene was the semen sample recovered from Marianne's body. Unfortunately, in 2014 the then Head of the NSW Unsolved Homicide Unit, Peter Lehmann, confirmed that the semen sample had been lost. It had never been tested. This must have been heart-breaking for Marianne and Christine's families, as if that sample could be located and analysed with today's techniques it may have been possible to obtain a full DNA profile.

This would have confirmed once and for all if Christopher Wilder was the Wanda Beach killer. And it is not too late, as although Wilder is deceased his two brothers are still alive, so their DNA could be taken to compare to a crime scene sample from Wanda Beach, which could either implicate or exonerate Wilder.

This could then be compared to the blood sample taken from the girl's clothes, which does still exist, and I would urge the NSW police to consider the option of retesting the available DNA now.

And that's not all. The police still have Marianne and Christine's clothing, which means they can go back to them as technology advances and look for smaller and smaller amounts of DNA, that may still be – or may in the future become – viable for creating a full profile of the offender, if he left any semen, blood, or other biological sample on the girls' clothing.

It's possible that evidence remains of the brutal double murder, and that it could provide the victims' families with the answers they so desperately crave after over five decades of waiting.

FORENSIC SCIENCE EXPLAINED: DNA SHEDDERS

Everywhere we go, we leave small traces of ourselves, genetic evidence that we have touched an item or been in a room. Contemporary forensic science techniques can detect and analyse ever more microscopic amounts of genetic material left at crime scenes. The amount of material left behind is important, but so is the quality. Is the sample pure (i.e. not a mixture from two or more people)? Could it have been contaminated, or the genetic material denatured (the DNA double strand broken down)?

Then there's the issue of 'secondary transference' of genetic material. In a forensic context this might mean that person A could shake hands with person B who then becomes a carrier, and person B could then pick up a knife and stab person C. It's possible that person A's DNA could also be recovered from the knife, not because they ever touched it but because their genetic material was transferred onto the knife from person B. Miscarriages of justice are known to have occurred as a result of secondary transference.

As an example, in 2011 a group of up to a dozen men attended a house in Adelaide armed with axes and gardening forks. The men split into two groups, with some forcing entry to the property through the back door, some through the front. Those men who had not brought weapons with them armed themselves with opportunistic items they picked up around the house. Two people inside the house were attacked; one, Kym Bruce Drover, was killed, and the other sustained serious head injuries. Two of the group of attackers, Daniel Fitzgerald and Grant Sumner, were found guilty of murder and aggravated assault causing serious harm with intent to cause serious harm. There was no direct evidence that either man had inflicted the killer blow to Drover or those blows that caused the second victim's brain injuries, but they were charged under joint criminal enterprise law – meaning that it is enough for the Crown to prove that there was a common plan for the group to either kill someone or cause serious harm. If the accused could be placed at the scene, that would be enough to charge them. There was not much evidence linking Fitzgerald to the attacks – six eyewitnesses to the crime failed to identify him as being in the group that entered the house. Many DNA samples were collected from the house, and only one small mixed sample taken from a blood sample found on a didgeridoo stored at the home matched Fitzgerald. This was enough to convince the jury Fitzgerald was guilty, and he received a life sentence with a non-parole period of 20 years.

Fitzgerald maintained his innocence, and in 2013 applied to the South Australian Court of Criminal Appeal, but his conviction was upheld. He didn't give up, however, and in 2014 the High Court quashed Fitzgerald's conviction, saying in its judgment 'it could not be accepted that the evidence relied on by the prosecution was sufficient to establish beyond reasonable doubt that the appellant was present at, and participated in, the attack' and that the DNA evidence against Fitzgerald could have resulted from the 'rare' occurrence of secondary DNA transference.

This was in the early days of our understanding of DNA transference. Previously it had been thought that if your DNA was found on an object then you had to have had direct contact, but, as Fitzgerald claimed all along, there was another explanation. Tracking the contact between Sumner and Fitzgerald it is possible to see how genetic transference occurred. Earlier on the day of the attacks Sumner and Fitzgerald had been to an amateur boxing match, and the men had shaken hands and Sumner had put his arm around Fitzgerald. The theory is that Fitzgerald shed genetic material that transferred to Sumner during that contact, and that Sumner then secondarily transferred the DNA to the didgeridoo during the attack in the house, resulting in the mixed DNA profile recovered from the scene.

The amount of DNA a person transfers to objects and people around them varies between individuals – people who pass on more of their DNA when they touch things are known as 'shedders'. It's possible Fitzgerald is a shedder. How much DNA a person leaves behind is also related to sex, in that men 'shed' more than women, and different body parts shed material at different rates, for example, the thumb sheds the most. Force of contact also affects how much genetic material is deposited.

Experts from Flinders University have developed a test that can help determine if someone is a shedder. This has implications for the criminal justice system, as defendants can be tested to determine if they are prone to shed genetic material or not. DNA evidence – like all forensic evidence – has to be interpreted within the context in which it's found. As we discover more about shedders, the analyses of evidence will become more sophisticated, reducing the likelihood of miscarriages of justice. It's likely that cases successfully prosecuted on DNA evidence from a mixed sample (such as in Fitzgerald's case) may well now be the subject of scrutiny, and convictions may be quashed as a result. This means that crimes that were previously considered solved may have to be fully reinvestigated, a further source of distress for victims' families.

However, no innocent person should be in jail, so scrutiny and transparency of evidential evaluation must be the cornerstone of the criminal justice system. If questions regarding the reliability of a conviction are raised, they must be addressed fully. A good rule of thumb is that one single type of evidence should not be used in isolation to prosecute someone; there should always be confirmatory evidence supporting guilt. If this had been applied in Fitzgerald's case, he would never have been convicted for the vicious attacks in Adelaide in 2011.

TWO

THE BEAUMONT CHILDREN'S DISAPPEARANCE - AN END OF INNOCENCE

In January 2018 I find myself standing on Glenelg Beach in Adelaide, South Australia, looking out at the Southern Ocean. It is a hot summer's day, pushing 40 °C.

The sounds of children playing are ringing through the still air as families splash around in the waves, seeking respite from the searing midday heat. There's no wind. The sea is calm, gently lapping the shoreline, glittering like diamonds in the sun.

Looking out over this idyllic scene, it's easy to see this as a slice of heaven.

As I stand here, taking it in, all is peaceful.

But I'm not here on holiday. I'm reinvestigating one of Australia's most baffling cold cases – the disappearance of the three young Beaumont children over 50 years ago.

I try to put myself in the frame of mind of the offender – I imagine a predator standing just where I am now. He would have observed a similar vista in 1966, but instead of seeing innocence and fun, he would have seen potential victims and vulnerability. I look out over the beach and try to see it through his eyes, try to understand him. Where I'm standing right now is where it all started, where the predator chose his victims, where he groomed them and enticed them away.

THE CASE

I wasn't born when Jane, Arnna, and Grant Beaumont were abducted from Adelaide's Glenelg Beach in 1966. But this case haunts me, partly because I was involved with the reinvestigation of their disappearance in 2018, and partly because this case – above all others – meant an end to childish innocence in Australia forever, marking a moment in national history when Australia realised it wasn't immune to the worst the world had to offer.

I have stood on the beach where the Beaumonts were seen playing and watched children frolic at the playground where they were spotted that fateful day. And, chillingly, I have stood on the pavement outside the main suspect's house, looking towards the beach and understood how easy it would have been to coerce those children away.

In this chapter I will go back to ground zero, looking at what is most likely to have happened to the children. Who could have been involved, given what we know today about child abductions. I haven't given up hope that one day we will know the fate of the three young Beaumonts, and be able to prove who was responsible for taking them.

GROUND ZERO – GLENELG, AUSTRALIA DAY, 1966

The seaside town of Glenelg is a beacon for holidaymakers, and on Australia Day 1966 it was hot, really hot, reaching almost 40 °C.

The beach was packed with families finding relief from the heat by swimming in the sea. The town was particularly busy with tourists that year as Adelaide was hosting the fourth Ashes test. Hidden amongst all of the people having fun on the beach that day, a predator was on the hunt. And he had nine-year-old Jane Beaumont and her sister Arnna, aged seven, and little brother Grant, aged four, in his sights.

For the three kids, Wednesday, 26 January started in an ordinary way. It was not a public holiday, as it is today. Instead, the anniversary of the 1788 arrival of the First Fleet of British ships at Port Jackson was celebrated the weekend after 26 January. All three kids wanted to go to the beach and make the most of the last few days of their summer school holidays. But Nancy, their mum, suffered in the heat and didn't like the beach, and their dad Grant 'Jim' Beaumont was away working in Snowtown (now infamous for being the site of some of the worst crimes in modern Australian history, known as the Snowtown Murders). It didn't matter, the family lived on the corner of Harding and Peterson Streets, Somerton Park, a short bus ride to the beach, and the eldest, Jane, was very mature for her age and certainly capable of taking her younger siblings on the bus to the beach. She had done it many times.

That day Jane wore a pink one-piece bathing suit with green shorts over the top and tartan canvas sandals. Nancy dressed Arnna in a red and white striped swimming costume, tan shorts and tan sandals, and Grant in green and white bathing shorts with green cotton shorts over the top and red leather sandals. Grant didn't wear a T-shirt, as Nancy knew he wouldn't keep it on; besides, the kids were only going to be gone a couple of hours so he wouldn't need it anyway.

Jane was responsible for looking after everything they would need for the short trip. She took with her a small white clip purse, into which she put the eight shillings and sixpence (around $10 today) Nancy had given her for the bus fares to and from the beach, as well as to buy lunch for them all before they came home. Nancy asked Jane to buy a pastie from the bakery next to the bus stop for her too. Jane also had a copy of *Little Women* with her, and three beach towels. All of this she put into a blue shoulder bag.

Nancy told them they had to be home by 12 o'clock, before the searing heat of the day really kicked in.

Just before 10 am Nancy waved the kids off, watching as they walked to the bus stop. Then she turned and went back inside, confident they would be fine.

We know the children got to the beach safely as there were several witnesses who saw them, people who knew them, including the local postman who said hello to them, and a schoolfriend of Jane's who saw all three swimming in the shallow water near Glenelg jetty, then going to play at Colley Reserve, which runs almost down to the beach next to the lifesaving club.

Jane's schoolfriend wasn't the only person to see the children playing at Colley Reserve. A 74-year-old local woman also saw them, but they weren't alone. They were playing with a man she described as a tanned 'surfie' type with wavy blond hair, athletic build, about 6 feet tall, and between 30–40 years old. He had a longish face with a high forehead. They were all still playing in a group when the woman left just before midday, when the children should have been heading home.

A little later an older couple who were sitting nearby with their teenage granddaughter spoke to the man. He approached them and asked if they had seen anyone touching 'their' things, as some money had gone missing. It is certain this man was with the Beaumont children because the woman was able to describe in detail what the children were wearing, as well as the blue bag Jane was carrying. The man was then seen helping all three children to get dressed – especially strange in Jane's case as she was nine years old and always dressed herself – and leaving the area.

As it was now gone 12, the children had missed their bus home. Anyway, they had no money for the fare because according to the mystery man it had been stolen. Later, people surmised that the man took the money himself, and speaking to the couple was a ruse to convince the children he was trying to help them. By taking their money he could step into the breach as their saviour, gaining both their trust and compliance.

The next sighting of the children was in Wenzel's Cakes, where they bought lunch. And they did this with a one-pound note (the Australian pound was replaced by the Australian dollar a couple of weeks later on 14 February 1966).

Where did they get this money? Even more importantly, the salesgirl remembers Jane saying that she was also buying 'a pie for the man'. No name, just 'the man'. The man Jane refers to must surely be the one seen playing with the children at the beach. The children were known in the bakery, as they regularly bought food there, but this particular day stood out precisely because of that one-pound note, which would be the equivalent of around $28 today, so a considerable sum of money for three young children to have. And not the money Nancy Beaumont had given them that morning.

Then the children left the bakery. And disappeared.

Just before midday, Nancy was expecting the children home. She'd been out at a friend's house but made sure she was home in time to welcome them off the 12 o'clock bus. But that bus came and went and the children weren't on it. She wasn't too worried, assuming they'd lost track of time at the beach, missed that bus and would catch the next one at 2 pm.

Again, the bus at 2 o'clock came and the children didn't get off. Now Nancy began to panic. She thought of going out to look for them, but if they'd walked home, they could have taken several routes, and she didn't want to miss them. So she waited for the 3 o'clock bus.

Nancy was already worried – what if something had happened to one of them at the beach, an accident? But if that were the case, she would have been contacted by now as one of the other two would have raised the alarm. Also, the beach and foreshore was packed; if the children were in trouble, surely someone would have helped them and again got in touch with her. She didn't have a phone at the house, but Glenelg Police Station was less than 100 metres from Colley Reserve, so if something terrible had happened the police would have come to tell her.

All these thoughts were whirling around in Nancy's head when Jim came home from work unexpectedly. He wasn't due back until Thursday, but the clients he had been visiting in Snowtown were away on holiday. Nancy told her husband that the children had failed to arrive home, and he went straight down to the beach to look for them. He didn't see a sign of his children, although he later commented that it was so packed that even if they had still been there he could have missed them.

Jim went home, hoping the kids would have gone back since he'd been out searching. They hadn't. So he and Nancy went out again, looking up and down the coast, but they couldn't find them. Just before 6 o'clock that evening, around six hours since they were last seen, the Beaumonts went to the police station and reported all three children missing.

There were two officers on duty at Glenelg Police Station, one of whom was Detective Constable Mostyn Matters. He took the original missing persons report and remembers how upset the Beaumont parents were that day. Full descriptions were taken of what the three siblings looked like, what they were wearing and the personal items they had with them, and then Mostyn called through to the main station in Adelaide, as Glenelg simply didn't have the resources to mount a large search unaided.

The police response was quick, although initially they thought they were looking for lost children or siblings who had run away. So they went through the usual motions, searching the house thoroughly to make sure they weren't hiding and ascertaining whether the children had taken anything else (such as extra clothes, food or money) with them.

The 10 pm radio and television programs were interrupted with the news that three young children had gone missing from Glenelg Beach. The police search continued all night, with worried neighbours and strangers joining in as the news spread throughout the community.

Thousands of people were still at the beach, trying to get some respite from the impossibly warm evening, so it was hard to search the area for three small children. But equally, if they had got into trouble in the water, or somewhere close to the beach, with that many potential witnesses, surely someone would have seen something?

At sunrise the next morning five boats from the Sea Rescue Squadron joined the search, checking a large expanse of ocean in case the children had been washed out to sea. Other police looked on land, checking caves, hollows and anywhere else three small children could be hiding, sheltering or have got stuck. Stormwater drains that opened onto the sea were also searched, but there was no sign of any of the children anywhere.

They weren't out at sea, they weren't on the beach. It was as if they had literally vanished.

By this point Jim Beaumont knew something was very wrong, as he believed his children would have come home if they were able to. The day after they disappeared, he gave an emotional press conference, saying that someone must be holding them against their will. Sadly, it seems he was right.

WHAT HAPPENED TO THE BEAUMONT CHILDREN?

There are only really three possibilities to explain the disappearance of the Beaumont children: 1) they suffered an accident at the beach or within close proximity to it; 2) they ran away; or 3) they were abducted. If we look at each in turn, we can narrow down the likely events of the day.

AN ACCIDENT

The police and local volunteers combed every ditch, shallow depression, sandhill and every other place the children could have accidentally ended up – either by hiding or having been injured or washed there by the sea. Alongside the land search was a thorough search of the ocean. No sign was found. Not only had the children disappeared, but so had their belongings.

People suggested that they could have been washed out to sea and their bodies never recovered. On the face of it, that is possible. However, a number of factors argue against it. Firstly, whilst Jane was a good swimmer, neither Arnna nor Grant could swim, and Jane would never have let them go out of their depth. Even if she had, or one or all of them had got into trouble in the water, perhaps been caught in a rip, there were so many other people on the beach and in the ocean, it is impossible that no one would have seen them. It also defies logic that all three children from one family would get taken out to sea by a rip, as no one else reported any problems with the currents that day. Even if we accept they were taken out to sea, their belongings should have been found on the beach where they would have left them. They weren't, so wherever the children went, they took their clothes and bag with them. And to discount the 'lost at sea' theory further, the children were seen alive and well at the bakery where they bought lunch and paid with that one-pound note, and that was *after* they left the beach and were, presumably, intending to head home.

THEY RAN AWAY

The police interviewed the Beaumonts and searched the house thoroughly, and the children left no evidence that they planned to run away. Jane was a sensible girl, and although she was only nine years old, she would have known that they would have needed extra clothes (especially as Grant wasn't even wearing a T-shirt when he left home), and money, and she would have packed snacks. Nothing was found to have been taken. The police also canvassed Nancy and Jim's adult friends, as well as Jane's schoolfriends, and no one knew of any reason the children would want to run away. Commonly children report running away to escape family conflict, violence or abuse, but no one reported seeing any evidence of this in the Beaumont home. Their family life was stable and the children happy.

Research on modern missing persons data (which includes information on those who leave home intentionally, such as runaways) shows that around 38,000 Australians are reported missing each year, around half of whom are young people (under 18 years old), whilst 0–12-year-olds account for only 8% of the total.

Data from the Australian Federal Police suggests that in 2015 98% of the 40,580 people reported missing that year were found alive, less than 1% were found dead and under 2% had not been located by the end of the year. Furthermore, around 65% of reports are resolved in less than 48 hours, and another 20% within a week of the report being made.

Someone is considered 'long-term' missing when their case lasts longer than three months. The Beaumont children have been missing over 50 years, and there is no evidence to support the hypothesis that they intentionally ran away from home, so we can discount that possibility too.

THEY WERE ABDUCTED

Now we get to the more sinister category: 'abduction'. There are a number of different types of child abduction that we need to consider: familial, acquaintance, and stranger. In Australia, half of all annual kidnapping/abduction investigations (comprising around 250–300 victims) are finalised by police within 30 days. This includes all categories.

The most common type of familial abduction is non-custodial parental, where one parent takes a child from the custody of the other equalling around 50% of all cases. Normally this happens following family break-ups, such as divorce proceedings, and women are more often the perpetrators than men. Children under six years of age are the most likely to be taken, and the site of abduction is often the family home. Victims of this type of abduction are unlikely to be harmed. In the Beaumont case there was no suggestion that either parent was involved – there was no marriage break-up on the cards or custody dispute looming. Nor was there any evidence to suggest another close relative would have taken the children, so a familial abduction can be discounted.

Acquaintance child abduction accounts for around a quarter of all cases. Juvenile perpetrators are the most common in this category, and the victims are often teenagers. This type of abduction usually takes place from homes or other residences, and is often associated with other crimes such as sexual assault. Victims in this category are injured more than any other. Included in this group are children kidnapped by extended family, as well as teachers, neighbours, scout leaders or anyone else the children might know, even superficially.

The remaining quarter of abducted children are taken by strangers. A common tactic is to lure the child into a car or house, usually with the promise of money, sweets or to see puppies or kittens – anything that might appeal to a young person.

On average across all categories, only about 1 child in every 10,000 reported to police as missing is not found alive; however, this number increases to around 20 in every 100 in the acquaintance and stranger abduction classifications. Sadly, the statistics show that of the abducted children that are murdered, around 75% are killed within three hours of being taken.

As we have discounted familial abduction in the Beaumont case, we are left with the last two categories: acquaintance and stranger. To determine which of the two is most likely to explain the children's disappearance, all we have to go on is the fact that the children were seen with a man they appeared to trust, and whom they were happy to go with. There is the possibility that he had met them before, but the children didn't say anything to their parents about intending to meet someone at the beach, so he would have been relying on luck to see them again. Nor had they mentioned to anyone interviewed by police that a man had previously befriended them, so acquaintance abduction seems unlikely, but we can't rule it out.

What appears most probable is that this predator was very skilled at getting children onside, perhaps by coming to their aid when their money was 'stolen'. Maybe this was enough to convince them to go with him. He could have coerced them with the money for lunch and then offered them a lift home. It fits the evidence of them simply disappearing, because if he had tried to forcibly abduct three children, someone would have seen or heard their cries for help.

Because we don't know if the offender was an acquaintance or a stranger, we can't establish if the children were specifically targeted that day because he had seen them before and possibly already begun to groom them, or if they were chosen at random as a result of their vulnerability; what we would call an opportunistic crime. My personal opinion is that this was a stranger attack, so whilst the man was likely on the hunt for one (or more) victims, he was random in his selection of victims.

Stranger or acquaintance, the result was the same; a man was seen with the children, they left the beach with him, and then they disappeared without trace and were never seen alive again.

SO WHO TOOK THEM?
BEVAN VON EINEM

Several people have been suspected of involvement in the Beaumont children's abduction over the years, notably Bevan von Einem, a child sex offender who raped and murdered 15-year-old Richard Kelvin. Around 6 pm on 5 June 1983, von Einem, along with other offenders who have not been caught, snatched Richard off a North Adelaide street, just 60 metres from his home. Witnesses heard Richard's cries for help, as well as car doors slamming and a car taking off at speed. Von Einem held Richard for five weeks, during which time the boy was given hypnotic drugs, tortured and raped. Finally he was murdered and his body left at an airstrip in the Adelaide Hills.

The police initially had few clues as to who could have kidnapped and murdered Richard; all they really had to go on were the hypnotic drugs in his system – Mandrax and Noctec – which would have required a prescription.

It was very easy to obtain Mandrax in Australia in the late 1970s and early 1980s, and the police started reviewing all prescriptions issued for these drugs. Von Einem's name came up. It stood out as he had been questioned previously over the deaths of three young men and the alleged sexual assault of a fourth. Von Einem's home was searched, during which the police found a bottle of Mandrax and a bottle of Noctec hidden in his wardrobe. Surprisingly, von Einem allowed the police to take samples of his blood and hair, as well as fibres from carpets in his home. A forensic comparison showed that 250 of the 925 fibres found on Richard's clothing matched those taken from carpets in von Einem's home (only 7 matched Richard's home). Von Einem was charged on 3 November 1983, and although he pleaded not guilty, he was convicted and sentenced to life with a minimum period of 36 years without parole.

The police thought that von Einem may be responsible for the murder of four other young men between 1979 and 1982: Alan Barnes, Neil Muir, Peter Stogneff and Mark Langley. In 1988 the State Coroner of South Australia ordered an inquest into the deaths of these four men. He stated that the circumstances and manner of death were very similar to that of Richard Kelvin. The police knew that von Einem had accomplices, and they continued to search for them. The group was dubbed 'The Family' in the media and, apart from von Einem, no other member of this tight-knit ring of male child sex offenders and murderers has been identified.

Von Einem became a person of interest in the Beaumont children's disappearance because he was known to have been active in Adelaide, and he targeted children and young people. In addition, an unnamed witness told police that von Einem had confessed to him that he had killed the Beaumont children, as well as Kirste Gordon (aged 4) and Joanne Ratcliffe (aged 11) who disappeared together from Adelaide Oval in 1973, in circumstances similar to the Beaumont abductions. The witness claimed von Einem had disposed of their bodies in Myponga Dam, south of Adelaide. Of course the dam was searched, but police divers did not find the children's bodies.

In 2007 von Einem was officially questioned as to his involvement in both sets of abductions but he refused to cooperate and he has not been charged with these offences.

A NEW SUSPECT

As with all high-profile cases of this nature, interest goes in cycles and is usually reignited when fresh evidence comes to light. That's what happened in 2006 when a woman named Angela Fyfe came forward with a compelling story after reading a book about the disappearance of the Beaumont children. Angela had been married to Haydn Phipps, son of one Harry Phipps, who died in 2004 when he was in his 80s.

Angela and Haydn had met when they were both living in Queensland in the 1990s and had remained married for 10 years, until his deteriorating physical and mental health, brought on by his growing alcohol and drug dependency, led to their divorce. During their marriage, it became clear that Haydn was a very damaged man. Haydn had grown up in Glenelg, in a house on the corner of Augusta and Sussex Streets, 300 metres from Colley Reserve and Glenelg Beach.

According to Haydn, as well as other members of the family, his father Harry had an obsession with satin. It aroused him sexually. This is known as a paraphilia, which is characterised by unusual sexual behaviours or impulses, intense sexual fantasies and urges that keep recurring. If the paraphilia causes the person distress or harm, or leads to the risk of harm to others, it is considered a paraphilic disorder.

Although Harry tried to keep his paraphilia secret, people knew not to wear satin around Harry as he became so aroused he could not control himself. Harry also got sexually aroused by dressing up in satin dresses that he made himself. This was not his only paraphilia, as Harry liked to cause pain and psychological distress in others. He was a sexual sadist. Harry acted on these impulses with awful consequences. According to Haydn, Harry would don one of his satin dresses late at night, get sexually aroused, and visit his son Haydn's room to sexually abuse him.

The only evidence we have directly from Haydn comes from an interview conducted by former South Australian detective turned private investigator, Bill Hayes, that was audio recorded shortly before Haydn's death in 2014. Bill had been tasked with investigating the children's disappearance by Stuart Mullins as part of his research for *The Satin Man*, published in 2013. Bill has maintained a strong interest in the case ever since and was a significant source of knowledge for the Channel 7 documentary about the case that aired in January 2018.

In the interview, Haydn vividly, and very disturbingly, describes hearing his father swoosh down the hall in his satin dresses on his way to Haydn's room. Haydn would hear that sound and know what it meant. Those memories haunted Haydn for the rest of his life. Of course, he could have been lying, but I have heard the recordings and, whilst Haydn was clearly very damaged as a result of the abuse he allegedly suffered at the hands of his father, I was left with the strong impression that he was telling his truth – by which I mean, he was honestly relaying experiences as he remembers them. Haydn said this abuse would happen about three or four times a week, beginning when he was around 2 years old and continuing until he was around 14.

One evening he and Angela were watching a program about the missing Beaumont children. Out of the blue he announced that he had always believed his father had had something to do with the Beaumonts' disappearance. At first Angela didn't think Haydn could be serious. Clearly Harry had caused Haydn a significant amount of psychological trauma, which he was still struggling to deal with over 30 years later, but surely it was a leap to think that Harry Phipps kidnapped the Beaumont children.

But Haydn was serious. Haydn even thought he knew where the children were buried. He said, 'They're in the pit.'

One reason Haydn thought his father could be involved in the

Beaumonts' disappearance was the fact that they paid for their lunch with a one-pound note. Phipps was known to carry wads of one-pound notes around with him. He would give one to Haydn and his friends on a Saturday, telling them to go and spend it at the side-shows. As we have seen, one pound was a lot of money in 1966, so it would last them all day. Which was what Phipps wanted. His wife, Haydn's mother, would be out at the tennis club all day, and, according to Haydn, Harry wanted the house to himself so that he could dress in his satin and act out his fantasies without interruption. Several of Haydn's friends have confirmed Harry used to give them one-pound notes on Saturdays. Of course they had no idea why he wanted them out of the house.

There was one final piece of evidence that convinced Haydn that his dad had harmed the Beaumonts: he claimed he saw them the day they went missing. At around 12.00–12.30 pm Haydn was in the garden playing when he saw his father come through the back gate with three children. They talked for a few minutes, too far away for Haydn to hear what they were saying, before Harry and the three kids went into the house. Haydn did not see the children again.

WHO WAS HARRY PHIPPS?

Harry Phipps was a man of influence. Wealthy, charismatic, well connected. Not the bogeyman the police had been looking for.

Phipps was a millionaire businessman who lived in Glenelg, just 300 metres from the beach and about the same from Wenzel's Cakes, the bakery where the Beaumonts were last seen alive.

In his younger days Phipps was blond-haired and athletic. He was around six feet tall, with a narrow face and high forehead. He would have been 48-years-old in 1966, which is slightly older than the man described by the witnesses as playing with the Beaumont children at Glenelg Beach, but Phipps fit the general description and was known to look after himself, so he may have appeared younger than his real age. When you look at the police sketch done in 1966 from eyewitness accounts of the man seen playing with the children, and compare this to Harry Phipps, the similarities are startling (figures 1 and 2).

The question remained, did Harry Phipps really have the personality type to commit these crimes? From the evidence presented by Haydn, it appears Phipps was highly controlling, was a sexual deviant and enjoyed causing harm to others. Haydn claimed his father was also violent to his mother, beating her at times. But Harry was never questioned about the Beaumonts' disappearance, he was never a suspect, and he had died by the time Haydn came forward.

Other people have been interviewed about Phipps's personality, and they say he was very charismatic, charming and highly influential. He also liked to be in control, liked everyone to recognise his importance and wealth, and enjoyed his high status around Glenelg.

Figure 1: The 1966 police sketch of the Beaumont suspect (© South Australia Police).

Figure 2: A young Harry Phipps.

I've stood on the corner of the street outside of the old Phipps's home. Straight in front is the beach, just out of sight, and to the left Wenzel's Cakes. I was struck by the geography of it, it is all so close together. I could easily imagine how it could have been done. After meeting and grooming the kids at the beach, he got them to go to the bakery to buy lunch, and Phipps tells them he can drive them home, they just have to walk the short distance to his house to get his car. The kids would follow him, up the back lane (which is very quiet), in the back gate into the garden, where Haydn sees them before they go into the house.

Once in the house, the children are at Phipps's mercy.

A short time afterwards, Haydn went into the house to see what was going on. The front door was open, but there was no one in the house. He assumed his father and the kids had gone out the front door, and thought no more of it.

Perhaps one of the children was his primary target; perhaps it was the thrill of taking all three. Either way, it is likely the offender would have killed two of the children quickly, as three would be hard to control. Jane would have done anything to protect her younger siblings, so it seems likely she would have been killed early on. From what Haydn said about his father, it is possible Harry Phipps would have sexually assaulted one or more of the children, then killed them all so that there would be no witnesses. Then he would have had to get rid of the bodies somewhere where they wouldn't be found. A site he could control.

There is more evidence. In 1966 two brothers, David (15) and Robin (17) Harkin, were asked to dig a hole at Phipps's Castal-loy Factory site in North Plympton. It had to be dug on the long weekend following the Beaumonts' disappearance and finished by the Sunday night. This arrangement had been made through Dave and Robin's father, who was a contractor for Harry Phipps, although their employer was not identified to them by name. They did see him, however. As they dug the hole, a man fitting Harry Phipps's description supervised them whilst sitting in his big American car. He told them where to dig and how deep.

It was made very clear to the brothers that the hole had to be two metres long by one metre wide, by two metres deep. It didn't strike the brothers at the time but it was essentially the shape and size of a grave. The man wanted straight sides, he was insistent on that. And the boys kept digging until the man was satisfied.

The man didn't speak to them unless it was to give them directions (like 'make it deeper'); otherwise he would just watch from a short distance away, drive off for a while, then return and resume his vigil.

The motivation for digging this hole in 40 ºC heat? Money. The well-dressed businessman was paying well – at least a one-pound note each, as Dave Harkin clearly remembers, good money for two days work. If it weren't for the money, the two boys would have been down the beach like everybody else.

The boys had no reason to wonder what the hole was for.

Until 2013. The brothers, now grown men, were watching a television program about the Beaumont children's disappearance. Harry Phipps was named as a suspect, and the Castalloy Factory a potential burial location because it had belonged to Phipps at the time the children vanished.

Dave Harkin recognised the site and remembered digging a hole right around the time the Beaumonts were abducted. He was also struck by how similar the photograph of Harry Phipps was to his memory of the man who watched them that day.

The hair literally stood up on Dave Harkin's neck.

He knew he needed to do something, so he reported the incident to South Australia Police.

The police took the brothers to the site and asked them to identify where they'd dug almost 50 years earlier. They did their best, but unfortunately the fence and gates onto the site, which they used to orientate themselves, had been moved in the intervening years, and this led to them choosing the wrong area. Unaware of this error, the police dug and found nothing. It later transpired that the area the police excavated didn't even belong to the Castalloy Factory site in 1966.

And for a while it seemed like the case had gone cold again.

AND THEN IN 2018 . . .

I began looking at Phipps as a suspect in 2018, when I was involved with a true crime program for Channel 7 called *The Beaumont Children: What Really Happened?* Initially I was sceptical when he was presented as a potential person of interest – so many people's names have been put forward over the years that it's hard to see the wood for the trees.

And my forensic training always leads me to begin with an assumption of innocence. In a practical sense, that means that I begin reviewing any potential suspects from the perspective that they are not involved. I am literally looking for evidence that will exclude them from the inquiry. If, once I've followed every lead, gone down every rabbit hole, I still can't exclude them, then, and only then, will I include them as a possible suspect.

After all my enquiries, I have to say that, in my opinion, Harry Phipps is the best suspect that has ever been put forward in the Beaumont case.

I'm basing this on a number of key factors. Firstly, we can't ignore the geography. We know from research into offender behaviour that predators work within comfort zones, so whoever targeted these children was either from, or at least familiar with, the area. Phipps was local, had easy access to Glenelg Beach and lived very close so he could take the children to his house easily whilst minimising the risk of being seen. He also worked for himself, keeping his own hours, and would not have been missed or had to explain any absences during the day.

EXPERT INSERT: GEOGRAPHIC PROFILING

Criminology tries to explain criminal behaviour, as well as why some perpetrators select certain victims. One aspect of this analysis is 'geographic profiling' – a technique for serial violent crimes that evaluates key locations in a connected series of crimes. Geographic profiling includes both physical and psychological elements of an offender's behaviour. Criminal behaviour and human movements are not random processes, so it is possible to develop a working model to map and predict a perpetrator's movements, something known as crime pattern theory.

Of particular interest to geographic profilers are a perpetrator's 'activity spaces'. These could be based around an offender's home or work, or a place where they engage in a particular hobby. Locations such as these are termed 'anchor points'. Within their activity spaces they may search for suitable criminal targets or victims; these are known as 'hunting grounds'. Activity spaces can be identified as those where victims are being abducted or personal effects or bodies being deposited.

In this way, geographic profiling draws links between an offender's criminal and non-criminal life, as people tend to commit crimes in areas they are most familiar with, within what are known as 'comfort zones'. The size of different offenders' comfort zones can vary very significantly, depending on an individual's upbringing, lifestyle and job history, as well as their personality as some people are simply better at adapting to new environments and are more confident than others. For example, an individual who has grown up in a remote town and has never travelled far is unlikely to develop a criminal comfort zone outside their pre-existing geographical limits. Contrast that with someone who grew up on military bases in various countries and as an adult becomes a long-distance lorry driver. They have the capacity to develop a very large comfort zone that may span areas across different countries. But that does not mean that their comfort zone is limitless. Even someone with diverse life experience and high levels of confidence will invariably commit crimes and dispose of victims close to familiar places as this provides a feeling of safety. The further away an offender feels from one of their comfort zones, the less likely they are to engage in criminal activity.

Importantly, there is also an area around an offender's home or place of work where they are more likely to avoid committing criminal activity, the 'buffer zone', as offending in this area may seem to them too risky.

Geographic profiling can help focus an investigation, manage and prioritise information, as well as suggest new strategies of policing. In essence this discipline is about understanding criminal behaviour in relation to spatial and temporal reasoning, whilst taking into consideration the significant variations that result from individual differences in psychology, comfort zones, and experience.

Colin Johnson, geographic profiler, UK

Secondly, the one-pound note. Witnesses confirm that the children had a one-pound note to buy their lunch, which their mother had not given them. Phipps was known to carry wads of one-pound notes around with him, and he gave them to children. Thirdly, the physical description of the man seen playing with the siblings at the beach before they disappeared was strikingly similar to pictures of Phipps from the time. Fourthly, according to Haydn's evidence, Phipps was a sexual sadist who predated on children.

What that list tells us, in an investigative sense, is that Phipps had means, motive and opportunity.

But where should we look for the children?

As part of the Channel 7 investigation we uncovered a rare photograph of the site, taken circa 1966. We took Dave and Robin Harkin back to the correct factory site, to see if they could use the map to orientate themselves. They could and were sure they'd identified the area they dug all those years earlier (figures 3 and 4).

GEOPHYSICAL TECHNIQUES APPLIED TO A FORENSIC INVESTIGATION

Our next challenge was to determine whether there was any evidence that a hole had been dug in the area pinpointed by the Harkin brothers and, if so, whether we could identify exactly the exact spot.

To answer this question I went to a specialist in geophysical techniques, Dr Ian Moffat, an archaeological scientist specialising in the application of geological techniques to archaeological research questions. Ian, conveniently based at Flinders University in Adelaide, had a variety of sensing equipment that could be used to image what was going on below the soil to a depth of around 10 metres. We weren't looking for the outline of bodies.

Figure 3: Map of the Castalloy site in 1966. Arrow on left shows the pit area mentioned by Haydn Phipps. Arrow on right shows the area of the 2018 dig.

Rather we were looking for an anomaly in the subsurface, something that stood out as being different from the surrounding area. The search was complicated by the site having been built up with additional soil after the 1960s, so it was necessary to image deeper and through a more complicated soil profile than is usual for most forensic investigations.

In January 2018 Ian and some of his students attended the Castalloy site and conducted two sets of tests: Ground Penetrating Radar (GPR) and Electrical Resistivity Tomography (ERT) (see page 68). Ian had a good idea which of the two techniques would be better at imaging deep enough to find any relevant anomalies, but he wanted to compare and contrast the two. To our knowledge,

Figure 4: Map of the Castalloy site in 2018. 'A' indicates main Castalloy building, arrow along Kinkaid Avenue indicates the area of the 2018 dig, and the arrow near Mooring Avenue shows the pit area mentioned by Haydn Phipps (© Google Maps).

this was the first time that ERT had been used in a forensic context, certainly within Australia. It was an exciting moment.

It took three days to scan an area 20 metres by 31 metres, and two more weeks for the data to be analysed. But by the end of January we had our answer. Ian had identified a rectangular area two metres long, by one metre wide, by two metres deep. It looked like a purposely dug hole, and to Ian it stood out as interesting (figure 5). It was directly adjacent to what looked like another, larger hole. Also of note was the fact that the holes didn't start at the surface but at a depth of about 1.5 metres, suggesting that they had been dug before the extra fill had been added to the site. Of the two, it was clear which correlated to the Harkins' testimony.

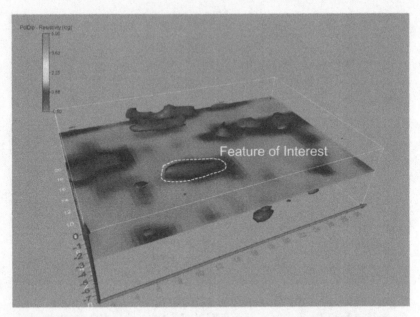

Figure 5: 3D representation of the ERT data from the Castalloy site showing the anomaly that was excavated (© Dr Ian Moffat, Flinders University).

EXPERT INSERT: GEOPHYSICAL TECHNIQUES

Electrical Resistivity Tomography (ERT) is a widely applied geophysical technique that can be used across a large number of scales, from millimetres to several hundred kilometres, depending on the research question. In that sense it can be used to survey large areas of land, and can even be used underwater. The process works by measuring how easily an electrical current passes between probes placed into the soil. Different materials are better or worse at conducting electricity and so variations in the results can be used to reconstruct what is happening under the site.

The main advantage of ERT for forensic investigations is that it can image to greater depths through sites with complicated soil profiles than other commonly used methods such as Ground Penetrating Radar (GPR). This was critical at the Castalloy site where at least 1.5 metres of soil was known to have been added to the site after the pit was dug by the Harkin brothers.

GPR is another geophysical technique, but instead of using an electrical current, it uses radar pulses to image the subsurface. The GPR antenna is often mounted in a cart which looks a lot like a lawnmower and is run over the area of interest. The radar pulses bounce off changes in the soil so these features can be mapped in 3D across the site. GPR is particularly useful because it is quick and it provides a lot of information about both the soil and any features buried within it. Unfortunately it can struggle to image below a metre or so if soil conditions are unfavourable. It has a range of uses, including by the military who use it to search for buried ordinance or hidden installations, and archaeologists who use it to search for ancient buildings or burial chambers. In an investigative context it has been used successfully to search for mass graves.

Both methods are non-destructive, in that you can image large areas without having to do any excavation or in any way disturb the subsurface, which is ideal in a forensic scenario. Neither technique is better or worse than the other; they each have their strengths and limitations.

Dr Ian Moffat, Flinders University, South Australia

'THEY'RE IN THE PIT'

I knew we'd followed the breadcrumbs. We'd found a suspect, and I'd done my best to exclude him, but I couldn't. We'd re-interviewed the Harkin brothers and confirmed through ERT that there was a hole just where they said, of the size they indicated. So far, so good.

We took our results to South Australia Police, who agreed the hole had to be investigated.

So on Friday 2 February 2018 the police undertook a full forensic recovery of the site. It only took one day, but it was extremely tense. The stress of the day was increased by the fact that it was 40 °C, just like the day the Beaumont siblings vanished.

The scene around the Castalloy site was a media circus; every news outlet was there, many with cherry pickers looking over the high fence onto the factory site and dig zone. And the public was there en masse. It was like nothing I'd ever witnessed before; people had brought chairs and packed lunches, the day had turned into an event.

And if you had watched this on the news and seen the crowds gathering, you may have been mistaken in thinking people were just being voyeuristic. But you'd be wrong. Time and time again that day people approached me to ask what was happening, and many others – mostly women – stopped me to give me a hug. It was as though the emotion of the situation was overwhelming, and people needed to reach out to one another. If I needed proof people genuinely cared about the Beaumont kids, I felt it in those hugs.

There was also a core group of people there who had committed years of their lives to this search for the Beaumont children, including Mostyn Matters, the ex-police officer who took the original missing persons report in 1966 at Glenelg Police Station. As the diggers got to work on the opposite side of the fence, Moss, now in his mid-80s, sat quietly in the shade, waiting. Also there was Bill

Hayes, former NSW detective, who has been heavily involved with the reinvestigation of the children's abduction, and Stuart Mullins, co-author of a book about Harry Phipps. Bill and Stuart are like chalk and cheese. Bill is a big, deep-voiced bear of a man, ex-military, martial artist and true gentleman. Stuart is a small, quietly spoken person. Very different men, but both feel the failure to find the Beaumont children keenly.

We all had a lot invested in the dig. We all wanted answers, and we all hoped that this would be the day we got them.

My one nagging concern was that the brothers had dug so close to the road – back in 1966 there had only been a hurricane fence, which anyone passing could have seen straight through. Although it was a quiet area, there was a chance that Phipps could have drawn attention to himself by getting the brothers to dig in such a visible spot. If he was really getting the brothers to dig a grave, why not get them to dig a hole somewhere out of sight of prying eyes? It was almost as if he wanted them to be seen. And remember, he hung around to supervise, again drawing more attention from anyone who happened to pass.

Considering how clever Phipps was, it didn't sit well with me that he would take that unnecessary risk.

Haydn's words were also playing around in my head: 'They're in the pit'. Where we were digging was rough ground, but it wasn't a pit.

There was a pit at the Castalloy site, around the back, near where an old cottage still stands (figures 3 and 4).

The excavation took all day. The police used a digger and I waited nervously for them to move to hand tools, as that would indicate that they were taking things more slowly as something of interest had been uncovered. A couple of times they paused and a forensic anthropologist (able to differentiate human from animal bones) moved something out of the hole, before the digger resumed the excavation.

By 4 pm virgin soil had been reached at the base of the anomaly Ian had identified using ERT. It was over.

The Beaumont children were not buried in the hole. All that had been recovered was some rubbish and animal bones.

People asked me if I was disappointed, knowing I had committed several months of my life building up to this moment. I wasn't sure. Part of me was disheartened, as I'd been hoping we would be able to give the family and community answers. But the other part was relieved, as until we find their bodies there is a chance (albeit a very small one) that Jane, Arnna and Grant may one day be found alive.

One thing I will always remember from that day as I was breaking the news to our small group that we hadn't found the missing Beaumont children. Bill, Stuart, Moss and I were standing on the pavement opposite the factory gates. Moss's response broke my heart. In his mid-80s and not in the best of health, he'd waited all day in the scorching heat as he needed to know once and for all what had happened to the children all those years before. He'd been there from the very start; he'd taken the original missing person report, and he still felt it was his job to see it through until the end and find them.

Without a word he simply turned and started walking slowly down the street. As he went I felt as if I was watching him physically shrink, almost as if he was being crushed by the realisation that we are unlikely to find the children in his lifetime.

THE AFTERMATH

Not surprisingly, the situation played on my mind. All weekend I wondered what we'd missed, and the more I thought about it, the more convinced I became that Phipps was involved.

Think about it. If Phipps was the man at the beach with the Beaumont siblings, he may well have been seen by someone he knew or someone who recognised him; after all, he was well known around town. He could easily explain that he was trying to help them find their money, but what if the police started looking at him more closely?

It's my belief that, being a cunning man, Phipps intentionally selected two boys to dig a hole that could be traced back to him (remember, the brothers were the sons of one of his contractors, so would not have been hard to track down). If Phipps had become a suspect and the brothers questioned, they would have told the police where they dug the hole and the police would have excavated it. Just as we did 52 years later.

Then it hit me. We had found his alibi hole.

Harry Phipps had outmanoeuvred us from the grave.

I wasn't the only one to reach this conclusion. Over the next few days I called Bill Hayes and Duncan McNab (ex-New South Wales detective, author, and television producer who was part of the team that worked on the documentary for Channel 7). Both had been obsessing about our failure to find the children and trying to figure out what we had done wrong.

And the answer was nothing. We had another piece of the puzzle, which to me strongly indicates that Harry Phipps dug that hole for a reason – as a red herring. And if he needed a red herring, he wanted to direct attention away from somewhere else.

But where? Because of Haydn's comment 'they're in the pit', some people think that the pit around the back of the site should be excavated; others think the pit in the garage at the old family home in Glenelg should be investigated. Both are certainly possible sites where Harry could have disposed of the children's bodies.

The problem is permissions. It was incredibly difficult to get permission from the site owners and the tenants to do the site search at Castalloy in 2018. After that, we had to convince the South Australian Police the intelligence was worth acting on. Whilst the police were amazing and took the dig as seriously as if the children had gone missing yesterday, it would take some very strong and specific information to convince them to dig anywhere else.

Harry Phipps died in 2004, aged 85. He was never questioned about his involvement in the Beaumont children's abduction and likely murder. And that also means he is not here to defend himself or offer evidence of his innocence. Saying all that, after everything I've learnt during our reinvestigation of the case, I consider him my number one suspect in this case.

WHAT ABOUT THE FAMILY?

After the North Plympton dig in 2018 lots of people got in touch with me, most offering tips or advice, others simply offering support. But some people were critical. The two main points were that a) we should stop looking and, as one lady put it, 'let the kids rest in peace', and b) we were retraumatising the family, raising their hopes only to dash them, and that was cruel.

To the first criticism I would say that if the children are deceased as we suspect, it is the living who cannot rest easily until the children are found and given somewhere we can go to pay our respects. We do this in honour of their memory. As for making things worse for the family, that is constantly on my mind when I'm going through these cases. However, I've spent a lot of time with the families of missing victims, and one thing they have in common is that they want to know what happened. They need a resolution, regardless of how long it has been since their loved one disappeared. The worst thing is the not knowing.

I am certain we did not make things worse for Nancy and Jim Beaumont by trying to find their children. How can I be so sure?

Well, the day we did the dig, Mr Beaumont reached out to the group from Channel 7, who had been investigating the case for over a year at this point, and thanked us for trying.

He said that he had never given up looking for his children and he hoped no one else would either.

FORENSIC SCIENCE EXPLAINED: HAIR ANALYSIS

Hair analysis has had a long association with crime scene investigation, with the microscopic study of hair being well established by the early 1900s. Hair is almost indestructible. It does melt when burnt, although healthy hair can withstand temperatures of around 230 °C or more. Hair does not decompose like soft tissue and remains available for study many years after death if a body is undisturbed. As it is hard to destroy, yet light and naturally shed, hair often transfers from victim to assailant or vice versa, or from scene to scene.

Aside from leaving a physical trail as to where someone has been and what they have been in contact with, hair also contains DNA – although the distribution and type of DNA in the hair sample varies. For example, nuclear DNA (nDNA, found inside the nucleus of the cell and containing 20,000–25,000 genes) cannot be isolated from the hair shaft as a result of the way hair forms; however, it is found in the root of the hair as well as the follicle (the sheath of connective tissues and cells that surrounds the root, which looks like a small grey–white ball at the base of the hair shaft and is visible with the naked eye). Nuclear DNA is inherited from both parents and allows identification of a person. Mitochondrial

COLD CASE INVESTIGATIONS

DNA (containing 37 genes) can be found in the hair shaft. Mitochondrial DNA (mtDNA) is passed down the female line, unchanged, to all offspring. Testing mtDNA allows an individual's maternal lineage to be traced back many generations. However, mtDNA cannot distinguish between people with the same maternal ancestor, as each copy is identical, but a person could be excluded on the basis that their mtDNA did not match a sample from a scene.

The aim in a forensic context, where resources allow, is to extract a full DNA profile as this yields the most information. Therefore, even when no root or follicle is available and only a single hair recovered, if the crime warrants it (for example in violent crimes), significant effort will be made to extract a full profile regardless of the fact that the probability of success is minimal without the root or follicle.

Hair can be analysed in a number of ways: visually, genetically, and chemically. To analyse hair visually it is normally dry-mounted on a glass slide under a microscope. A visual examination can determine whether the hair is human or animal in origin; if it's human what ancestral group the person came from, whether it fell out or was pulled, as well as the area of the body the hair came from. It is also possible to see if the hair has been dyed or otherwise treated. For DNA analysis, the hair is cut into lengths and digested in a reaction agent, after which the DNA can be extracted. For chemical analysis, the hair matrix is disintegrated into solutes in liquid form that can then be further extracted or analysed.

Hair is not only used to identify a person, but can also be used to detect drugs, if the concentration is high enough. Hair has become increasingly valuable for this purpose, and is now

77

the third most important biological material for drug testing in forensic toxicology, after blood and urine. We know that human head hair grows at around 1.25 millimetres per week. This allows hair to be analysed segmentally, which facilitates the provision of information regarding historic exposure to drugs.

An early example of hair analysis leading to a criminal conviction occurred in Melbourne in 1922. In December 1921, 12-year-old Alma Tirtschke was strangled, raped and murdered. It was around 2.30 pm and Alma had been sent on an errand. Her body was located the next day wrapped in a blanket in Gun Alley, an area of the city well known for prostitution. Cars were a rarity in Melbourne in the 1920s so the police hypothesised that the offender had to be local. Several witnesses who had seen the child were found, including Colin Ross, the owner of a local bar. A number of police interviews with prostitutes from the area were conducted, and the police identified Ross as a suspect, although no one actually saw Ross and Alma together. The police, however, were sure they had their man – especially as Ross had previously stated that he had a predilection for young girls. The police searched Ross's house and found long red hairs on a blanket. These were identified by new experts in the field to be human and, moreover, to match the colour and length of the victim's hair. Ross confessed to two people that he had killed Alma, although he said her death was unintentional, but he was charged with murder. At trial, the defence challenged the hair analysis evidence, but the expert was able to identify several hair samples by way of demonstration. This was enough to convince a jury the evidence was reliable and that there was indeed a link between Ross and Alma, and therefore the murder. Ross was found guilty and was sentenced to death and hanged at Old Melbourne Goal in April 1922. However, recent forensic analysis of the hair found on the blanket has shown that it was misidentified, and that Ross was almost certainly innocent. In May 2008 Ross was pardoned posthumously, 86 years after he died.

THREE

ASHLEY COULSTON - THE KILLER WITH A FLAIR FOR THEATRICS

Most of us have been there – either we've posted an advertisement for a housemate or we've answered one. Sometimes we vaguely know the person we are considering living with, other times they will be complete strangers. And we open our homes to these people, let them sleep in the bedroom next to ours, without thinking twice.

In 1992 two young women placed an advert in the local paper for a housemate. Several people probably answered the ad. The girls would have met the prospective housemates, had a chat, tried to sound them out to see if they felt they could live with them. They'd have offered them tea or coffee, sat on the sofa and, as with all strangers trying to see if they get on, made small talk, trying to find interests in common to begin to build rapport.

This scenario is one we can all relate to. It's predictable and unexceptional.

Never in their wildest nightmares would these young women have imagined that one of the strangers they invited into their home would be a violent predator, that a man would see their advert and plan to kill them, taking his murder bag with him to fulfil a violent fantasy. But that's what happened, and we still don't know why.

And to think this was just bad luck. One simple, innocent act sealed the fates of these young people, and there was nothing they could have done to avoid becoming targets.

THE CASE

A murderer with no motive. That is the hardest to catch.

But Ashley Coulston, triple murderer and serial rapist, was caught. Maybe because of his bravado. Or stupidity. Or laziness. For whatever reason, in 1992, five weeks after brutally murdering three young people in Victoria for no reason that has ever been determined, Coulston used the same shotgun in a brazen attempt to abduct two other people, right outside the National Gallery of Victoria, on Melbourne's busy St Kilda Road. He was caught that night, but more through luck than anything else. Until his arrest, the police had no clues as to whom they were hunting for the triple homicide five weeks previously.

But how did quiet, small-town boy Ashley Coulston go from living on a dairy farm to being a triple murderer? Not in one fell swoop, that's for sure.

We know about some of Coulston's violent crimes. I'm re-examining Coulston because there are gaps in his criminal history, which makes me wonder how many cold cases he might be responsible for. Coulston certainly isn't telling.

It all began in 1971 when Coulston was just 14 years old and he audaciously abducted two adult teachers at gunpoint in his own home town of a few hundred people. It ended in 1992 when he was caught. But how do we explain the gap in his criminal history in the middle. Where was he, and what was he doing between 1971 and 1992? What crimes took place around him, and could he be responsible for any of them?

I'm going to call on two different disciplines to help unpick this case. The first is geographic profiling, which was introduced in chapter two. As you'll remember, this is a criminal investigative technique that evaluates key locations of a connected series of serial and violent crimes. The second technique we will apply is criminal profiling, an investigative tool that combines the behavioural sciences of psychology and criminology, as well as crime scene analysis, to identify likely suspects in a crime (see Criminal Profiling, on page 97). Together these disciplines will assist us to determine which, if any, cold cases Coulston could be responsible for, by looking at where he committed crimes and whether any cold cases fall within his comfort zones, as well as the victims he chose and how he went about perpetrating his crimes.

We will also consider Coulston's psychological profile. Do some of the cold cases fit a pattern of criminal escalation? Coulston's first crime, the abductions, was showy, brazen, bold. This is a trend we see repeated throughout his known criminal career and may help narrow down the cold case list.

BORN BAD

Born on 10 October 1956, Ashley Mervyn Coulston was a country boy who grew up on a dairy farm in Tangambalanga, a small, quiet town in northeast Victoria. There is no evidence that his home life was anything other than ordinary. There were no claims of abusive parents or maltreatment at the hands of a teacher or priest.

Coulston is one of four siblings; the others are all without murderous proclivities, but the warning signs were there with Coulston from an early age. One of the indicators that someone may go on to have violent tendencies in adulthood is harming animals, and as a child Coulston enjoyed torturing animals. Worse still, he fantasised about harming people, specifically taking victims to small dark rooms. We suspect Coulston had violent imaginings about what he would do if he managed to get these victims into dark and confined spaces. Criminologically, we would call this 'violent ideation' or, if taken to the extreme, 'homicidal ideation', a term for thoughts or fantasies about murder that range from vague ideas through to fully planning the actual crime but stopping short of going through with it.

Case history has shown us that violent fantasies shouldn't necessarily ring alarm bells, as they may simply fulfil a psychological function whereby the fantasist is substituting violent thoughts for violent behaviour and never plans to harm anyone.

However, a minority of people who have violent fantasies act them out. Coulston is one of those people. This was in the days before true crime programs and books, so Coulston wasn't inspired by real life events. What he did came from his own imagination.

Coulston also had problems at school. Old schoolfriends reported that Coulston struggled to read and write, and that he may have been dyslexic, but it is doubtful he was formally diagnosed as such, as in the 1960s and 1970s, when Coulston was at school, little was known about the condition. As a result of his difficulties, Coulston could only find acceptance in the company of much younger children.

Now we know far more about the problems those with dyslexia have with language and words, and the subsequent frustration that can result from learning in different ways to other people. Coulston certainly expressed his frustration in the classroom. Tony Shelper, Coulston's former teacher, told the *Herald Sun* in 1995 that

Coulston struggled to cope at school, and that sometimes his anger would boil over in explosive outbursts, expressed by him ripping his shirt off in class or smashing up rulers and pencils.

Coulston's behaviour outside school also deteriorated, and by the time he was 13 he had started breaking into local buildings, was involved in low-level theft, and he was suspected of setting small fires on his family's dairy farm. Together with torturing animals, fire-starting can be another signal that a person may be suffering from psychopathic personality disorder, and may hint at problems to come.

In April 1971, the inconspicuous Coulston began to show his true colours, in what was a bold and sensational crime, especially for a young and inexperienced boy. He started stalking two primary school teachers from his home town, 20-year-old Halinka Wilson and 21-year-old Carol Scott. After two weeks of his covert activity he was ready to pounce. One Sunday evening, armed with a .22 calibre shotgun, Coulston entered the flat the young women shared and abducted them at gunpoint. He then made them drive across the New South Wales border towards Sydney. At 5 am the next day, and having travelled over 200 kilometres, the women saw a chance of escape and talked Coulston into stopping for supplies at a roadside café in Gundagai. The women raised the alarm and Coulston was arrested.

Interestingly, one of the women would later say, 'Even when he put the gun to the back of my head, it was never as frightening as when he first turned up. *He just seemed so ordinary after that* [my emphasis]'.

This act was premeditated but poorly planned. The crime of a boy yet to hone his skills. But the intent was there, as was the showmanship as there was nothing shy about this offence. What interests me particularly about this attack is that research suggests it's natural and common for boys to start sexually fantasising in their teens, yet few have the courage to act their fantasies out. This sets Coulston apart as a very confident offender from a young age. Even if I didn't know about his later history, this situation would have rung serious alarm bells for me.

Coulston's case was heard before the children's court. He received a three-month sentence in a Melbourne boys' home. We can get an insight into Coulston's mind from this period of incarceration, because whilst there he shared his fantasies with another inmate about what he would do when he got out – his plans to abduct women, to take them to a cave, and to rape them. It appeared the abduction of the two teachers was his first foray into making his fantasies a reality.

THE APPLICANT FROM HELL

Fast forward just over 20 years to 1992. It's 8.30 pm on a cold Melbourne evening, and students Kerryn Henstridge and Anne Smerdon were waiting to meet a stranger who had applied to an advert they'd placed in the *Herald Sun* newspaper for a housemate. With them is Peter Dempsey, Anne's 27-year-old brother-in-law, who was staying at the flat that night as he was in town on a training course.

Coulston appears to have selected the victims randomly as a result of the tenancy advert. Leaving his home at Westernport Marina, Hastings, where he lived on his de facto wife's yacht, he drove over 60 kilometres to Melbourne. He had his 'kill kit' in a bag: long cream cable ties, his .22 calibre sawn-off shotgun and ammunition, as well as a home-made silencer crafted from an old oil filter.

Gaining entry to the flat at 14 Summit Road, Burwood, was no problem. Coulston had called ahead and arranged the viewing. Peter's presence would have been a surprise, but armed with a shotgun Coulston managed to control all three victims, using the cable ties to bind his victims and also gagging them. Anyway, he may have been expecting three people because there was a third regular tenant, a man in his 20s, but he was away visiting his family. A lucky escape for him, but sadly not for Peter.

In a further act of cruelty, it was Kerryn's mother who found the victims. She went around to the house the next day, and when she couldn't get an answer to her knocks she became concerned and broke in. The sight that greeted her would have been unimaginable. Amongst the signs of domestic normality – the dirty dishes were still in the sink from the previous night's dinner, the iron and ironing board were out, the TV and lights were still on – was a scene of carnage.

Coulston had made the victims move into three separate rooms, placed a towel or other cloth over their head and then shot each one in the back of the head at close range, execution style. Kerryn's mother found her daughter dead in the bedroom with a towel over her head. Anne was in the hallway naked from the waist down with a white dressing gown over her head; her hands had been bound with three plastic ties and there were two more around her neck. Peter was found dead in the lounge, lying face down with his hands tied behind his back and a blue dressing gown draped across the top of his head, partly covering it. He too had a plastic tie around his neck.

This was a scene no one, let alone the mother of one of the victims, should ever have to see.

From the evidence at the scene it was obvious that this was not Coulston's first crime. Not the work of an amateur.

Coulston knew how to handle multiple victims and appears to have been 'forensically aware', meaning he considered what evidence might be collected by the police and took steps to minimise the signs of his presence. The only items left behind were the three bullets fired into the head of each victim and the cable ties used to secure them.

The crime appeared motiveless. Around $200 was stolen, but other items of value were left, so robbery was ruled out. The victims weren't sexually assaulted, and none of them had any links to illicit or criminal activity.

The selection of victims was random, but the murders were premeditated and well planned, and executed by a cold, cruel and calculating person. There was no emotion evident in the crime scene. No overkill. The single shot to the head spoke of a detachment unusual in murders committed for the offender's gratification.

The media went crazy, fuelled by the fact that the police had turned to the press in the search for leads. Stories ran on an almost daily basis. And the public were horrified that such a brutal and motiveless crime could happen in quiet and unassuming Burwood. A wave of fear swept the neighbourhood – how could three young people be brutally executed without cause? It didn't make any sense.

The police established a base outside the Burwood flat in an attempt to gain more information, and the devastated families of the victims made heart-breaking pleas for help from the public.

The police worked every angle but were baffled. No credible suspects were identified and the case went cold.

Coulston was not an extrovert, being described by those who knew him as shy, quiet, calm. But there is a certain showman-like quality about his crimes. He might not have wanted the spotlight on him, but that the country's press and public were focused on something he'd done would have been exhilarating for him.

A BRAZEN MISTAKE

Coulston had got away with three murders and the police were no closer to tracking him down. Perhaps revelling in the excitement and emboldened by the feelings of power, nearly five weeks later Coulston, the introverted egotist, went hunting again.

On 1 September 1992 Coulston made the same trip from Hastings to Melbourne, this time choosing a more brazen and less private place to attack.

Around 8.45 pm a young married couple, Anne and Richard Shalagin, were getting into their car, which was parked on Government House Drive, off busy St Kilda Road. Before they could drive off, a man wearing a balaclava stepped out of the shadows, appearing suddenly at the passenger window. Silently he knelt by the side of the car and pointed a sawn-off .22 calibre shotgun at them through the window. He didn't say a word. The couple assumed the motive was robbery, so they thrust a few $50 notes at him, hoping he would take the money and leave. They were wrong, and whilst he did pocket the cash, that was not his prime incentive.

Instead of leaving, the attacker forced the couple from their car and motioned for them to move towards a darker part of the Botanic Gardens, to an area in shadow under a large tree. He told Anne to lie face-down on the ground. He reached for his bag and took out a long cream cable tie to bind her hands. To do this he had to put the gun down. In that moment Richard Shalagin knew that if he didn't do something they were going to die. He launched himself at their assailant, grabbing him from behind around the neck, snatching at the gun as he did so and throwing it a metre or two away. He shouted at Anne to run. Anne did run, into St Kilda Road. Richard saw her go and took his chance, throwing his attacker aside and making a break for it, running for his life after his wife.

Two security guards, Paul Sycam and Graeme Loader, heard the couple's screams for help and called the police. Clearly still terrified, the couple briefly told the guards what had happened, and the silhouette of a man in the shadows of the trees was still visible.

He was the only person in the park. The security officers approached the balaclava-clad attacker, who pulled a knife before picking up the discarded gun, taking a crouching stance and shooting at the guards seven times. Although he fired directly at the guards, because the barrel of the shotgun had been shortened, the gun was not firing in a straight line, meaning the bullets were spiralling off to the left. But one bullet did find a mark, hitting Sycam in the hip.

Coulston now attempted to run from the scene, desperately seeking an escape route. He attempted a car-jacking at gunpoint but failed, then kept running. Despite his injury, Sycam chased the shooter. A police officer arrived and Coulston stood his ground, pointing the sawn-off straight at her. Sycam knew that Coulston was willing to kill, so he charged at him, tackling him from behind and forcing him to the ground.

Paul Sycam would later say in an interview that the look in Coulston's eyes was 'the most evil and sinister look I've ever seen' and that 'he was there to kill people'. He was right. Coulston had taken his kill kit with him that evening, containing the same accessories as those recovered from the Burwood murder scene: the sawn-off .22 calibre shotgun and high-velocity cartridges, the home-made silencer, and cream cable ties. In his kill kit the police also found handcuffs and thumb-cuffs, a knife, gloves, a balaclava, and a pack of ten condoms.

That Coulston wore a balaclava and took additional items like handcuffs gives us some insight into how he was able to control and dominate his three adult victims in his earlier murderous attack.

It was the recovery of the shotgun that led to Coulston being named as the man responsible for the triple murder in Burwood. Two different forensic techniques tied the gun to the execution of the three young people almost five weeks earlier. Firstly, a ballistics expert confirmed the gun in Coulston's possession the night he attacked the Shalagins had fired at least two of the shots that killed the Burwood victims (the third bullet was too badly damaged to undertake a comparison). Secondly, blood recovered from the gun's makeshift silencer was matched to that on the dressing gown that had been put over Anne Smerdon's head, and the blood spatter pattern on both was consistent with a weapon being fired at close range. The absence of gunshot residue on the dressing gown was consistent with a silencer having been used.

If Coulston had used a different weapon he could not have been linked to the Burwood homicides.

Was Coulston too bold and sure he would not be caught? Is that why he made the critical error that led to his being arrested? I am inclined to think so, as again there is an air of the showmanship about this brazen assault. St Kilda Road is busy, there would have been lots of people around, making the crime even riskier – but the thrill bigger.

Now the police were sure they had their man for the Burwood killings, but they were no closer to understanding why he did it, as in the initial interview Coulston refused to answer all of the police's questions. A couple of days later, on 4 September 1992, Coulston was willing to go on record with regards to one issue – the gun – attempting to deflect suspicion onto a man named Rod Davis, who allegedly had asked Coulston if he could borrow the gun the week before the Burwood murders and requested he shorten the barrel. In court, Davis would later give evidence that he did not know Coulston, and had in fact been in New Zealand when the Burwood killings took place.

Coulston accepted his part in the attack on the Shalagins. How could he not, he was caught at the scene wearing a balaclava and carrying the gun and cable ties. So he decided to offer some explanation as to his actions, in an attempt to convince the police he did not intend to murder the Shalagins. During the police interviews he admitted to buying the gun in Devonport, Tasmania, as he was afraid of sharks (he spent a lot of time on boats). He also said that the barrel had been shortened 'sometime in the middle of last month' (meaning August 1992). Coulston went on to describe how he had fashioned the silencer for the shotgun from an old oil filter and altered the barrel of the rifle to accommodate the addition. In terms of the cable ties used at both crime scenes, he said he had bought them anything up to a year before and used them on boats. He said he had come to Melbourne the evening the Shalagins were assaulted to visit his de facto wife, Jan McLeod, who worked at the National Gallery on St Kilda Road, and brought the gun and other items because he hoped to find someone to rob.

He was therefore claiming that whilst his motivations were hardly legal and could not be argued to be nonviolent, he would rather be thought of as a mugger than a murderer. However, had this been the case, when the Shalagins threw cash at him he would simply have taken the money and left, or possibly asked them to hand over any other valuables. But he didn't. He forced them at gunpoint from their car and proceeded to try to tie them up. His lies weren't stacking up.

He kept trying though. Coulston offered an alibi for the time of the Burwood murders. He said he was visiting Jan McLeod in Frankston Hospital (a 40–50 minute drive from Summit Road where the murders took place) where she was recuperating from surgery. McLeod confirmed this story, saying Coulston was with her between 8.00 pm and 9.15 pm on 29 July, the window of time during which the Burwood three were shot.

This alibi was not accepted by the police, or indeed the court, and it remained a mystery at the time of Coulston's trial as to why a man who seemed generally socially well adjusted – he could function on a day-to-day basis and was in a stable relationship with McLeod – would commit such random acts of brutality.

Regardless that there was a lack of motive offered by the prosecution, in January 1993 the strength of the case against Coulston was assessed during an eight-day committal hearing at the Melbourne Magistrate's Court. The court heard of the stalking and abduction of the two young teachers in 1971, as well as an incident of stalking a woman he worked with. The case against Coulston was considered strong enough to continue to trial, and Coulston was put on trial for murder at Victoria's Supreme Court in front of Justice Bernard Teague.

The criminal trial began in August 1993 and ran for almost four weeks. Coulston, now 36, stood charged with the Burwood triple murders as well as 11 other charges relating to the assault on St Kilda Road, including the attempted murder of the security guards and armed robbery of the Shalagins. Jan McLeod maintained her support of Coulston, repeating her evidence that he could not have committed the murders as he was with her at the hospital until after 9 pm. The prosecution accepted that Coulston had visited McLeod that evening, but alleged that Coulston had left earlier than she stated, giving Coulston time to get back to the marina where he picked up his kill kit, and continued on to Burwood.

There was also more evidence linking Coulston to the Summit Road murders. Found at Coulston's house was a street directory, and on the page that covered Summit Road was a fingerprint, marking the location of the address. And he had opportunity, as Coulston was seen back at the marina by witnesses, but not until around 10.30 pm that night giving him time to drive back after the murders in Melbourne.

The case against Coulston was compelling, and at trial in 1993 he was found guilty of three counts of murder and two of false imprisonment. He was acquitted of the two attempted murder charges and found guilty of the alternative charges of reckless conduct endangering life. Ultimately he was also found guilty of two counts of armed robbery, one of assault, one of intentionally causing injury and one of using a firearm to resist arrest. At sentencing he was given three life sentences, with a minimum of 30 years without parole.

Coulston is nothing if not persistent. Two years later, in 1995, he was granted a retrial and the three murder charges were quashed on appeal on the grounds that a joint trial for both the Burwood murders and St Kilda Road attacks risked prejudice to the defendant. It was considered that this could have led to a miscarriage of justice, and the Supreme Court determined that some of the evidence heard during the original trial regarding the assault on the Shalagins was inadmissible, and that the suggestion there were similarities between the two crimes 'might well have been beguiling to the jury'. A retrial was subsequently allowed. The Supreme Court set a two-year minimum sentence for the St Kilda Road charges and said Coulston should have been granted a separate trial on these charges to avoid prejudice against him. They also set aside the three murder convictions and ordered a retrial.

In August and early September 1995, Coulston was tried again for the three Burwood murders in front of Justice Norman O'Bryan. This time the defence took aim at the main evidence linking Coulston to the deaths – the gun. To undermine the Crown's case, the defence lawyers viciously attacked the credibility of Senior Constable Ray Vincent, the main prosecution witness and the ballistics expert who determined the same gun had been used at the Summit Road and St Kilda Road attacks. They went as far as to suggest that Vincent had exchanged the three bullets recovered from the deceased Burwood victims for different bullets, so that he could give evidence that the same gun was used in both incidents. This struck at the heart of the Crown's case, which accepted that if the jury had any doubts over the reliability of Vincent's evidence, they would have to acquit Coulston of the triple murders.

Sadly for the defence, but luckily for those wishing to seek justice for the victims, there was no evidence to support the hypothesis that Vincent had faked any evidence. The judge was scathing of this defence tactic and took the opportunity in open court to fully support Vincent's undoubted integrity.

The judge was also contemptuous of Coulston's continued refusal to give sworn evidence, saying, 'I infer you remained mute out of fear of self-incrimination'. Given Justice O'Bryan's clear view that Coulston was guilty of the triple murder for which he stood accused, it is no surprise – even given the separation of the charges of murder from those related to the attack on the Shalagins – that the original outcome was upheld.

More damning still was the judge's concluding remark that because of the 'wicked nature of the crimes, and the absence of remorse of any kind on your part . . . In my opinion, you have forfeited forever your entitlement to live outside the confines of a prison. I am of the opinion that you should never be released'. Coulston was then sentenced to life imprisonment without the possibility of parole. He will die in prison.

Justice O'Bryan also mentioned the impact statements prepared by the Burwood victims' families. He noted how severely the families had been traumatised, not only by the initial murders but by the two subsequent trials and appeals process. The judge offered the families his sympathies.

Coulston did not share the judge's sympathy towards his victims' families, again challenging his sentence, early in 1996, which failed, and again later that same year. Coulston then submitted a special leave to appeal against his convictions. As part of this review, the judges again looked at the issue of Vincent's evidence and whether he tampered with the bullets taken from the three Burwood murder victims and then subsequently perjured himself in order to state the bullets were fired from the same gun used to attack the Shalagins. Justice Bleechmore put it directly to the defence: What possible motive did Senior Constable Vincent have to manufacture a false case against a person he had never met?

Clearly Vincent had no motive to lie, and the appeal was refused on the grounds that it 'would enjoy no prospects of success'.

Coulston had exhausted all his avenues of legal redress. But he was not done yet. In 2009, under freedom of information legislation, he sought access to hand-drawn plans of the house where the Burwood murders had taken place and all photographs taken at the scene by the investigators in 1992. This request was directed to the Office of Public Prosecutions (OPP) Victoria, and was denied following an internal review. Coulston then requested that a tribunal examine this decision; he also confirmed he was not seeking access to the images showing the deceased victims. The reason he wanted access to these items was, in his own words, as a 'continuation of my inquiries into the particulars of my conviction, and the methods used by both members of the Victoria Police and members of the OPP itself, who have engaged in deceptive strategies, and/or criminal activities to reach a conviction in my particular case'. His request was again denied.

Coulston, however, is clearly not a man to give up. In early 2017 the State Coroner of Victoria refused to grant Coulston's request to reopen an inquest into the deaths of Peter Dempsey, Kerryn Henstridge, and Anne Smerdon. In 2018 Coulston again sought to appeal to the Supreme Court against the determination of the state coroner, and again he was refused.

LOOK AT ME

To this day Coulston has never spoken about his crimes or offered any kind of explanation. Perhaps his silence is all part of his power game.

Former Victorian Homicide Detective Mick Stefanovic, who was part of the original investigation into the triple Burwood murders, described him as a 'bland, nothing of an individual'. One of the teachers Coulston abducted as a 14-year-old boy said he seemed 'so ordinary', and the police officer who questioned him following the attempted murder of the Shalagins described him as bland.

I was struck by the juxtaposition between his blandness and the bold nature with which he perpetrated his crimes. Was Coulston fighting his ordinariness, wanting to be more? Craving fame, or rather infamy? Answering questions like these is all part of the process of criminal profiling. I suspected that outwardly unassuming Coulston was empowered by the attention his crimes achieved and he enjoyed the fear and notoriety from afar. But I wanted a second opinion.

EXPERT INSERT: CRIMINAL PROFILING

Also known as offender profiling, criminal profiling is an investigative tool that combines the behavioural sciences of psychology and criminology, as well as crime scene analysis, to identify likely suspects in a crime. The basic principle is that a person's personality is reflected in their behaviour, and that an advanced understanding of criminal behaviour can be used by experts in a criminal investigation to deduce information about an offender. It can be used in a number of ways: to narrow suspect pools, to direct investigations, and to link serial crimes by the same perpetrator. It can also help predict what an offender might do in the future, based on their past activity.

The evidence used by experts to compile a criminal profile comprises crime scene evidence (including photographs of

---

the scene and victims, together with what physical evidence was left by the perpetrator and where), together with witness statements and an evaluation of 'victimology'.

Victimology literally means the study of victims. In an investigative context, an analysis of victim selection can tell us a lot about the offender – was the choice of victim random, or was the victim or victim-type selected purposely? If the victim was chosen for a particular reason, what might that reason have been? This type of analysis can be especially useful when trying to identify an offender in serial crimes, as well as informing the public about which specific individuals may be at heightened risk of victimisation at a particular time in a specific location.

Similar crimes will also be reviewed, to see what lessons, if any, can be learnt.

The data will be collated and evaluated, to make predictions about the offender. This will include psychological information (for example, does the offender exhibit evidence of an antisocial personality disorder, or are they likely to be suffering from a psychopathology such as schizophrenia that may lead to delusions or hallucinations), as well as personal characteristics (including likely age range, sex, and the areas in which they may feel comfortable to conduct criminal activity).

The information will also be used to determine likely lifestyle factors that may help identify the perpetrator (for example, whether they live alone or are married, if they are likely to be employed), as well as situational factors (such as whether the crime is committed in a domestic setting, or what time of day or night the crime occurs) that are known to be highly influential on behaviour.

Offender profiling was originally used largely to assist in serial sex crime investigations but developed to include all serious serial crimes, including murder, burglary, arson and terrorism.

One of the key features of a criminal profile is the categorisation of offenders into 'organised' or 'disorganised'. According to this dichotomy, an organised offender who commits serious crimes plans their crime carefully, and the crime is premeditated, which means they leave less evidence at the scene. These offenders are often of above average intelligence, educated, married and in stable employment. They are also often suffering antisocial personality disorder but are not legally insane, so they know right from wrong. With these offenders there may be multiple crime scenes to consider; in a murder, for example, where the victim met their attacker, where they were killed and where the offender disposed of the body. Mr Cruel would be a good example of an organised killer (discussed in chapter four), or Ivan Milat (discussed in chapter five).

Disorganised criminals, on the other hand, often leave significant amounts of evidence at crime scenes, as they are more reactive to situations, and commit crimes on the spur of the moment in a blitz-style attack. This makes them easier to catch. There is normally just one crime scene with these offenders; using murder again as an example, this type of individual is likely to kill someone and leave the body in the one place. The ultimate blitz-style disorganised murderer would be Jack the Ripper.

Tim Watson-Munro, criminal psychologist

I arranged to meet and chat with Tim Watson-Munro, consultant criminal psychologist and author, about his thoughts on Coulston. Tim was the perfect person to ask, having risen to prominence as a pioneering prison psychologist at Parramatta Gaol. During the 1980s and 1990s he gave expert evidence in some of the country's most notorious court cases, including mass murderer Julian Knight who shot and killed 7 people, injuring a further 19, in 1987 in Clifton Hill, Victoria, in a crime that became known as the Hoddle Street Massacre. Tim is a wealth of useful insights due to his very significant experience with serial violent offenders; in fact, he has been interviewed many times by the media about the Coulston case.

We met in a coffee shop on Sydney's north shore. The sunshine and warmth jarred with the topic under discussion.

Tim told me, 'In my view, had Coulston not been detained and arrested at the Domain Gardens in Melbourne, he in all likelihood would have continued and escalated in terms of his offending behaviour. At the time of his court case, a journalist from the *Herald Sun* approached me for comment, arising from him investigating a significant number of cases where women had vanished or had been raped and murdered in various parts of Australia. Whether it be coincidence or something more insidious, Coulston had lived in each of these areas at the time of these offences occurring. These crimes were thoroughly investigated by the police and, as it eventuated, he was not charged'.

I also asked him about Coulston, his psychology, and the motivations behind his crimes. 'There appears to be no motive beyond the thrill of the kill at that time. Although described by those who knew him as being shy, quiet and calm, it is clear that he craved the attention which his crimes created.'

It looks like I was right.

TRIPLE MURDER – HOW DID HE GET THERE?

From a criminological perspective, how did 14-year-old Coulston advance from a poorly executed but incredibly bold, impulse-driven abduction (with potential murderous intent) to a triple homicide as a 35-year-old man?

It is the intervening years we're interested in. Is there anything to suggest Coulston may have been involved in other crimes that have not been solved?

Because of the publicity surrounding the abduction case in 1972, the Coulston family left country Victoria a year later and moved to northern New South Wales. By 1979 he had settled in southern Queensland, near Tweed Heads, and in 1980 he moved states again, this time to live in Sydney.

What was he doing? Is it possible he was hunting more headlines?

THE BALACLAVA KILLER, THE RETURN TO THEATRICALITY?

In the summer of 1979 and into 1980, the Gold Coast and Tweed Heads were in the grip of terror. A monster was on the loose, responsible for a series of rapes and at least one murder. It is unclear exactly how many attacks there were, but it is suspected there were a minimum of six separate incidents.

The first took place on 15 December 1979. A 30-year-old female was attacked whilst approaching her car in Tugun – a little over 7 kilometres from Tweed Heads where Coulston's family owned a farm. Her assailant threatened her with a Glenfield .22 calibre rifle and pushed her into the boot of her car. The offender then drove her to the Gold Coast hinterland where he raped her, after which he put the woman back into the boot of her car and drove to Tugun Beach, abandoning the car and his victim there.

A few days later, on Christmas Day, Coulston struck again. This time the targets were a Cabarita couple, attacked whilst parked in their car, by a man wearing a balaclava. The male victim's hands were secured using the car windows, before the woman was sexually assaulted and the man made to watch.

Three days later, on 28 December, another couple was attacked. This time the victims were inside their secluded farmhouse at Cudgen, in the Tweed Shire. A man wearing a balaclava entered the house. The female was forced to bind her partner's hands before the female was raped. Again the male victim was forced to watch the sexual assault.

The next assault didn't take place until 25 January 1980. A man wearing a balaclava broke into a house in Burleigh Heads, surprising a married couple. Just like in the previous attack, the woman was told to bind the male victim's hands. In a twist on the previous incidents, however, the woman was not raped – she pleaded with her assailant not to hurt her as she was pregnant. The masked man left the house without causing further injury to either victim.

The next attack saw things take a violent turn, and was one of the boldest yet. On 2 February 1980, Jeff Parkinson and Lorraine Harrison were on a date. Around 1.30 am the couple were leaving the Twin Town Services Club in Tweed Heads. It was summer, so although it was late there were lots of people still around. The club was very close to Tweed Heads Police Station, the largest police station in the area that operates 24 hours a day. Not the time or place a shy offender would choose to commit their crime.

Jeff and Lorraine came out the back door of the club, crossing a small park to where Jeff had left his car. Jeff opened the passenger door for his date, before walking around the car and getting in the driver's side. Before he could drive off, a man appeared out of the dark wearing a balaclava. The assailant jumped into the back seat of the car and ordered them at gunpoint to drive to a secluded spot at Cobaki Creek, a 10-minute drive away. To get there they had to drive past Tweed Heads Police Station at gunpoint.

Once at the secluded spot the attacker, true to form, tried to get Lorraine to tie Jeff's hands, but Jeff took the offender by surprise. He fought back. Lorraine took her chance whilst the two men fought; she ran, attracting the attention of a passing motorist. They heard five gunshots. Jeff was later found dead, lying in the grass beside his car. He had been shot three times.

There was then a long gap between incidents. The murder of Jeff Parkinson was in all likelihood an accident, and the surprise may have caused the offender to take a break from his activities, because the next attack didn't come until 31 October 1980. On this occasion a woman was assaulted at gunpoint in her own home at Burleigh Waters, on the Gold Coast. The assailant fled the scene on a motorbike.

The attacker was described by the witnesses as having blue eyes and bushy eyebrows and dark brown hair. Some described those blue eyes as 'steely', others as 'evil'. The attacker was believed to be in his 20s, of athletic build, and around 177 centimetres tall. No further description was available as his face was hidden by the balaclava.

Although the attacks themselves were brutal, and one victim was killed, the offender was oddly polite to his female victims – often apologising to them. They all also described him as being well spoken with a soft voice.

Coulston is in the frame for this series of unsolved rapes and murder because of a number of factors. Firstly, we can't ignore the similarity between these attacks and the assault on the Shalagins, as well as the Burwood homicides. They're almost identical: the man wore a balaclava and carried a .22 rifle. Importantly, he also attacked couples, which is unusual and speaks to the offender's confidence in his ability to control the situation, as well as his desire to feel the power that comes from dominating and subduing more than one person simultaneously. Imagine the power a sex offender would feel making another man watch him sexually assault his male victim's partner but be unable to intervene.

Secondly, there's a theatricality to these crimes that reminds me of Coulston.

This also fits with what we know about serial violent offenders, including murderers. Some murderers focus on the process of killing; what is important is the build-up to the murder which serves to fulfil a fantasy, such as torture or sexual gratification. Others focus on the act of killing, with the murder being the end in itself.

I was in two minds about Coulston – he seemed to murder without remorse, enjoy sexually assaulting women in front of their partners, but then he chose not to harm a pregnant woman. Was that consideration for the woman, or something else? The behaviours appeared to be paradoxical.

I asked Tim Watson-Munro if he thought Coulston was a psychopath. Tim cut straight to it. 'It's clear from his behaviour that Coulston was both a narcissist and a psychopath. He lacked empathy for his victims and the cold-blooded manner in which the three people were killed in Burwood speaks to this issue.

'In general terms, psychopaths are well oriented in time, place and person. They do not suffer a "disease of the mind" in that they are well aware of the nature of their actions and the consequences which will accrue. They have a very high threshold for anxiety and consequently undertake crimes and behaviours which would cause most to break out in a cold sweat. Psychopaths have no remorse and this, in conjunction with an absence of empathy, suggests that they are not likely to respond to treatment.'

Coulston had the opportunity to commit these crimes, as he was living with his family at a farm near the country town of Kyogle, around 100 kilometres from the Tweed Shire. The police would later search this rural property whilst investigating Coulston for the Burwood murders, and some of the things they found were disturbing, including; a .22 calibre shotgun (which he'd bought under a false name) as well as a .22 calibre rifle, American real crime magazines that detailed cases of serial killers and rapists, as well as motel room keys from all over New South Wales. They also found an old oil filter, similar to the one Coulston would later fashion into a home-made silencer for the shotgun used in the Burwood murders. In a trinket box they discovered two fired .22 calibre bullets.

Coulston also had the means – he loved motorbikes (the method of transport the offender largely used to flee the scenes of his attacks). As to motive, given that he was fantasising about raping women as a 14-year-old boy, these sound like exactly the type of crimes we might expect him to be committing.

But in 1980, just as suddenly as they had started, the attacks stopped. Coincidentally, at the same time Coulston moved from the Tweed Heads area to Sydney. And in Sydney's southern suburbs in the 1980s . . .

THE SUTHERLAND RAPIST – AND COULSTON IS ON THE SCENE

Some killers like to make a statement. Making partners watch. Attacking in busy places where the risk of being caught increases.

The man terrorising Sydney's southern suburbs between 1985 and 1987 had the mark of a showman about him. For a start, the attacks happened in broad daylight.

The offender struck at least five separate times. He became known as the Sutherland Rapist. Just like the attacks in Tweed, the assailant wore a balaclava and threatened his victims with a sawn-off shotgun, attacking single women and couples and restraining them.

The similarities to the Balaclava Killer's MO were immediate and striking.

In his mid-20s at this stage, Coulston had returned to New South Wales in early 1980, shortly after Jeff Parkinson was murdered in Tweed Heads and coinciding with the end to the attacks in that area. He chose Cronulla, a southern Sydney suburb, as his base. Cronulla is less than 10 kilometres from Sutherland.

Coulston had a few jobs, one relevant one was at Hertz Rent-a-Car, where he worked as a car detailer. Later, in 1992, a young woman who had been a colleague of Coulston's at Hertz gave evidence to police in preparation for his committal hearings for the Burwood murders. She said she had made complaints to management about Coulston's behaviour. She said he had started stalking her to and from work after she had declined his invitations to go on dates. But that wasn't the only misdemeanour – he was taking hire cars off the lot and stealing fuel. The woman's complaints of harassment and his taking fleet cars without permission led to Coulston being sacked in 1986. Whilst he was employed by Hertz, just when the rapes were happening, Coulston had access to any number of different cars, making it very difficult to track which vehicle he may have been in at any given time. As a criminal, this is a great way to avoid detection.

For whatever reason, the rapes in Sydney, just like in northern NSW a few years before, stopped as quickly as they had started.

AN OFFENDER RAMPING UP HIS MO

Coulston didn't return to Melbourne until 1989. There he lived on a yacht at Westernport Marina, Hastings. The yacht belonged to Jan McLeod, his new girlfriend, whom he'd met shortly after getting fired from Hertz in 1987. If Coulston is the Sutherland Rapist, perhaps his new relationship with McLeod helped to temper his violent urges. At least for a while.

It would be another four years before McLeod would be confronted with the shocking truth that behind Coulston's quiet exterior lurked a monster. To this day, however, McLeod remains Coulston's loyal supporter, refusing to believe he committed the triple Burwood murders, regardless of the significant evidence stacked up against him, as well as his violent and sinister history of stalking and harassing women.

Years after Coulston was sentenced to three life sentences without the possibility of parole, McLeod still keeps his belongings safe at her house. Amongst them, several balaclavas.

But if Coulston is the offender in both Tweed and Sutherland, why did he go from a serial sex attacker to a triple murderer?

I believe he was escalating (which is common in serial violent offenders), that the sex attacks simply weren't giving him the same thrill any more. He wanted to test himself, step it up. So he decided to assault multiple victims simultaneously, both males and females, and bend them to his domination. In his everyday life he was unexceptional, ordinary, known to be quiet, withdrawn, a loner. He wanted people to take notice, to acknowledge his power, and I guarantee that when he pointed his gun at people they took him very seriously indeed.

WHAT NOW?

DNA was in its infancy in the 1980s, and the most police would have been able to determine from any of the offender's DNA left at the scene of the murder and other attacks would be blood type. And regardless of how forensically aware the offender may have been, he would have needed a crystal ball to know that within a few years the DNA he left on his victims could be compared to a suspect's DNA and a match made.

It seems an obvious step to take Coulston's DNA and upload it to the national database to see if he can be forensically linked to any other crimes. And in September 2000 Victoria Police obtained a court order to do just that. At the time of writing, however, I am unable to determine whether Coulston's DNA profile was ever uploaded to the national DNA database, as Victoria Police were not in a position to confirm or deny this had taken place. Whilst I understand the investigative limitations under which Victoria Police function, were Coulston's DNA to be added to the national database, we may at last be able to say for sure if Coulston was both the Balaclava Killer and the Sutherland Rapist, as many believe. If this proves to be the case, Coulston would be one of Australia's most prolific and violent serial offenders of modern times.

Even today we are making huge advances in DNA technology. For example, since 2015, DNA phenotyping (an advanced technique that predicts appearance from DNA based on observable and somewhat predictable physical characteristics) has been available and it is revolutionising cold case investigations. This method has been employed across a wide variety of cases – from identifying offenders in rape and murder cases, to helping to identify long-term unidentified persons.

Today it is possible to read the sequence of millions of pieces of DNA from a tiny quantity of sample, even one that may be degraded or contain genetic material from more than one person. Because such huge amounts of data are being produced, a large proportion of the genomic variation between people is also captured, and geneticists are gradually decoding the DNA sequence. Some of this information relates to how our DNA affects how we look. One phenotyping system developed by a US company, Parabon NanoLabs, Inc., has had great success in this area. They have developed a technique that takes information from a sample of DNA from an unknown person and transforms that information into predictions of physical appearance (including eye colour, skin colour, and hair colour, as well as the shape of the face). The technique also predicts ancestral, or familial, relationships.

It's hard to imagine, so here's an example. In 2018 I had my phenotype predicted from a saliva sample. The result is given in figure 6, which shows my projected facial appearance at age 25 and with a BMI of 22. You can compare it to a photo of me taken at a similar age (figure 7) to decide if you think it looks like me – remembering the image on the left is created solely from a DNA sample.

Even more recently, in 2018, genetic genealogy (GG) rocked the forensic DNA world. Genetic genealogy is the combination of genetic analysis with traditional historical and genealogical research into family history. For forensic investigations, it can be used to

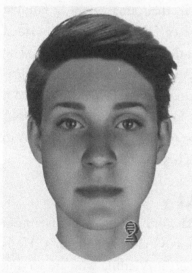

Figure 6: Phenotype prediction of what the author looks like from her DNA sample (provided by FHID Pty Ltd, © 2018 Parabon NanoLabs, Inc. All rights reserved).

Figure 7: Photo of the author at a similar age for comparative purposes.

identify remains by tying the DNA to a family with a missing person or to point to the likely identity of a perpetrator.

The Golden State Killer, East Coast Rapist, Diamond Knot Killer. All of these names, devised by the media to describe a monster prowling California between 1974 and 1986, are alleged in current criminal proceedings to apply to one man – Joseph James DeAngelo. He is alleged to have murdered at least 13 people, raped over 50, and burglarised over 120 others. The case is still before the courts and he is entitled to a presumption of innocence, but if convicted he would be confirmed as a prolific and eclectic offender. DeAngelo is also an ex-police officer, who was only charged after the police, almost randomly, uploaded the offender's genomic sequence to a public genealogy database, GEDmatch, which is normally used to help people research their family trees. To their amazement, a familial match came up, meaning a relative of DeAngelo's had uploaded their DNA onto the database when doing an ancestry search. The person who had donated their DNA was traced, and the investigative path led the police to DeAngelo. The police then obtained a warrant to covertly monitor DeAngelo and collect 'discarded' DNA samples (such as drink cans he threw away) to compare his DNA to those taken from the crime scenes. They matched.

IS COULSTON MR CRUEL?

Coulston is held at HM Prison Barwon, a high-risk, maximum security prison for males located near Geelong in Victoria. He is now one of just a handful of prisoners in Victoria who are serving life sentences with no minimum – his crimes deemed so monstrous that he will die in jail.

Disturbingly, Coulston has allegedly shown interest in other infamous crimes. According to one newspaper report he applied to the state coroner for access to files in relation to the Mr Cruel case.

This unsolved case involved the abduction and sexual assault of at least three schoolgirls in Melbourne between 1987 and 1991, and the murder of a 13-year-old who was shot execution-style in the head, just like Coulston's Burwood victims.

The identity of Mr Cruel is one of Australia's most notorious and haunting crime mysteries and the police have considered that Coulston might have been the offender.

So is Coulston teasing us, wanting people to wonder if he is Mr Cruel and again basking in the reflected 'glory', as he would see it, of the infamy that would bring?

Or should we consider him seriously as a suspect in the Mr Cruel case? This is a question we will look at in chapter four.

FORENSIC SCIENCE EXPLAINED: BLOOD GROUPS AND DNA TYPING

Humans have distinct blood groups – A, B, AB and O – classifications based on genetically determined antigens (sugars that live on the walls of our blood cells), which are either A and/or B, or O group (no antigens), and each can be either positive or negative totalling eight blood groups. Blood groups are inherited and comprised of genetic contributions from both parents.

Forensic scientists have long used blood types to rule persons of interest (POI) in or out of criminal activity. However, a match in blood group only provides a statistical likelihood that the POI may also be the crime scene donor – for example, 45% of Caucasian individuals have type O blood, therefore if the blood is type O from the crime scene it could have come from the suspect, but also any other O-group individual. However, if the suspect and crime scene samples represent different blood groups, generally speaking they did not originate from the same person. Blood groups are useful in a forensic context as they are not affected by any environmental factors (such as living conditions, diet or drug use) or disease. However, although a person's blood group is normally stable throughout life, under specific circumstances it can change (for example, following a liver or bone marrow transplant, but this is very rare).

Blood groups were in the news in 2017 when an eminent Australian scientist, Emeritus Professor Barry Boettcher (a blood expert who found errors in the evidence presented as part of the prosecution case against Lindy Chamberlain) raised concerns over a murder conviction. The case in question was the murder of Celia Douty, a 40-year-old British woman who was killed on Brampton Island, Queensland, in September 1983. Although blood and semen was found on a red beach towel covering Celia's body, DNA analysis was in its infancy in the early 1980s and the retrieved samples did not facilitate an identification of the offender. However, by the early 2000s technologies had advanced significantly. This allowed the police to re-examine the DNA evidence and confirm that the semen found on the towel belonged to Sydney businessman Wayne Butler, who had long been a suspect in the murder for various circumstantial reasons. The prosecution successfully argued that the DNA extracted from semen left on the towel was a match to a blood sample taken from Butler, and the jury only took 90 minutes to find him responsible for Celia's brutal murder. Butler was the first person to be found guilty on the basis of DNA testing in Australia.

However, Boettcher has long claimed that there were errors in the DNA testing that led to Butler's conviction. In 2009 a second court of appeal upheld Butler's conviction. However, in June 2017 Boettcher again claimed that the DNA on the towel was not Butler's, and that a recent sample of Butler's semen demonstrated that Butler was blood group B, whereas the semen on the towel was blood group O. Therefore, in

Boettcher's opinion, the semen on the towel could not be Butler's. Boettcher made an application to the attorney general in Queensland requesting a pardon on Butler's behalf. At the time of writing Butler remains in prison, awaiting the attorney general's response.

In the forensic space, blood group testing was supplemented with DNA typing in the 1980s because of its ability to individuate between people as opposed to simply grouping them. Today tests based on antigen-antibody reactions are still used for excluding non-donors; this can be done en masse, and then DNA profiling techniques applied to compare specific samples from a reduced number of persons of interest. Together, these methods are known as forensic serology; the study of semen, blood, saliva, and other body fluids as part of the medico-legal process. Forensic serology has a number of applications, including DNA typing for both POIs and victims, semen identification in cases of sexual assault, blood spatter analysis, identification of unknown stains, blood typing, and paternity testing.

Forensic serology comprises a core element of contemporary police investigations. Many of the processes are now automated and the Forensic Biology and DNA team from New South Wales Health Pathology process 40,000 DNA samples per year. The unit also provides a fast analysis capability to NSW police for critical incidents, with the capacity to report 'cold hits' on the DNA database in less than 12 hours from sample receipt. Degraded and mixed samples (containing genetic material from more than one person) can now be analysed in smaller and smaller quantities, meaning the science of DNA analysis continues to advance, providing an invaluable resource for police across the world.

FOUR

MR CRUEL -
THE CAREFUL PREDATOR

When I look at a case, I attempt to get inside the mind of the perpetrator, as dark a process as that is. I need to understand what motivates them to commit the crimes they do. But getting inside the head of the man who attacked at least four young girls in Melbourne in the 1980s and 1990s was always going to be particularly hard, not only because of his crimes but because we know so little about him.

One thing I could do to get a sense of Mr Cruel was to be in his space, the zone he hunted in and therefore where he felt most comfortable. So, on a trip to Melbourne in late 2018, I decided to take a drive around the areas where the girls were taken or released. As I drove through the quiet suburban streets it was hard to imagine a man stalking young girls here. But that's what happened. Somewhere around here, innocent children, just like the ones I could see playing in the parks, caught his attention. He must have watched his victims, planned how to access them. Watched and waited.

All the time, he was thinking how to fulfil his fantasies without getting caught. He was clever, but he was also lucky. And cunning, rat cunning. Hard to see these kids as prey, but that's what Mr Cruel's eyes would have shown him, and that's how I needed to think to understand this predator.

I don't know what he looks like; he was very careful not to let his victims see his face. But after reviewing predacious crimes where males have stalked and attacked young, vulnerable victims, I feel like I know this man. And to know him moves us one step closer to catching him, and men like him.

THE CASE

It began on 22 August 1987. At 4 am a man wearing a balaclava broke into a family home in the Melbourne suburb of Lower Plenty. He removed a window pane in the lounge and made his way straight to the parents' bedroom, where they were forced at gunpoint to lie on the floor on their stomachs. He also had a small knife. The parents were tied up and surgical tape was put over their eyes, before they were made to get into a wardrobe. Their six-year-old son was blindfolded, gagged, and tied to his bed. The intruder told the family all he wanted was money, clothes and food. But he lied. His real target was their 11-year-old daughter. He told the girl to clean her teeth and then assaulted her. Afterwards he told her to count slowly to 100 and then to free her parents. To give himself extra time before the police could be called, the offender cut the phone lines.

Their attacker was in no hurry to leave, spending about two hours in the house altogether, even taking the time to make himself a meal. He searched the house and stole records and a coat. He also pretended to make a phone call and used the term 'bozo' to refer to the person on the other end, saying that the other person needed to move their children otherwise they would be in danger. Later the police checked and no call had been made. The conclusion drawn was that this was an attempt to hide his true motives, as was the theft of the personal items – a ruse to distract and confuse the police.

Was this his first offence? From the practised and bold nature of the crime, it seems unlikely. Whoever did this built up to it.

The offender waited 16 months before striking again. The second confirmed attack came on 27 December 1988, in Ringwood, a working-class suburb of Melbourne. John Wills, father and husband, hadn't been able to sleep and had stayed up until about 5 am doing a jigsaw puzzle downstairs. Eventually he went upstairs to bed. What John didn't know was that someone was watching, waiting for the house to go dark. The offender gave John enough time to get off to sleep, waiting until 5.30 am before breaking in through the back door.

Wearing blue overalls and keeping his face covered with a black ski mask, the intruder went straight into the parents' bedroom, bursting in loudly and turning on the light. As with the first incident, he was armed with a knife and gun. Julie, John's wife, woke to find the man standing over her, pointing the gun at her. She started to scream, telling her four daughters to get out of the house. The gunman told her to stop screaming, putting the gun to John's head as he did so, asking John if 'he was going to be a hero'. Fearful for his family, John shook his head. The offender made the couple lie on their bed and tied their hands with copper wire. He said he wanted all the money they kept in the house, taking $35 in cash from a bedside table. He then gagged them. Mr Cruel cut the phone line before going into the girls' bedroom. All four siblings slept in one room, on two sets of bunkbeds. Ten-year-old Sharon, the intruder's target, was cowering in one of the top bunks pretending to be asleep. The girls had been woken by their mother's screams, and they were all terrified when the intruder walked into their room. The offender called Sharon by name. He bound her, covering her mouth with masking tape and also covering her eyes. He then picked her up and carried her off into the night.

It took around 15 minutes for John and Julie to free themselves. Finding Sharon missing, John ran to a neighbour's house to raise the alarm. Victoria Police's Major Crime Squad quickly took control of the scene. The immediate area was searched, but there was no trace of Sharon, and no witnesses were discovered to offer any clues as to who had taken Sharon and where he might have gone.

Initially the idea was floated that the motive for the abduction might be financial, as the intruder had taken what little cash was in the house. But no ransom demand was made, and this was not a wealthy suburb so not an obvious choice to target for extortion. The police thought the intruder took the money as a diversionary tactic, to make it look like that's what he wanted, and Sharon was the real target.

All the next day the family waited for news. But nothing. There was no evidence to analyse, no leads to follow. The family, police, and community just had to wait, and hope.

At 11.15 pm on 27 December, 18 hours after Sharon was taken, a white Commodore Vacation sedan drew the attention of a motorist in Bayswater (7.5 kilometres from Ringwood) because the driver was driving suspiciously. The car had its lights turned off even though it was dark, and as it turned from Jersey Road into Mountain Road it almost hit another car. The motorist followed the Commodore and stopped next to it at a red light. He tried to talk to the male driver, the sole person visible in the car. The Commodore driver didn't want to engage, turning away as though not wanting to show his face. The lights turned green and the Commodore pulled away, turning right towards Bayswater High School. The motorist didn't take the Commodore's licence plate.

Just 45 minutes later Sharon was found outside Bayswater High School when a passing motorist saw her alone and stopped to check she was okay. She was wearing a man's shirt and green bin bags.

Sharon was able to provide the police with a significant amount of information about her abductor – and the extraordinary lengths he had gone to in order to ensure they were both clean. Just like in the first attack, he told the little girl to shower and to brush and floss her teeth. Sharon also told police that her assailant had given her food even as she was being assaulted. She was kept blindfolded for the entire 18 hours of her ordeal.

Detective Chief Inspector Des Johnson spoke to the press. 'We can only dread what the man would have done if the girl had pulled off the blindfold and seen his face. It is that close to being a homicide.'

The first attack had been big news, now Mr Cruel was a household name and was causing a wave of fear felt by all parents across Melbourne.

The third assault occurred 3 July 1990, 18 months after the attack on Sharon. The assailant broke into a house in Canterbury, 17 kilometres west of his last attack in Ringwood. It was 11.40 pm and 13-year-old Nicola Lynas and her 15-year-old sister, Fiona, were in bed asleep. The two girls were home alone. Brian and Rosemary Lynas were out for dinner with friends. A man wearing a black balaclava and dark clothes broke into the house through a back window. He moved silently through the house to the girls' bedroom. He woke them and threatened to harm them if they didn't do as he said. He was carrying a knife and a handgun. He tied Fiona up and told her to tell her father that he wanted $25,000 for Nicola's safe release. He made Nicola go into another room and collect her school uniform; she was a pupil at Presbyterian Ladies College. The offender put the school uniform and some underwear into a bag, before stealing the car keys to a rented car that was parked on the drive. He again cut the phone lines and searched the house for money. When he was done, he forced Nicola into the car and left. It would be 40 minutes before Brian and Rosemary would get home to find one daughter bound and gagged and the other gone.

The police were called, and discussions began about the ransom as the parents were prepared to pay. But the kidnapper had not left instructions on how it should be paid, or when he would make contact. The police pleaded with the abductor via the media to make contact with them or the family.

The car the intruder had taken from the house was found abandoned a few streets away at 3 pm the following day. The kidnapper had driven the short distance and then changed to a second vehicle, to avoid his own car being spotted at the scene. There was no sign of Nicola.

At 2 am on Friday 6 July, Nicola was being driven around by the offender. They drove for hours before the man stopped the car and told her to get out. He chose to release her at a power substation in the suburb of Kew, 6 kilometres west of the original attack site. She had been held for 50 hours. Like Sharon she was blindfolded, and was left wrapped in a blanket. Before dropping her off, he had given clear instructions – she was to sit down with her head between her legs, then she had to wait 10 minutes. She then made her way to a nearby house to raise the alarm.

Nicola was unable to tell the police much about her abductor, or the house at which she'd been held. She was, however, able to describe how careful he had been that they were both clean, meticulous. He had told Nicola to wash herself thoroughly, to brush her teeth really well. Mr Cruel sexually assaulted her. As with Sharon, he gave Nicola food and water throughout her ordeal. Although the sexual abuse was clearly awful, the offender was not overtly violent, in that he did not beat or otherwise harm the girls.

He also took an interest in the media coverage, watching a press conference held by Mr Lynas and commenting to Nicola about it.

Together victims and their families provided a good description of the man, as far as they could, given that he kept his face covered. Mr Cruel was Caucasian, spoke with an Australian accent, was between 30 and 50 years of age, and 173–180 centimetres tall and was of medium build with a small pot belly. He had fair or sandy hair and eyebrows, and sometimes had a ginger beard. He also used specific phrases, including 'worry wart', 'bozo', and 'missy' during the attacks.

The captives, Sharon in particular, were also able to provide details of the house they were held in, and they told police that they could hear planes flying overhead and were even able to narrow down the flight times. This information was valuable as it allowed aviation experts to determine that the house was somewhere on the flight path to Melbourne's Tullamarine Airport, and a large residential area around the airport was investigated. This means that the offender had another anchor point, a house or place of work, around the airport where he felt safe to take his captives.

The girls were also able to provide enough detailed information to convince the police that a serial child sex offender was active in the area. And the police also knew by this time that the offender had been trying to confuse them – the theft of petty personal items and fake phone calls at his first crime scene, theft of money at Sharon's house, and the demand for a ransom (that was never followed through on) during Nicola's abduction. This again speaks to a level of planning and organisation.

The press went wild with speculation – who was this man, and where would he strike next? The public were frantic. People weren't safe in their own homes, and parents felt helpless, unable to protect their own children.

And Mr Cruel was listening and watching the panic spread. His reign of terror wasn't over.

The last suspected attack came nine months later, on 13 April 1991, in Templestowe. This was sticking right within the offender's comfort zone: Templestowe is 11 kilometres from his last attack site and only 5.5 kilometres from Lower Plenty, his first known offence location. Clearly, the offender had an anchor point close to where these attacks were taking place.

This incident was the most violent yet. It was 9 pm. Three young siblings, Karmein (aged 13), Karlie (aged 9) and Karen (aged 7), were home alone; their parents, John and Phyllis Chan, were working at their Chinese restaurant. Mr Cruel came in through the garden, after tampering with a security gate and scaling a high brick wall that surrounded the house. Once on the property, he went to one of the cars on the drive, and wrote in white spray paint *Payback More to come* and *Asian drug deal*. Armed with a large knife and with his face hidden by a balaclava, the intruder entered the home quietly through an unlocked door or window. He made his way upstairs as the girls watched TV in a bedroom. The girls heard a noise, and when Karmein and Karlie went to investigate they were confronted by Mr Cruel in the hall. He forced the girls back into the bedroom, where Karen was cowering behind the door. Mr Cruel threatened the girls with a knife, and forced Karlie and Karen into a wardrobe, pushing the bed up against it to stop them getting out, telling them he only wanted money. He told the young sisters that after he had gone Karmein would open the door for them. He was lying. He dragged Karmein away by her hair, and she was never seen alive again. Interestingly, Karmein went to the same school (Presbyterian Ladies College), as Nicola Lynas, his third victim.

About 9.45 pm, Karlie and Karen managed to get out of the wardrobe, immediately calling their parents at the restaurant and telling them what had happened. When the police were told of the circumstances of Karmein's abduction, they immediately saw the parallels with the previous three attacks. A huge search took place, involving sniffer dogs and a helicopter, and whilst a sniffer dog did follow a scent to a nearby street, the trail went suddenly cold, no doubt indicating where Mr Cruel had parked his car away from his intended victim's house.

Karmein's parents made heartbreaking appeals for information, as well as begging Mr Cruel to let their daughter go as he had done with the other girls, and offering money for her safe return. But no one answered their pleas and Karmein was not let go. As the timeline of the other captives' releases came and went, hope waned. The family were shattered, waiting endlessly for the news that never came.

Just like Karmein, Mr Cruel had disappeared.

Whoever the offender was, and for a reason we can't explain, the attacks stopped after Karmein was abducted. For a long time the public feared more abductions, but as the days became weeks and the weeks became months with no new crimes attributed to Mr Cruel, the fear he had caused gradually dissipated and his crimes faded into the background.

That all changed on 9 April 1992, when, four days before the one-year anniversary of Karmein's abduction, her badly decomposed body was found by a dog walker on an isolated track at a State Electricity Commission terminal station in Thomastown, 16 kilometres from her home. Part of the area had been used as a landfill site and had recently been levelled by earthworks. The dog walker found a human skull near Edgars Creek. He called the police, and their subsequent search uncovered a number of other bones in a shallow grave that had been disturbed by the recent earthworks. Although a lot of evidence had been lost because of the passage of time, police were able to establish that she had been shot three times in the head and her body had been left at the landfill site. Where she had been taken before being killed and how long she had been held remain a mystery, although the then head of the Homicide Squad, Detective Chief Inspector Peter Halloran, suggested that the body had probably been in the shallow grave for almost 12 months – meaning she had been killed and buried very soon after her abduction – and that whoever buried her was familiar with the area. (It should also be noted that although we are including Karmein amongst Mr Cruel's crimes, the detectives that investigated this spate of attacks had doubts about whether she was part of the series.)

There were problems with the investigation into Karmein's abduction from the beginning. Unfortunately the police work was not as thorough as it could have been – when the police set up a command in the hours after Karmein's abduction, they established it inside the house before it had been forensically examined. This meant that dozens of people were tramping backwards and forwards, potentially destroying any evidence that may have been left behind. This is a huge problem, as forensic evidence is transitory, meaning that it loses its evidentiary value if it isn't protected and suitably preserved. Had the offender left footprints outside, or fingerprints in the house, fibres from his clothes, all of this could have been damaged or destroyed in the first few hours.

Even though evidence was in all likelihood lost in those early days following Karmein's disappearance, we do have information to go on. For example, what is very clear from these incidents is that the offender either worked or lived in the area immediately local to the attack/abduction and release/body deposition sites. If you look at the map showing where the crimes happened (figure 8), in incidents two and three (Sharon Wills and Nicola Lynas respectively) the abduction site was very close to the release site (within six or seven kilometres). Going by what we know of perpetrator patterns, it is likely the offender had a base (such as a house) within the grey-dot triangle triangle, possibly near the centre. Karmein's body was buried outside of this zone, which for this offender is a deviation from his MO

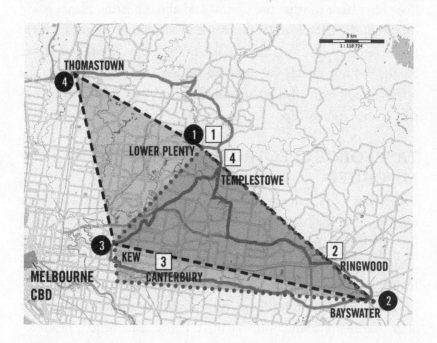

ATTACK AND ABDUCTION SITES

●●●● Likely Mr Cruel living radius

▬ ▬ Attack/abduction sites

① Release sites

[1] Attack/Abduction sites

▬ Directions by road

Figure 8: Map showing abduction, release, and body deposition sites.

and may indicate that he intentionally disposed of the body outside his normal activity area to avoid detection. Regardless, he would still have left her body somewhere he knew, as the police acknowledged when she was found, and this selection of deposition site again speaks to the fact that the offender was local and had ties to the area. If we refer back to what the victims said about hearing planes going overhead, the choice of Thomastown to dispose of Karmein's body makes sense, as it is roughly equidistant from the airport and Lower Plenty, the first attack site. I would suggest that this is a route the offender took regularly and he probably drove past the landfill site as part of that regular trip.

TASKFORCE SPECTRUM – TO CATCH MR CRUEL

When Karmein Chan was abducted, news that a serial child predator was haunting Melbourne made national headlines. The police used the public's interest to try to generate new information and leads. They were concerned that there may have been other victims that hadn't yet been linked to Mr Cruel.

The case took on a life of its own and, as a result, four weeks after Karmein's abduction, Victoria Police established Taskforce Spectrum, headed by Detective Inspector David Sprague. The remit of this taskforce was to identify and catch Mr Cruel. In total, 40 staff were attached to Spectrum, which ran for almost 3 years and cost $3.8 million.

One of the major initiatives undertaken by Spectrum was to publicise all three cases together (the three publicly identified victims linked to Mr Cruel) as they knew this would have the largest impact and generate the most interest and therefore potential leads. They produced a poster entitled *Child Abductions* and it was published in newspapers and displayed in public places. Leaflet-sized versions were delivered to every home in Victoria, as well as some homes in New South Wales and South Australia – 1.4 million homes in total. No police force had attempted anything of this scale in Australia before. It produced a new surge of information to the police.

Yet Mr Cruel remained elusive.

This did not mean that the taskforce did not have successes. All unsolved sex crimes came under the taskforce's intense scrutiny. As a result thousands of persons of interest were reinvestigated. This led to a number of cases totally unrelated to Mr Cruel being closed and offenders being brought to justice, including 74 people who were charged with offences involving rape, incest, blackmail, attempted bestiality, possession of child sexual abuse material, threats to kill, making obscene phone calls, and firearm offences.

The police determined that Mr Cruel was potentially responsible for attacks on and the abduction of up to 13 girls over the course of a decade. And the taskforce established that the same offender was almost certainly responsible for a series of earlier attacks in Melbourne's southern suburbs in the mid-1980s. This might have been the key to identifying him, but, again, critical evidence had been lost – including a piece of tape used to bind one of the victims. It is just possible that Mr Cruel unwittingly left his DNA on the inside of the tape, which it would now be possible to collect and process, possibly leading to a full genetic profile of this offender. Who knows how many other crimes would have been linked through this invaluable evidence once it was uploaded to a national database.

Unfortunately it wasn't a case of being a little bit slack with police procedure, this was a major problem. When the investigators on Taskforce Spectrum sought information, such as exhibits and criminal record sheets for POIs, they were told these had gone missing. This seriously hampered any efforts to assess whether Mr Cruel was responsible for any other crimes. The officers of the taskforce made such a fuss about not having access to proper records from earlier sex crimes that their complaints prompted a review of investigative procedure by Victoria Police, the result of which was the introduction of minimum standards for all future major crime investigations.

As well as professionalising crime scene management, exhibit handling, report writing, storage and so on, Taskforce Spectrum's work led to the Victorian Government strengthening legislation regarding sex offenders lingering in areas frequented by children, as well as the possession of child sexual abuse material (the term 'child pornography' should not be used as pornography relates to adults engaged in (usually) consensual sexual activity; as it is not possible for a child to consent to sexual activity of any kind, the term 'child sexual abuse material' is more appropriate).

Spectrum was Victoria Police's largest ever operation. Dozens of known sex offenders were interviewed, and every lead was followed. The taskforce was disbanded in January 1994 after eliminating over 27,000 persons of interest from their inquiries into Mr Cruel crimes and conducting interviews in the US and UK. During the 3 years of Spectrum's operation, the police searched 30,000 houses across 15 northern Melbourne suburbs that could have been used to hold the abducted children.

When Spectrum was closed, there were still 32 people who could not be discounted as suspects, but unfortunately there was simply not enough evidence to charge any of them.

Still Mr Cruel eluded capture.

TASKFORCE APOLLO
In May 2010 Mr Cruel came to the fore again as new information was provided to police: a name had been put forward by a credible witness. As a result Taskforce Apollo was formed to see if the Mr Cruel case, amongst others, could be progressed.

In addition to looking at Mr Cruel's cases, Apollo was also tasked with reviewing cold case sex crimes in Victoria more generally. All of the information collected by Spectrum had to be uploaded into a digital format (previously it had all been paper-based, which made cross-referencing and checking very time-consuming and difficult). The taskforce also had to reinterview key POIs from the original Mr Cruel investigations, trying to establish if their alibis were reliable and therefore if they could be excluded. This proved impossible in most cases.

Again, Mr Cruel slipped beneath the police's radar, and the probe ended in 2013 without an arrest. No new or compelling evidence was uncovered and the named person was eliminated as a suspect, for the Chan murder and the other unsolved cases that were the focus of Taskforce Spectrum.

MR CRUEL'S MO – WHAT CAN WE LEARN ABOUT HIM?

We know that an offender's MO is related to their personal attributes, such as intelligence, impulsiveness and self-control. However, it can change in response to situational factors that arise during the commission of a crime (for example, if a victim fights back unexpectedly). We also know that individuals demonstrating a greater sexual interest in nonsexual violence (such as Mr Cruel) show a higher level of organisation.

This fits with Mr Cruel, who shows a pattern of organised offending as his crimes are premeditated and well planned, helping him to leave less evidence at the scene. He also created multiple crime scenes: where the children were abducted, where they were held, and (if he is responsible for Karmein Chan's murder) where he disposed of the body.

Over this series of attacks, Mr Cruel can be seen to evolve, by which I mean he learnt from his earlier crimes and adapted and improved his method. He also grew bolder. The first known attack, in Lower Plenty, happened late at night. It was well planned and well executed. The offender took with him the items he would need to subdue and control multiple victims simultaneously: the surgical tape used to cover the parents' eyes, and the knife and gun. He also hid his face, wearing a balaclava, so identification would be difficult.

This crime was too well planned and executed to be a first offence. The method exudes confidence. Mr Cruel was totally in control.

EXPERT INSERT: FORENSIC PSYCHOLOGY

Forensic psychology, or criminal psychology as it is also known, is the application of psychological theory and knowledge to the criminal justice system. It focuses on understanding the thoughts, feelings and behaviours of criminals.

Pre-trial psychologists are asked to assess suspects to determine whether they are fit to be questioned or stand trial (known as competency, meaning they understand the charges against them and the implications of the process, as well as being able to assist their defence counsel prepare their case). During the prosecution process, practitioners are often called as expert witnesses to explain the mind of a criminal to a jury, and to comment on whether they were of sound mind at the time of the offence (and consequently, whether they are criminally responsible for their actions).

Psychologists are also asked to evaluate offenders to determine the likelihood that they will reoffend. This will often include clinical judgement but will be combined with statistics on the probability of events happening – based on research and past cases.

Forensic psychologists have an advisory role within police investigations. In relation to offenders, a psychologist will be able to describe how a certain type of offender is likely to behave in the hours immediately following an offence. In a series of serious crimes, forensic psychologists can assess evidence to determine whether the offender is devolving (beginning to break down mentally, as a result of which their crimes may become more violent or occur more frequently) or evolving (learning from their past behaviours).

Forensic psychologists can also comment on any ritualistic elements to a crime, which can comprise what is known as the offender's 'signature'. A signature may involve repetitive behaviour; for example, items that are left or taken from a scene, or specific victim selection (based on characteristics such as age, gender, or physical characteristics). A signature reflects an offender's emotional connection to an activity and psychological needs. This is different to an offender's modus operandi, which is practical in nature; it is the process by which an offender commits his crime. As part of a criminal MO, an individual may take specific items with them to a scene, but there is no personal significance to those items – they are simply a means to an end. For example, a gun to shoot victims in a murder. Therefore, criminal activity will always have an MO but will not always have a signature.

Forensic psychologists also compose criminal profiles. Compiling an offender profile relies on two types of reasoning: deductive and inductive. A deductive analysis is case-based and aims to extrapolate offender characteristics from an evaluation of the evidence gathered at a scene or a set of linked scenes. In this circumstance, the expert is drawing a conclusion from facts they already know. Inductive reasoning looks at 'average' or 'typical' offenders, whereby the expert will make inferences from information they have. In this situation, a person compiling a profile won't reach conclusions per se, because they are making suppositions about the premises they are basing their analysis on. Both deductive and inductive reasoning techniques are essential elements of the process of creating an offender profile.

Tim Watson-Munro, criminal psychologist

Many sex offenders build on minor 'nuisance' crimes, such as stealing underwear from washing lines, peeping in windows, taking covert photos, working up to more violent offences. In Mr Cruel's case it is likely that there would have been incidents of harassment or stalking in his past, as well as indecent assaults and sex attacks, perhaps on adults as well as children. But that does not mean he had ever been investigated or charged with anything; he's smart, so he may well have evaded attention.

By the second attack Mr Cruel was acting out his fantasies with even more confidence, this time being self-assured enough to take the child and keep her for a protracted period before releasing her. He wanted more time alone with the child (18 hours) than staying in the house would have afforded him, as the risk of being caught would increase the longer he remained there. He again kept his face covered the whole time and so wasn't concerned about being identified. The third assault was another escalation. It happened earlier in the evening, and this time Mr Cruel took even longer with his victim (50 hours) before releasing her.

Although there is no specific forensic or other evidence to connect Mr Cruel with Karmein Chan's abduction and murder, I would include it amongst Mr Cruel's crimes, as this feels to me like the final act in this particular sequence. We can't ignore how tidily this offence fits within the geographic spread of the other crimes. Mr Cruel knew and felt comfortable in this area. The first and fourth attacks are so close together that it is likely the offender lived close to where these incidents happened.

However, I don't think this was an acceleration in MO (from sex crime to murder); it seems more likely that Karmein's death was unplanned. The offender was confident to return the girls to their families when they couldn't identify him. Maybe he kept Karmein too long or something went wrong when he planned to release her and she accidentally saw his face, which could have led the offender to break from his pattern and kill from necessity.

We know that Mr Cruel was watching the media reports and enjoyed reading articles about his crimes in newspapers, as he talked to some of his other victims about the media attention. He would have seen the heartbreak he caused the Chans when they made distraught appeals for information on the news. Did Mr Cruel feel something like empathy for the Chans? I don't think so: remember, he left her body at a rubbish tip. That is not a respectful place to leave a young girl's body. My sense is that he killed Karmein when a situation arose that meant he had no choice, and afterwards he was too afraid of being caught to offend again.

This offender had a specific interest in children, particularly those between the ages of 10–13 years. He selected children at a specific developmental stage; people grow and develop at slightly different rates, so one 13-year-old girl can look very young, more like a 10- or 11-year-old, whereas another can look 16. This offender specifically targeted children in their prepubescent stage (before they go through puberty and develop secondary sexual characteristics).

I was interested to know whether Mr Cruel was a paedophile in the true sense of the word. This term is often incorrectly used interchangeably with 'child sex offender', but it has a specific meaning. A paedophilia is a psychiatric condition whereby an adult is specifically attracted to prepubescent children.

I knew criminal psychologist Tim Watson-Munro had worked on this case, so I asked him what he thought.

Tim said, 'No, Mr Cruel wasn't an exclusive paedophile. Prior to him gaining national prominence for his infamous crimes, he was active in Melbourne. I had been retained by the Victorian Police to profile his offending, which exposed me to the full range of his actions. These included the rape and confinement of an elderly nun in a Melbourne northern suburb, with him brazenly taking her car and her ATM card in order to drive to the local bank and steal her savings. There were a number of other crimes involving the detention and rape of adult women'.

So, even though Mr Cruel's later victims were all female children, this could have skewed our profile, as I was unaware of his earlier criminal history until talking to Tim.

I asked Tim why he thought Mr Cruel's victim selection had changed.

'It may well be the case that with the effluxion of time, as is often the case, he became desensitised to the extreme sadism and brutality he inflicted on these women, with the situation then escalating to him abducting and sexually abusing children. From that time onwards he selected households with a young girl which fitted his specific criteria. They were always his main target.

'Mr Cruel's offending demonstrates that he was both predatory and opportunistic. The nature of his offences, however, mitigate against him being impulsive. His precision planning, the lack of evidence obtained at crime scenes and the fact that he is yet to be identified speaks to a high level of organisation, prior, during and subsequent to his offending behaviour. As with most sexual offenders it is probable that he accessed child sexual abuse material.'

Perhaps most important and enlightening from the police's perspective is the fact that this offender was so careful at not leaving behind any forensic evidence – even over 30 years later we are no closer to identifying him. This is extraordinary, as in 1987, when the first known attack took place, DNA analysis was in its infancy. There is no way this child predator could have predicted the scientific advances that would later help identify offenders in so many cold cases. Perhaps Mr Cruel was intelligent enough to know that any trace he left could one day lead back to him, or perhaps (even more worryingly) he was aware of core forensic principles. Was he a trained investigator with knowledge of Dr Edmond Locard's famous 'exchange principle' that 'every contact leaves a trace'?

Or was it luck, and had the evidence been correctly protected, collected and stored, we might have been able to identify this dangerous offender?

When I was investigating this case I also spoke to retired Detective Chris O'Connor, who had been part of the Mr Cruel taskforce from 1987 and had spent years of his career looking at this case. Chris wasn't convinced all the attacks were perpetrated by the same person. 'The problem the police had was that we couldn't debrief Karmein Chan. If we could have done that, we would have known for sure.' We also don't know for certain what the motivation was behind Karmein's kidnap and murder, as her body was too decomposed to provide evidence of sexual assault, or (as importantly) that sexual assault didn't occur. We know Mr Cruel was motivated by sexual gratification, but was Karmein's abductor? Without knowing the 'why', we can't figure out the 'who'.

As Chris eloquently put it, 'You could write a book about everything we don't know in this case'. I could hear the frustration in his voice. The police, and Chris specifically, spent years looking at every detail of Mr Cruel's crimes, and they remain committed to getting a resolution for the families of the victims. Having spoken to other ex-police, I know it's hard for them when they leave the force with a case like this unsolved. But we need heroes like Chris working cold cases, never giving up, chasing every lead, as without them the Mr Cruels of this world would never be brought to justice.

Chris, who worked on hundreds of sex offender cases during his career, said that Mr Cruel struck him as 'a street-smart offender, rat cunning, but not necessarily highly educated'. He knew how to minimise the risks of being caught, was patient and single-minded, but then he took risks removing the girls from their homes and transferring between more than one vehicle. Another risk Mr Cruel took, if we accept he is responsible for Karmein Chan's murder, is the site he chose to dispose of her body. Chris described the scene as it was in 1992, telling me, 'It was just too open. Too exposed. With houses on one side and nothing to hide his activity as he would have needed to dig the grave and move the body. No trees. It's not a good spot to have chosen'.

Was he careless or fearless? Or are we looking at two offenders – one committing the original abductions and assaults, and one abducting and murdering Karmein Chan?

The more I delved into this case, the more questions I had. What I could say was that Mr Cruel was an intelligent, meticulous and callous offender. He was also patient and disciplined. And someone who would have blended in. If he lived in the small area identified in figure 8, he would have been considered a good neighbour.

Probably a nice guy. He was meticulous and would have been known for being detail oriented. Perhaps quiet, even introverted, he is likely to have been involved in community-based projects, may have helped out at local sports clubs or at church. He may even have worked at a local school. Whatever his job or hobbies, he would have had access to children in one part of his life.

There is nothing deranged about his behaviour, his attacks are not the result of mental illness – instead, they are reasoned and ordered.

This man did not have horns and a tail.

Which is why the nickname 'Mr Cruel' is a bit misleading, as in his everyday life he would come across as anything but cruel.

LINKS TO OTHER CASES

In 1991 the attacks stopped. Did the perpetrator die, was he arrested and incarcerated, or did he simply move on?

In chapter three we raised the possibility that Ashley Coulston and Mr Cruel could be one and the same person, and we know that Coulston is one of the most violent serial offenders in recent Australian history. There are a few reasons why Coulston could be in the frame, but let's consider whether his criminal MO fits with the crimes against the four young girls.

There are a number of similarities between Coulston's sex crimes and the murder of the three young people in Burwood and Mr Cruel's attacks. They all happened in Melbourne and both perpetrators carried a knife and a gun, although Mr Cruel carried a small handgun, not a sawn-off shotgun. Karmein Chan was shot execution-style in the head, just like Coulston's Burwood victims. However, this is an efficient way of killing someone and does not necessarily indicate a signature. They both wore balaclavas, although this is a fairly common way for an offender to hide their face, so that alone cannot link the crimes. Both offenders were intelligent, organised and well-practised.

But there are too many factors that don't fit.

From looking at the victimology and methodology of the Mr Cruel crimes, I don't think Coulston is a good fit. Coulston attacked and sexually assaulted adults only; Mr Cruel targeted a range of victims, abducting female children and raping an elderly woman, and he did not make the adult male watch the sexual attack. Coulston did not take his victims to quiet locations to assault them over a long period of time, instead he liked to attack more than one person, to dominate and control his victims, and often make the male victim watch him assault the female. Coulston was also comfortable to travel around an hour from his base (either working or living) when hunting, unlike Mr Cruel who stayed very much within a small comfort zone of only a few kilometres. Mr Cruel used wire to bind his victims, and Coulston cable ties.

Mr Cruel was also meticulous, not just in how he went about his crimes, but also in his obsession with making sure the girls were clean. This is a compulsion that would have carried over into his private and professional life. This obsession with hygiene is a signature, and was not evident in the Coulston crimes.

Another factor that likely rules out Coulston is that, in the first three cases, Mr Cruel probably did not (in his mind) harm the children. If he was responsible for Karmein Chan's death, it is likely that this was accidental, and that she either saw his face or attempted to flee and he killed her out of desperation. This fits with what Phyllis Chan said about her daughter – that she would not allow herself to be abducted easily and would escape if she got the chance. The police had stated publicly after Sharon Wills's abduction how dangerous it would be for any of his victims to see his face, that it would be enough for him to commit murder, as ultimately his own safety was of more value to him than the life of a child.

There are other differences between the two. For example, the experience of Karmein's murder could have been disturbing enough to Mr Cruel that he did not offend again. At least for a while. If he did reoffend, he is intelligent enough to have modified his MO to disrupt the pattern the police were starting to identify. Coulston, on the other hand, intentionally escalated into murder, likely after rape no longer brought him the excitement he sought.

Taken together, the difference in victimology, Mr Cruel's obsession with hygiene and Coulston's intentional escalation to murder, indicate to me that these two offenders are not one and the same.

If I were the investigators I would discount Coulston as a suspect and would instead look for an offender who lived in the Lower Plenty/Templestowe area. It's unlikely this person's name would have come up during their initial scan for child sex offenders or other sexual predators known to be in the area as he would have blended in, although he may have been amongst those 27,000 people interviewed as part of Taskforce Spectrum. Crime is solved by people, and it is the people in Mr Cruel's life who hold the clue to his being identified. Perhaps he has shown too much interest in activities that include girls aged 10–13 years, at sporting groups or other community-based activities. Perhaps he makes the girls or parents uncomfortable. Although maybe he is clever enough to keep his true intentions and desires to himself. But his family, if he has one, would know about his obsession with cleanliness and hygiene. Maybe that will be the key to his undoing even now.

WILL WE EVER KNOW?

One of the difficulties police have in identifying suspects is that Mr Cruel was meticulously careful not to leave behind DNA. He also never let the victims see his face. Added to that, he was lucky in that the police did not do a good job of preserving and collecting what little evidence he did leave behind. There have never been any fingerprints; there is no DNA to upload to a database. This case is totally devoid of forensic evidence.

All is not lost, however. The young girls Mr Cruel assaulted, now grown women, remember the incidents clearly and would make compelling witnesses should anyone ever be taken to court. What the police need is a strong lead, a name they can chase down. If the suspect can't be excluded (i.e. they don't have a reliable alibi), can they be placed in the area? Did they live/work around the attack sites? Did they have a tie to the airport or a house located very close? And crucially, do they have an obsession with hygiene and cleanliness? If someone can give the police the clues they need, then I have no doubt a strong circumstantial case can be built.

And there is a significant incentive for someone to come forward if they do have evidence that could help. In 2016, on the 25th anniversary of Karmein Chan's abduction, Victoria Police increased the reward from $300,000 to $1 million for information that leads to the arrest and conviction for her murderer. Importantly, the police also announced that the Office of Public Prosecutions would consider granting anyone with information on the case indemnity from prosecution if they came forward. After all this time, this is really the last chance the police have to catch – or identify, if they are deceased – this man.

As he spent so many years investigating this case, I thought it appropriate to leave the last word to Chris O'Connor: 'I haven't given up hope that we'll still identify Mr Cruel. And the police are determined, if he's alive they will bring him to justice'.

FORENSIC SCIENCE EXPLAINED: FINGERPRINTS

Fingerprints are one of the oldest methods of forensic identification. One of the pioneers of fingerprint identification
was Dr Henry Faulds (1843–1930), a missionary doctor
from the United Presbyterian Church. Whilst stationed in
Japan, Faulds became interested in archaeology and noticed
that when ancient pottery was recovered the fingerprints
of those who created it were sometimes still visible. Faulds
was intrigued and began to study modern fingerprints and
their potential uses. In late1880 he published a letter in the
prestigious multidisciplinary journal *Nature* entitled 'On the
Skin-Furrows of the Hand', in which he described loops,
whorls and lines, as well as the way that they branch 'like
junctions in a railway map'. Faulds eventually collected over
8000 sets of fingerprints.

The first documented use of fingerprints in a criminal
case occurred in 1892, when two children were violently
murdered in their home in Argentina. Initially the police had
no leads, but a bloody fingerprint was found at the crime
scene by Police Inspector Alvarez (who had been trained in
fingerprint identification by another pioneer, Juan Vucetich).
Alvarez's comparison between Francisca Rojas, the children's

mother, and the bloody print were a match. Rojas confessed, saying she had staged the crime and tried to shift the blame to her neighbour – the motive was that Rojas's boyfriend had said he would marry her, except for the children. Rojas was subsequently found guilty of both murders and sentenced to life imprisonment.

Independently, Englishman Sir Edward Henry established his own system of comparison. In 1901 he was appointed Assistant Commissioner of Police at New Scotland Yard (Metropolitan Police, UK), and by the end of the year had established a Fingerprint Office. The first conviction by a British court on the basis of fingerprint evidence occurred in 1902.

In Australia, the relevance of fingerprint identification was first recognised by Sam McCauley, Deputy Controller of Prisons and Inspector of Prisons in New South Wales in 1901. Inspired by what he learnt during a secondment to New Scotland Yard, on his return to Australia he recommended that fingerprint identification be initiated in NSW prisons. After it was successfully introduced in NSW, the system was rolled out to other states and territories in Australia as well as New Zealand.

In 1980, 100 years after fingerprints first became recognised for their significance in human identification, the first computerised databases were established. Known as AFIS (short for Automated Fingerprint Identification Systems), today the databases hold almost 700 million individual fingerprints, and thousands of people are added across the world on a daily basis. To date, no two finger-prints have ever been found to be identical, even after many billions of computerised comparisons, and the science of fingerprint identification is the basis for establishing identity and criminal history at every police agency on the planet.

Fingerprints can be lifted from almost any solid surface, including human skin, and the method of visualisation and recovery depends entirely on the surface on which they have been left. There are three types of fingerprints – those deposited on surfaces that create a three-dimensional effect (such as a bar of hand soap), or flat prints, which are either visible (patent), such as those left in blood, or invisible (latent). Latent prints can be detected using alternative light sources, chemicals or dusting powder.

Although fingerprints are one of the oldest methods of human identification, that does not mean that they aren't impactful in helping to solve cold cases as techniques improve. In 1983, 21-year-old newlywed Linda Reed and her new husband, Robert, had their whole lives ahead of them However, on 13 December 1983, Linda vanished during her lunchbreak, whilst working at a shopping centre on the Gold Coast. Linda's body was found three days later, along with her car, in bushland in Gaven, a 20-minute drive from where she disappeared. A witness came forward to say they had given a lift to a hitchhiker in their van, and a fingerprint was lifted from the van's passenger window, but this print did not match any of the police's suspects. Almost 35 years later, in August 2018, a person (who can't be named for legal reasons) was arrested for Linda's murder. As a result of advances in forensic print comparison technologies, the fingerprint from the van's window was reanalysed, and this time the police got a hit, which put the person in the area at the time Linda was abducted. Police have alleged that the person took Linda from the shopping centre and made her drive to Gaven where she was raped and murdered and her body abandoned. In addition to the fingerprint evidence, the person has allegedly been implicated in Linda's murder through DNA found on Linda's body. A great example of forensic technologies and good old-fashioned policing working in unison. The person will be back in court in 2019 but is, of course, entitled to the presumption of innocence. Neither fingerprint nor DNA evidence is infallible – and, of course, prosecutors generally have to prove their case by producing more than forensic evidence alone.

Fingerprint identification has come a long way from humble beginnings. Today a number of police forces in Australia are using portable fingerprint scanners, capable of verifying a person's identity and checking their criminal history in minutes. In 2018 the New South Wales police announced that they were purchasing as many as 1000 smartphone-compatible fingerprint scanners, the next generation of the technology. We live in an increasingly technologically advanced world – many of us unlock our mobiles and laptops with fingerprint or facial scans – and we can expect to see expanded uses of biometric technologies like fingerprint readers in the future, both in policing and in our personal spheres.

FIVE

IVAN MILAT - AUSTRALIA'S MOST INFAMOUS SERIAL KILLER

'It would be naive to think the seven backpackers were
his only victims.'

Retired Chief Inspector Bob Godden, NSW Police Force

There's always something sad about standing where victims of violent crimes have died, regardless of how much time has elapsed. It's almost as though their deaths have left a stain on the atmosphere. There's something palpable in the air, almost like electricity but heavy and stale. Of all the murder scenes I've been to, Belanglo State Forest has to be the most oppressive. Even in bright daylight it feels dark and foreboding.

Standing here I can't help thinking of all the terrible things that have happened in this place, amongst them the violent deaths of seven backpackers at the hands of Ivan Milat. I've come to Belanglo to research this chapter, doing the drive between the forest and Newcastle, where some of Milat's potential additional victims disappeared, to get a sense of the spaces we know Milat was comfortable operating in. As I drove here I was reminded how vulnerable people are, waiting at bus stops, hitchhiking. But unlike Milat, I didn't see the people I passed as potential prey. Now I'm here I can't wait to leave, painfully aware that seven young backpackers never had the chance to get out, that this was the final place on earth they saw.

On my way home I detour past Jenolan Karst Conservation Reserve, where another of Milat's potential victims, Peter Letcher, was found. Are there more deceased Milat victims yet to be found? I believe so, and after researching this chapter and getting some insights from an expert in geographic profiling, I know where I would start looking.

THE CASE

Backpacking used to be a rite of passage for many young people. And so it was in Australia, at least until the disappearance and murder of seven young backpackers between 1989 and 1992. Ivan Milat, serial killer, violent psychopath, was found guilty of all seven murders in 1996, as well as of the abduction and attempted murder of British backpacker Paul Onions, who would have been Milat's third victim in sequence if Onions hadn't managed to escape.

Even before the bodies were found, the disappearances of seven young people made the news, both nationally and international-ally, as two of the missing were Australian, three German and two British. The name Ivan Milat has since become synonymous with the brutal murder of the seven travellers, all of whom were found in Belanglo State Forest (BSF). All seven had been backpacking around Australia and were last seen in Sydney or the surrounding areas. The victims were stabbed and/or shot, and one was decap-itated; the violence of these crimes has meant that Ivan Milat is considered Australia's most infamous serial killer.

That does not explain, however, why I've included this case in a book of Australian cold cases. Let me clarify: although there is overwhelming evidence that Milat is responsible for the seven back-packer deaths (even though he still claims his innocence), there is some question as to whether there may be more victims not yet attributed to Milat.

In this chapter we will briefly look at the seven murders for which Milat has been found guilty as they tell us a lot about him as an offender. We will also look at the single case of a person known to have escaped Milat. Next we will look at another six possible victims to consider whether any can be discounted on logistical or other grounds and, if not, if there is sufficient evidence for Milat to be considered a strong person of interest for these crimes. We will also plot their disappearances against Milat's known movements, applying the technique of geographic profiling to determine his likely involvement.

THE BACKPACKER VICTIMS
JAMES GIBSON AND DEBORAH EVERIST

The first of Milat's victims were reported missing on 15 January 1990 by their parents. James Gibson and Deborah Everist, both 19 years old, had left their homes in Melbourne on 28 December 1989, with a plan to first travel to Sydney, where James had friends, before heading for Walwa in Victoria, travelling partly by train and then hitchhiking the rest of the way along the Hume Highway (the main road between Sydney and Melbourne). They made it to Sydney, stayed two days, leaving again on 30 December, but somewhere between Sydney and Walwa they disappeared. A day later, a walker found James's camera abandoned at the side of the road at Galston Gorge, 120 kilometres north of Sydney. James had written his name on the outside flap but this had been

147

cut off; however, he'd also written his name inside and this was still intact when it was found. The walker did not report this find straightaway, as he was unaware of its potential importance, and it was not until a month later when the media was publicising the news of James's disappearance and the fact that his missing backpack had been found that the walker reported finding the camera to police.

James and Deborah's remains were found almost 3 years later, on 6 October 1993, in a particularly remote part of Belanglo State Forest (1 hour and 30 minutes south of Sydney, see figure 9).

Both had been violently murdered. James had been stabbed eight times, and his spine had been severed, meaning that he would have been paralysed. Deborah had been beaten to death and had sustained two fractures to her skull and her jaw was broken. She had also suffered one stab wound to her back and others to her forehead. Their remains were located around 20 metres apart and had been partially covered with forest debris. The rest of their property, such as backpacks, were missing.

SIMONE SCHMIDL

Almost exactly a year after James and Deborah disappeared, 22-year-old German Simone Schmidl was reported missing by her mother. Simone was a seasoned traveller, having already visited Yugoslavia, Alaska, Canada and New Zealand, before arriving in Australia on 19 January 1991. Simone stayed at a friend's in Sydney's west, before leaving for Melbourne on 20 January. The morning she disappeared, Simone had intended to catch a bus to Liverpool and hitchhike from there to Melbourne to meet her mother, Erwine Schmidl, who was flying in from Germany to join Simone for a camping holiday. When Simone didn't meet her mother at the airport on 25 January 1991 as planned, Erwine raised the alarm.

Simone would be the fifth victim found, on 1 November 1993. Again there had been some attempt to hide the body under sticks and leaves, and Simone had been subject to a knife attack, suffering at least eight stab wounds (although, due to the level of decomposition, there may have been more that were no longer in evidence on her remains). Simone's spine had been severed in two places.

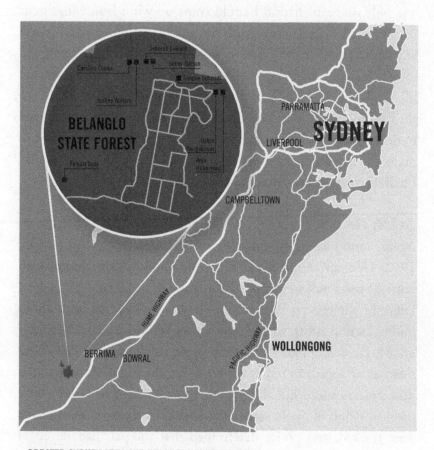

GREATER SYDNEY AREA AND BELANGLO STATE FOREST

Figure 9: The drive between Sydney and the Belanglo State Forest, passing Wollongong.

This was clearly a purposeful act by the perpetrator to disable his victims. Clothing was found with Simone's remains, but it was not hers, and later it transpired it belonged to another of the victims, Anja Habschied.

When I realised this, my breath caught. As you will see, Anja Habschied was still alive for a year *after* Simone was murdered. So how could Anja's T-shirt be found with Simone's remains? There was only one explanation I could come up with: Ivan Milat went back to the kill sites. This struck me as a revelation, as I can't recall anyone ever noticing this before. But of course it makes sense if you look at Milat's psychology. Milat loved taking trophies, so it follows that he would also go back to revisit his murder sites to relive the thrill he got from his crimes, the power he had over his victims even in death. Even so, I was taken aback that, after all this time and so many experts dissecting everything about Milat and his behaviour, I had discovered something new about Milat's signature.

ANJA HABSCHIED AND GABOR NEUGEBAUER

Again, almost exactly a year after Simone vanished, on 30 January 1992, German couple Anja Habschied and Gabor Neugebauer, both 22 years old, were reported missing to the Australian Federal Police by the Federal Republic of Germany. They had been hitch-hiking around Australia and had flights booked back to Germany on 24 January. Anja's father had gone to the airport to collect them as arranged, but they were not on the flight. After making numerous unsuccessful attempts to contact Anja and Gabor, their parents reported them missing. Anja and Gabor's movements were tracked, and police determined that the pair had stayed at the Original Backpackers Hostel in Sydney's Kings Cross for a few days, before leaving on 26 December, when they planned to hitch-hike to Adelaide. They needed to be in Darwin on 1 January 1992, as they had flights booked to Indonesia. The couple were not seen alive again after leaving Sydney. Anja and Gabor were the last of the confirmed Milat victims to be discovered, two days after Simone on 3 November 1993. Discovered 50 metres apart in shallow graves, Gabor had been shot six times in the head and once in the chest, and a gag had been placed over his mouth. Anja had been decapitated and, despite the police undertaking an exhaustive search, her head was never recovered.

JOANNE WALTERS AND CAROLINE CLARKE

A few months later, on 29 May 1992, 22-year-old British backpacker Joanne Walters was reported missing by a woman she had worked for. Joanne's concerned parents in the UK had contacted people their daughter had known in Australia as they hadn't heard from her since early April. Joanne had been travelling with another young British woman, 22-year-old Caroline Clarke, who was subsequently also reported missing by her family in the UK. Like others who had disappeared, the girls had been staying in Sydney's Kings Cross, at Bridge North Apartments. On 18 April they'd left Sydney for Mildura, a regional city in northwest Victoria, over 1000 kilometres away. They had planned to hitchhike and were last seen asking directions to the Hume Highway. That was the last sighting of the girls alive.

Caroline's body was discovered on 19 September 1992 by a couple on an orientating training exercise in Belanglo State Forest, and one day later Joanne's body was also found, 30 metres away. Both had been brutally murdered: Joanne had suffered 14 stab wounds, including the characteristic one to her spine that would have paralysed her, and Caroline had been shot 10 times in the head, and 10 fired .22 calibre cartridge cases were recovered from near her body. From the positioning of the injuries, it looked as if

Caroline had been used for target practice. Their bodies had been deposited near a network of fire trails that crisscross the area and partially buried under leaf litter. Their personal property had also been taken.

SIMILARITIES AND WHAT THEY TOLD US ABOUT THE OFFENDER

By the time all seven victims' bodies had been recovered from Belanglo forest, a number of factors common to all four scenes had become clear. All the victims were young, aged between 19–22 years; all had been hitchhiking when they disappeared; Liverpool was a common location linking their disappearances, and was in all likelihood where they had all been picked up. There was a high level of violence in all cases, and six of the seven victims had been stabbed or had cut clothing, and two had also been shot (Caroline and Gabor); analysis of bullets found at the scenes indicated that the same .22 calibre Ruger rifle had been used. All of the bodies had been laid face down, superficially hidden; all of the victims had been tied up (either with cable ties, rope or both), and trophies comprising of the victims' personal property had been taken.

From the victim selection we could also tell a lot about the offender. Whoever had abducted and murdered the backpackers was confident, evidenced by the fact that they took couples – which is obviously much harder than abducting people on their own. It was clear that they were organised and the crimes were planned, as the offender had brought the weapons and ties with him. Taking pairs of victims is unusual and initially it was thought this could mean that the police were hunting for more than one offender working together (known as a joint enterprise). There was also a heavily ritualistic nature to the murders; for example, all of the victims had been positioned face down with their hands tied behind their backs. Several of the victims, both male and female, showed evidence of sexual assault, although it did not appear that this was the offender's primary focus; rather, whoever abducted and murdered these young people enjoyed the feelings of power and control the crimes gave him. As the property taken was of limited monetary value, it is more likely that the offender liked to relive his crimes and had kept the victims' belongings as mementos. The offender also seemed to be spending increasingly more time with each victim or pair of victims, again showing increased confidence, as he did not fear getting caught. There was other evidence that linked the scenes – as well as the same calibre bullets and casings, beer bottles and cigarette butts also littered the scenes.

There was evidence of fires close to where the bodies were left, supporting the idea that the offender had been with the victims for a significant amount of time, even camping at the crime scenes. What I have now come to realise is that these fires and other evidence may also indicate that the offender went back to spend more time with his victims. That he left his victims in the open with very minimal attempts to hide them suggests a confidence as he knew people walked through the bush but he was not concerned that the bodies would be discovered. It may also have allowed him to go back and see his victims again, showing that he was still in charge as he had almost left them on show.

The offender clearly knew the forest well, as the victims had been murdered and deposited not far from a fire trail in open but secluded areas, and off main access routes – not places you would come across randomly. This suggests he may have preselected some suitable places to take his victims before the abductions occurred, again speaking to his level of organisation, preparation and premeditation. Given he clearly planned to abduct couples, and could not risk driving around with two living abductees in his car for any longer than absolutely necessary, he needed to know where he was going, somewhere he would not be disturbed. This also told police that it was likely the offender was driving a four-wheel drive, as he clearly needed a vehicle that could traverse uneven terrain.

Belanglo State Forest is not somewhere tourists go for picnics. It is about 3800 hectares of planted woodland, mostly pine, 3 kilometres off the Hume Highway. It's eerie, strangely quiet, and once amongst the trees you feel very isolated, especially at night.

WHY IVAN MILAT?

All seven murders were clearly the work of one person or possibly a pair of killers, and as serial killers in Australia are rare, the police had little experience dealing with this kind of case. In addition, a number of elements were working against investigators. The fact the victims were backpackers meant that it would be more difficult to pinpoint their precise movements immediately prior to their disappearances, the length of time between their disappearances and the discovery of the bodies resulted in high rates of decomposition that limited what the forensic pathologist could say regarding time and manner of death, and physical evidence would be lost or have degraded at the crime scenes. The remoteness and scale of the crime scene also meant that the likelihood of finding witnesses to the offender's movements in and out of the forest was unlikely.

Ivan Milat was mentioned as a person of interest early on in the investigation, more because there were a number of brothers in the family and they had a reputation for being violent than for any specific evidence linking him to the victims. The police began to collect more and more intelligence, much of which came via a hotline they had set up, and callers did ring and give Ivan Milat's name as he drove a four-wheel drive and was known to own a lot of guns and was heavily into shooting. This was still just gossip and innuendo; however, the Milat brothers in general remained of interest to investigators, and whilst nothing tied any one brother to the crimes, the police were beginning to think one or other of the brothers could have been involved.

Ivan Milat became of specific interest to investigators as a result of the abduction and attempted murder of another backpacker, 23-year-old British man Paul Onions, in January 1990. Onions had been hitchhiking from Liverpool to Melbourne along the Hume Highway and had been picked up by a man in his early 40s, with a big moustache and black hair, in a white four-wheel-drive Toyota Land Cruiser. He had given his name as Bill, a name Ivan Milat was known to use, although there was another Milat brother called Bill. They drove for about an hour before Milat stopped the car near the entrance to Belanglo State Forest, pulled a gun on Onions and got a bag of rope from underneath his seat. Paul fled the car, abandoning all of his possessions, and flagged down a passing car. He called the police and left a statement about the attack. The driver of this car, Canberra woman Joanne Berry, also reported the attack to police. Neither of these reports were followed up when they were made in 1990, and it was not until 1993 when the murdered backpackers were making headlines all over the world that both Paul Onions (now back in the UK) and Joanne Berry called the police again, concerned that the man who had killed the backpackers was also responsible for the attack on Paul.

To give this context, at the time Paul was attacked by Ivan Milat, two of the seven backpackers had been murdered and their bodies left in Belanglo, but five were yet to be killed. Paul's evidence became crucial in identifying Ivan Milat as a viable suspect for the back-packer killings. But the police no doubt didn't want to move too quickly and arrest Ivan Milat, as at this time they could only charge him with the crimes relating to Paul's abduction and attempted murder – they needed more if they were going to link him to the Belanglo killings.

When Ivan Milat's criminal records were checked it transpired that he had a criminal history going back to 1964, which included break, enter and steal, car theft and armed robbery. The records also showed that Ivan Milat had been accused of the abduction of two women, Margaret and Greta, and the rape of one of them, in 1971, although he had not been found guilty of these charges. However, the abduction and rape accusation mirrored the murder of the backpackers in some key ways – firstly, the two victims Milat allegedly abducted were 18-year-old females who had been hitchhiking. Milat had picked them up at Liverpool (the location central to all the murdered backpackers' travels) in April 1971 and had offered to drive them to Canberra. Milat then pulled over to a secluded spot and told the girls he wanted to have sex with them. When they refused, he tied them up and threatened to murder them, and so Margaret complied if Milat agreed to let them live. Milat then drove to a petrol station and the girls managed to escape. At trial, Milat claimed the sex was consensual and that he dropped the girls at the petrol station. The jury believed him. Although clear parallels could be drawn to the backpacker killings, this was still circumstantial evidence, but it does help to build a picture of the type of man Ivan Milat is.

Following further in-depth investigation of Ivan Milat, the police obtained search warrants, not just for his house but also properties that belonged to family members and to which he had access. The search teams were given a list of more than 100 items to look for specifically, including all of the personal items missing from the victims, as well as items that the killer had taken to the scene to either restrain or murder his victims (such as tie cords and the Ruger rifle). The amount of evidence collected during these raids was overwhelming; incriminating or suspicious items were found in almost every room of Milat's house. Key pieces of personal property that had undoubtedly belonged to some of the Belanglo victims included Simone Schmidl's water bottle, with the name 'Simi' scratched in two places, her sleeping bag and cover, and a headband identical to one around Simone's head when her body was found. Milat admitted all of these items belonged to Schmidl. Some of the items in Paul Onions' backpack, abandoned when he jumped out of the car and ran for his life, were also found at Milat properties.

In addition to the many other personal items identified as belonging to Milat's victims were dozens of boxes of ammunition (some with the same batch numbers as those at the crime scenes), as well as weapons – including a silencer that would fit a Ruger .22 calibre rifle. Some of these parts for the Ruger had been hidden in a cavity between the inner and outer walls at Ivan Milat's house. Milat denied ever having seen the gun parts before; however, amongst these items hidden in the wall in his house was a breech bolt that was quickly identified by a police ballistics expert as belonging to the Ruger rifle that had been used to murder Caroline Clarke. Following further tests, a second weapon belonging to Ivan and found at his brother Walter's house, a .22 calibre Anschurtz rifle, was also linked with the backpacker murders.

Milat had been arrested immediately prior to the raids.

The searches of the various properties took eight full days, and the sheer amount of evidence recovered – over 800 potential exhibits – clearly indicated Ivan Milat was in all likelihood the backpacker killer. However, the police still had a lot of legwork to prove that each of the items recovered belonged to victims or were otherwise involved in the killings (such as the cable ties used to restrain the victims). The guns also had to be matched to the bullets from the scene and the cartridge cases examined and compared, and as literally thousands of bullets and cartridge cases had been recovered from the various properties (as a number included shooting ranges), the police still had a lot of work to do before Ivan Milat could be charged and the case progressed to court.

Ivan Milat's trial began on 11 March 1996 and ran for 15 weeks. Although the case was circumstantial as no forensic or other evidence linked Milat directly to the murders (such as his DNA being recovered from one of the victims, or his fingerprints being found on items at the crime scenes), the evidence against him was overwhelming. On 27 July the jury returned its verdict. Milat was found guilty of all seven murders and was given seven life sentences. He was also found guilty of the abduction, false imprisonment and attempted murder of Paul Onions, for which he received six years for each count. All the sentences were to run concurrently, without the possibility of parole. Milat has unsuccessfully appealed his conviction twice and he will remain in prison for the rest of his life.

THE OTHER POTENTIAL CASES

The violent murder of seven backpackers between 1989 and 1992 rocked the country, but what other murders could Ivan Milat be guilty of? In 1993 the police launched a nationwide probe, Task-force Air, led by then New South Wales Assistant Commissioner Clive Small, which continued to investigate allegations against Ivan Milat and his associates. The task force case inclusion criteria encompassed all unsolved disappearances, murders and attempted murders, and other violent crimes where victims were between 17 and 40 years old, who had disappeared between 1970 and 1992 in New South Wales. The aim was to learn as much as possible about the victims and their movements, to see if they fit Milat's criminal pattern of behaviour.

Searches looking at key aspects of the Belanglo murders were included in the analysis. For example, because of the combination of weapons used on the known Milat victims, the list of inclusion criteria also included crimes where a .22 calibre rifle and/or knife had been used. Particular attention was paid to incidents where the victims were travelling, including backpackers and hitchhikers.

The investigators' search was not restricted to New South Wales; all police and state forces were contacted for assistance. The taskforce identified 16 unsolved murders and 43 missing persons cases that warranted further investigation before Milat could be discounted as a potential suspect. Included in this list were travellers and backpackers from New Zealand, the UK, Germany, Italy and the US, although the majority were Australians in their late teens and 20s – exactly the type of victim targeted by Ivan Milat. Following further examination, this list was significantly reduced; for example, nine of those listed as missing were found, and in other cases no evidence was found that linked Ivan Milat to the incident.

When Clive Small and Tom Gilling published *Milat: Inside Australia's biggest manhunt. A detective's story,* they looked at the remaining potential victims. Taking into consideration the results of the taskforce's search, the authors concluded that in three unsolved murders (Leanne Goodall, Robyn Hickie and Amanda Robinson) Milat could be considered a suspect, but there was not sufficient evidence to proceed to prosecution – either of Ivan Milat or anyone else. However, the authors state that one of the remaining unsolved murders was almost certainly a Milat victim: Peter Letcher.

And there are likely more. Of those who have been suggested, there appear to be two other victims (Gillian Jamieson and Deborah Balken) that fit Milat's MO, where he can also be placed in the area at the time of the disappearances.

POTENTIAL VICTIMS 1, 2 AND 3: LEANNE GOODALL, ROBYN HICKIE AND AMANDA ROBINSON

On 23 March 1998, two years after Milat was convicted and sent to prison, Strike Force Fenwick was established at the direction of Assistant Commissioner Clive Small. The purpose of the taskforce was to look specifically at the disappearance of 10 young people across the Hunter region of New South Wales between 1978 and 1993. The reason this region was of interest was because between 1978 and early 1979, Ivan Milat was known to have stayed in this vicinity.

One aspect of the strike force's job was to capture as much information as possible regarding the missing young people, and to upload this intelligence into a computerised information management system. This process allowed the police analysts to cross-reference details to determine if any of the cases could be linked; a significant step forward, and impossible at the time of the original disappearances.

During this process it became clear to investigators that three of the ten cases had a number of similarities, including two young women and a schoolgirl, all of whom disappeared between December 1978 and April 1979 during the time Milat was known to have been working in the area. Because of the likelihood that the young women had met with foul play, and the obvious similarities between the girls' disappearances (all three vanished whilst at bus stops along a stretch of the Pacific Highway outside of Newcastle), all three were referred to the New South Wales Coroner, John Abernethy. The cases were heard simultaneously at an inquest in 2002, over 20 years since the girls vanished.

The first young woman to go missing was 20-year-old Leanne Goodall. Leanne was last seen heading for the Star Hotel in

Newcastle on 30 December 1978. She was planning to travel to Sydney by train for New Year's Eve celebrations. She was at a bus stop on her way to the train station when she disappeared; she was never seen alive again and her body has not been found. There was no criminal investigation into Leanne's disappearance, and her case was not considered as a potential homicide or reported to the state coroner until Strike Force Fenwick's reinvestigation. The initial investigation into Leanne's disappearance would later be described by Coroner Abernethy as 'a failing of extreme magnitude'.

The second girl to vanish was Robyn Hickie, an 18-year-old who left her family home in Belmont, 19 kilometres south of Newcastle, to meet a friend at the Belmont Hotel on 7 April 1979. She never made it. Like Leanne, Robyn vanished from a bus stop. Robyn was known to hitchhike, and the police only opened an investigation 17 days after she vanished. A significant amount of effort was then made by officers to investigate her disappearance; this lasted for about two weeks, after which little appears to have been done and the original investigative leads were not followed up. After October 1979 no further attempts were made to find Robyn and no report was made to the coroner. The police in essence dropped her case, considering her a likely runaway. This remained the status quo until Strike Force Fenwick was established.

The last to disappear was 14-year-old Amanda Robinson, who vanished just 13 days after Robyn, on 21 April 1979. Just like Leanne and Robyn, Amanda had been on her own, travelling home by public transport. Amanda took a bus home after a school dance in Gateshead, 12 kilometres south of Newcastle; she got off at a stop and, just like Leanne and Robyn, disappeared (see figure 10). An extensive search was undertaken by police, but no trace was found and the case was listed as a missing person.

161

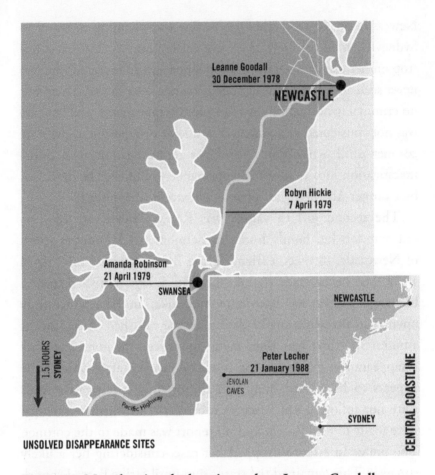

Figure 10: Map showing the locations where Leanne Goodall, Robyn Hickie and Amanda Robinson were last seen, and where Peter Letcher's body was found.

At the time of the girls' disappearances, the response to missing persons reports by the New South Wales Police Force (NSWPF) was largely nonexistent, and no follow-up was made. Missing persons, especially young adults, were largely dismissed by the NSWPF as family or social issues, not under the remit of the police. This remained the case until the late 1980s, after which a considerable effort has been made to respond more appropriately to missing persons reports, particularly if the person is identified as being at risk of violent crime. Coroner Abernethy concluded in the coronial inquest that, should a person disappear under similar circumstances, the contemporary response and investigation would be much improved.

The inquest into the disappearances of the three young women heard evidence from around 160 witnesses, but it did suffer from a number of limiting factors. As with any cold case that is decades old, the biggest enemy was time – the girls had vanished over 20 years before the hearings took place, as a result of which there were a number of discrepancies in the witness evidence compared to statements given in 1979. Some witnesses were called to give evidence at the coronial inquest who had not been interviewed when the girls disappeared, and other potential witnesses had died during the intervening period or were otherwise unable to give evidence. Add to this the lack of satisfactory record keeping during the original investigations and the inquest was fraught with challenges.

A number of males had come to the attention of Strike Force Fenwick. Investigators developed a system of reviewing and categorising these males in terms of how likely they were to have been involved (based on factors such as previous convictions and whether they were known to have a pre-existing relationship with one or more of the victims). Following a thorough analysis, and rejection of many as being uninvolved, the names of the remaining persons of interest were considered during the coronial inquest to determine if any could have been involved in the assumed abduction and murder of the three girls. One of these people was Ivan Milat.

In June 1998 Milat was questioned by investigators at the supermaximum-security prison in Goulburn, where he remains to this day. Milat denied any involvement in the disappearances of Leanne, Amanda, and Robyn. He was the first person named as a POI in the coronial investigation and was called to give evidence; State Coroner Abernethy stated that Milat was 'a major person of interest'. This was in part due to the fact Milat was known to have been working in the Hunter Region of New South Wales, and most of the places Milat stayed whilst working there were either on or were close to the Pacific Highway, or were near the locations where the missing girls lived or were seen. This included the Star Hotel (Leanne Goodall's destination when she disappeared), as well as numerous other hotels in the immediate area. Milat also had personal connections to the region, in that his girlfriend, Karen Duck (who later became his wife before divorcing him in 1984), lived at Buff Point, a town 51 kilometres south of Newcastle on the Pacific Highway; he visited her there on weekends during 1978 and possibly into 1979. When questioned at the inquest, Milat denied that his girlfriend lived at Buff Point, or that he had ever been there, but evidence from other sources corroborated this as accurate. Witnesses were called who gave evidence that they had seen Milat in the area around the time some of the girls vanished.

Milat made several key admissions whilst giving evidence, including that he had owned a large number of firearms and other weapons, and that he had stayed in the relevant areas at or around the time the girls disappeared. Milat also admitted that he had picked up around 15 hitchhikers over the years, but claimed not to have done so in the Newcastle area.

The coroner concluded his report by stating that Leanne Goodall died on or shortly after her disappearance on 30 December 1978, as the result of a homicide. Robyn Hickie is believed to have died on or around 7 April 1979, again as a result of murder. Finally, Coroner Abernethy stated that Amanda Robinson died on or around 21 April 1979 after being abducted, and was subsequently murdered. The Coroner was satisfied all three girls were deceased, despite their bodies never having been found. He also said that the likely perpetrator remains unknown. Although Coroner Abernethy stated that there was no evidence to indicate Milat was directly involved, he concluded that Milat's involvement could not be discounted in any of the girls' disappearances.

Given the passage of time between the girls' disappearances and the initiation of the strike force and subsequent coroner's inquest, it was always going to be a significant challenge to source information that could lead to a successful conviction. However, Milat has to remain the key suspect in relation to Leanne, Robyn and Amanda's disappearances.

POTENTIAL VICTIMS 4 AND 5: GILLIAN JAMIESON AND DEBORAH BALKEN

Gillian Jamieson and Deborah Balken were both 20 years old when they disappeared together on 20 June 1980. The friends were last seen at a bar in the Tollgate Hotel in Parramatta, Sydney. Deborah had phoned a flatmate to say that she and Gillian had got a lift to a party in Wollongong. This was not out of character for the pair, as they were known to hitchhike. Although more than 40 sightings of Gillian and Deborah were reported to the police, the girls were never seen alive after leaving the pub in Parramatta, and their bodies have not been located.

Ivan Milat was interviewed about the girls' disappearances, as he was known to have been at the Granville depot of the (then) Department of Main Roads, and Granville is only three kilometres south of Parramatta.

Two separate coronial inquiries were held back to back on 22 May 2006 into the disappearances. In both cases Deputy State Coroner Carl Milovanovich concluded that Deborah and Gillian were dead, and that they died sometime after 12 July 1980. The deputy coroner was unable to determine, from the evidence presented to him, the precise date, time, place or manner of death for either woman. The coroner's office stated that there is no written copy of the full findings on file, so I could not review it – and Milat cannot therefore be ruled out as having been involved.

POTENTIAL VICTIM 6: PETER LETCHER

Peter Letcher was 18 years old when he disappeared. He lived in Bathurst, 200 kilometres northwest of Sydney, and had been to see his girlfriend in Busby, near Liverpool. About a week later, on 13 November 1987, he was returning home and had hitched a lift from Busby to Liverpool, where he planned to catch a train to Sydney and on to Bathurst. He was not seen alive again.

Peter's body was found by bushwalkers nine weeks after he disappeared, 15 metres off a fire trail in a cleared section of Jenolan Karst Conservation Reserve. His body was face down in a shallow depression and covered by leaf litter and other forest debris – the same body positioning as the Belanglo seven. The violence and manner of Peter's murder also mirrored that of the victims found in Belanglo. Although his body was badly decomposed, evidence suggested that he had been bound, blindfolded, stabbed multiple times in the back and shot in the head five times.

Four .22 calibre bullets were recovered from the scene, and a ballistics expert determined that three of the four bullets were fired from the same Ruger .22 calibre rifle that had been used to kill Gabor Neugebauer and Caroline Clarke. The fourth bullet could not be linked to the Belanglo victims as it had deteriorated too badly. Besides the similarities in terms of the MO, the location was also interesting, as Ivan Milat was known to have been working in the Jenolan Caves area at the time Peter had been visiting Busby. Despite the similarities and links to the Belanglo murders, Milat was not charged with Peter's murder.

I have spoken to Clive Small many times about Ivan Milat and his crimes, and asked him about this, and Clive has no doubt that Milat is responsible for Peter's abduction and murder.

WHERE THE OTHER POTENTIAL VICTIMS FIT

To give this context, during the 1980s Milat's marriage to Karen Duck was beginning to deteriorate. Milat was getting more obsessed with weapons, including large knives and guns, and he was beginning to frighten Karen. Between 1989 and early 1990 Milat was working as a New South Wales road surface sprayer, a job that – like his other occupations – took him all over the state, to the Blue Mountains, the Hunter Valley and the south coast. This would be classed as Milat's geographic comfort zone.

Karen Duck would later tell investigators that Milat took her to Jenolan Caves, where Peter's body was found, as well as to Belanglo State Forest on four occasions. The similarities between the two sites are undeniable. As noted by Clive Small in his book, when Milat was in a settled and stable relationship he did not commit murder. However, when he had suffered a relationship breakdown the emotional circumstances triggered his desire to torture and kill others: in 1987 Karen Duck left Milat, which could have acted as a trigger for Peter's murder.

So did Milat move on from murdering these six victims to the known Belanglo seven? He could be argued to have motive, as, like all serial violent predators, Milat thrives on power – and he gets his sense of dominance from torturing and controlling others, by literally having their lives in his hands, deciding how and when they die. He enjoys playing God. Milat also had means and opportunity, he was familiar with the locations and was known to be in the area. From a criminological perspective, he is a strong suspect, as the additional victims disappeared before any of the Belanglo State Forest victims;

potentially indicating he had another multi-victim deposition site that has yet to be discovered. And they do seem to fit a pattern, both in terms of the cause and manner of the disappearances or murders, as well as the locations at which the victims were last seen.

It could therefore be suggested that we simply haven't found Milat's other deposition site (or sites) yet, as Belanglo State Forest was carefully searched. During one of my conversations with Clive Small, he told me that the police searched over 43 kilometres of fire trails, as well as the areas just off the trails to a maximum of around 100 metres. They used natural borders to restrict their searches, so did not search into dense bush as all Milat's body deposition sites were in areas of open ground, and so I do not believe the five missing girls are in Belanglo.

In addition, the five missing girls appear to potentially comprise a group, separated geographically in terms of where they disappeared, and it is probable that Milat had more than one area he used to dispose of his victims' bodies, one for the earlier five missing girls, and a later one he moved on to for the Belanglo seven. Jenolan Karst Conservation Reserve, where Peter Letcher's remains were discovered, could either represent a third site, or alternatively that Milat used this area for people's murders but at some point rejected it – perhaps he was nearly caught or was otherwise disturbed. All this is supposition, but it is possible to inject some scientific analysis into this process through geographic profiling.

A GEOGRAPHIC PROFILER'S THOUGHTS ON THE EXTRA VICTIMS

I wanted to try to narrow down an area Milat might have selected as a suitable site to dispose of the five missing bodies, so I discussed the case with Colin Johnson, a British geographic profiler (we met Colin in chapter two when he explained his work). I provided the information I had regarding the geographical location of the known victims and personal items, and details regarding the Australian landscapes we were talking about.

Colin shared his extensive experience and gave me permission to include some of his insights in this book:

A recurring theme in Milat's solved murders saw him target backpackers/hitchhikers. This may have occurred opportunistically, when he was going about non-criminal routine activities, or in a more focused hunt. His victims were likely to be in streets, roads or main highways known to and used by him. We know Milat disposed of his victims' bodies in rural, forested type locations, hence vehicular movement was essential. Assessment of many other murderers highlight that even if deposition sites are remote, isolated locations, they will invariably be known and familiar to their killers; body deposition sites are not randomly chosen. This is noteworthy when considering Milat. His known body deposition sites were close to areas where he has been described as having worked, lived and/or otherwise frequented previously; hence part of his 'mental map'.

Milat is known to have disposed of murdered victims' bodies relatively close to one another, in Belanglo State Forest. In effect, he developed a body deposition 'comfort zone', with a level of locational consistency, e.g., wooded and remote, yet significantly accessible using his truck. It is also significant to appreciate that he did not dispose of the bodies over a wide area of the forest, but relatively close together. This is an independent factor revealing the likelihood of one serial offender, not different killers.

Milat's deposition sites would almost certainly be ones he knew already. Moreover, their remoteness and the delay in others finding them would confirm to him the value and safety of repeatedly returning to dispose of subsequent victims nearby.

In the above context, if there were earlier Milat murders, using the later known deposition pattern, another similar, yet different deposition area becomes much more likely. This would reflect Milat's earlier personal geography. Therefore, the distinct similarities existing in the Peter Letcher murder and the type of body deposition location used by his killer becomes significant. This would bring into sharp focus the area of Jenolan Karst Conservation Reserve where Peter's body was discovered. Independent to this we also know that at the time of Peter's disappearance Milat worked in the Jenolan Caves area and so it was a familiar area to him. He's also noted as having taken others there.

Overall, this provides a deposition area frequented by Peter Letcher's killer to the north of Sydney, known to Milat. If in turn he had committed earlier murders he may have already developed awareness of where to leave victims' bodies to avoid them being found. It also places much more interest in the potential connection between Milat and the other earlier disappearances you highlighted.

We know Peter Letcher's body was found nine weeks after he disappeared. It is strongly suspected his murderer was Milat. Particularly if Milat was responsible for other earlier killings, this body discovery would have been viewed by him as a failure. Therefore, it comes as little surprise that if responsible, Milat never knowingly chose the area associated with the finding of Peter's body in any subsequent murder he was convicted of.

You explore many of the interesting links between Milat's own geography during particular periods in his earlier life, not least pertaining to several unexplained disappearances. In particular, developing a very detailed timeline for Milat around the outstanding missing person cases is seen as fundamental. Although modern technology greatly enhances the opportunities to link a person to a place (such as through mobile phone cell-site analysis and CCTV), this doesn't prevent it being done in older cases. One of the most notorious child serial killers, Robert Black [a British delivery driver convicted of abducting and murdering four young girls, as well as the sexual assault of two others, and a suspect in other cases], *was ultimately convicted, in no small part, by timeline evidence. This was gathered some 30 years ago, much more akin to the period being considered in relation to Milat.*

Research suggests that geographical classifications involving the offender and victim remain relatively consistent throughout a linked murder series, even though different offenders utilise different movement methods.

Milat is described as having knowledge of parts of both the Belanglo State Forest and Jenolan Karst Conservation Reserve. Geo-profiling principles would further suggest this would extend to him having personal familiarity with the actual deposition sites. It has also been indicated Milat probably revisited some of these sites post-offence. As these forested areas are both vast and remote, it would be interesting whether any of the deposition sites were ones that others knew Milat was familiar with, such as work colleagues.

The expectation is, if Milat is responsible for other serious crimes, such as some or all of those explored in your chapter, these are very likely to bear distinct behavioural similarities to those he's already been convicted of. This is especially so if any unsolved murders he may have perpetrated predated his known killings.

THE TIMELINE OF MILAT ATTACKS (CONVICTED AND SUSPECTED)

04/1971: Margaret and Greta, alleged abduction and rape, picked up at Liverpool

30/12/1978: Leanne Goodall, vanished from Newcastle

07/04/1979: Robyn Hickie, disappeared from a bus stop south of Newcastle

20/04/1979: Amanda Robinson, went missing from Gateshead

20/06/1980: Gillian Jamieson and Deborah Balken, disappeared from Parramatta

13/11/1987: Peter Letcher, vanished from Liverpool, found in Jenolan Karst Conservation Reserve

30/12/1989: James Gibson and Deborah Everist, abducted somewhere between Sydney and Walwa, found BSF

01/1990: Paul Onions, abduction and attempted murder, picked up along the Hume Highway

20/01/1991: Simone Schmidl, disappeared after hitchhiking from Liverpool to Melbourne, found BSF

26/12/1991: Anja Habschied and Gabor Neugebauer, disappeared after leaving Sydney, found BSF

18/04/1992: Joanne Walters and Caroline Clarke, last seen asking directions to the Hume Highway, found BSF

ARE THERE ANY MORE?

Looking at the timeline we see there is a gap between June 1980 and November 1987. What we know in general about serial killers is that they do not simply stop committing crimes for extended periods of time for no reason. If they break their pattern, it is usually for one of three reasons: they died, they were imprisoned or otherwise physically prevented from continuing, or they moved areas.

The police identified that there were 16 unsolved murders between 1970 and 1992, but apart from the cases we have discussed, the police found no evidence to implicate Ivan Milat in the remaining 12. So what could explain the gap in Milat's attacks? It led me to consider whether there were yet more victims we either haven't included because they didn't fit his standard pattern, or perhaps we don't even know about them as their bodies have not been found yet.

One recent example that may help fill that gap came to light in September 2018 when a British man named Colin Powes claimed in a UK newspaper interview that he had been hitchhiking near Katoomba, west of Sydney, in 1982, when he was picked up by someone he believes was Ivan Milat. The driver of the car began to ask Powes questions such as 'How long have you been in Australia?' and 'Who knows you're here?' Powes told him he had only been in Australia a couple of days, didn't know anyone in the country, and that no one knew his travel plans. Shortly afterwards, Powes says the man driving the car turned down a dirt track, before getting out of the car and attacking him with a hammer. Powes says he was only saved as cars were driving towards them, and Powes pushed past his assailant and ran off. Powes returned to the UK and it was not until he saw a documentary about Ivan Milat and his victims that he made the link between his experience in New South Wales in 1982 and the notorious serial killer. If Milat was the driver of this car, it gives us insight into how he selected his victims, based on whether, and how quickly, they would be missed.

This potential encounter between Powes and a man who could have been Ivan Milat does mirror Onions' attempted murder in 1990, excepting that Powes's attacker had a hammer and Onions' assailant a gun. This may be a reflection of the offender's evolving MO, or a chance spotting of a potential victim when not specifically searching for one. As with everything, practice makes perfect. When serial predators develop their skills to manipulate and control their victims, they learn through practice what works, what questions to ask, how to reduce the likelihood of getting caught.

So does this demonstrate an evolution of Milat's skills as a predator? Perhaps the offender learnt that it was easier to control his victims with a knife or gun rather than a hammer, and knew to have the means to bind them ready at the time of the initial attack. And if Milat was the man who attacked Powes, perhaps Milat's methods had already evolved from his earlier crimes. By 1982, had he already learned to avoid high-risk victims such as the young women he may have taken between 1978–1980? Had he started hunting out of cities and looking for victims who would not be immediately missed, such as backpackers? We will never know; however, this evolution in planning fits the pattern of an intelligent and committed violent serial predator. Like Ivan Milat.

SIMILARITIES WITH OTHER OFFENDERS: CHRISTOPHER WILDER

Rod Milton, a forensic psychiatrist brought in to provide a criminal profile of the offender shortly after Caroline Clarke's and Joanne Walter's bodies were recovered, was initially convinced that there were two killers involved with the Belanglo murders, due to the fact that the victims were killed with two different weapons and in different ways. It's also more difficult to abduct and control two adults. Although this could be the case, Clive Small, then New South Wales Assistant Commissioner and the man that led Task Force Air, discounts this as a possibility.

The evidence backs up the solo offender theory. We know that Milat acted alone in abducting the two hitchhikers, Margaret and Greta, in 1971, as well as potentially Colin Powes in 1982 and certainly Paul Onions in 1990. In fact, every survivor of Milat was attacked by Milat alone; no one has ever stated he had an accomplice.

And he is not unique in his criminal behaviour of being capable of abducting and controlling more than one adult simultaneously.

In fact, there are significant similarities between the Milat murders and the criminal behaviour of another Australian serial killer, Christopher Wilder, who we discussed in chapter one in relation to the Wanda Beach murders.

Christopher Wilder was born in Sydney in 1945, the son of an American naval officer and his Australian wife. He had dual citizenship and was used to moving around as a result of his father's job. He began his violent criminal career early. In 1962, at age 17, he was part of a group that raped a young girl at a quarry in Sydney, and he appears to be the main protagonist. Wilder married in 1968, but the arrangement lasted just one year. His wife found pictures of other women in their underwear or bikinis in Wilder's possession, and Wilder made sexual approaches to her mother and sister. The final straw was Wilder being taken in for questioning over a sexual assault on a young nursing student in early February 1969. At this point the police suggested to his wife that she go home to her parents and never return. A few days later she, along with her mother and sister, gave statements to police outlining his behaviour. This event is likely to have prompted his move to the US in 1969, where he settled in Florida.

At this stage he further utilised his interest in photography, which he used as a technique to engage with young women and girls. His MO was to approach his target, telling her he was a photographer and he could help her develop a modelling career. This led to him taking her somewhere secluded, where he raped her. Despite several convictions for sexual and violent offences, Wilder never went to prison. Wilder didn't limit his later activities to the US. During a visit to his parents in Australia in 1982, he raped two 15-year-old girls he picked up at Manly Beach using the photographer scam. He took them shopping to Balmoral, blindfolded them, terrorised them, then took them to a motel in Kings Cross where they were sexually assaulted. He dropped them off at Central Railway Station and told them he'd ring their parents to sort a modelling deal.

In 1984, Wilder was connected to the abduction and assault of two young sisters in Florida, aged 10 and 12 years old. This was the beginning of a six-week crime rampage, which covered Florida, Texas, Kansas, Utah, California, and New York before his self-inflicted death in a shoot-out with police in New Hampshire on 13 April 1984. The ultimate powerplay. During that month and a half leading up to his death, Wilder is known to have murdered ten young women and attacked three who survived, although the true number of his victims may be much higher.

Christopher Wilder is an exception to most offenders, who stick to one discrete geographic area to commit their crimes, but we can explain why. His upbringing as a navy child meant he moved around all the time and was used to quickly adapting to new environments. Everyone – including his surviving victims – described Wilder as charismatic, intelligent and charming, and he was able to very quickly draw in the young women he targeted, gaining their trust. However, once alone, they said he turned, became very dominant and aggressive, taking total control of them. This ability to control his victims is exemplified by one of his Sydney victims, Phionna Parsons, whom Wilder approached at Manly Beach, Sydney, in his photographer persona. Literally within minutes she says she had 'fallen under his spell'. His personality appears to have been almost magnetic to some women, and he was a master at selecting those his charms would work on. This was how he became such a prolific predator, as those around him had no idea what he was really like. Like all violent, sexually motivated psychopaths, he was able to hide in plain sight.

One of Wilder's other victims was 16-year-old Tina Marie Risico, over whom he had a particularly strong hold. Wilder abducted Tina on 4 April 1984, in Torrence, California. He held her for a week, during which time he tortured and terrorised her. During her captivity, Tina assisted Wilder in abducting 15-year-old Dawnette Wilt by approaching her in a shopping centre and introducing herself as Tina Marie Wilder. Tina lured Dawnette to the carpark, where Wilder was waiting. They abducted her and Wilder raped her at gunpoint and then stabbed her, leaving the girl for dead, but Dawnette managed to survive and get help. Wilder and Risico then abducted 33-year-old Beth Dodge, whom Wilder shot and killed, before leaving her body in a gravel pit.

Some women had escaped Wilder, but Tina didn't have to. In a turn of events totally out of character for the serial predator, Wilder simply let Tina go. He even drove her to Boston Logan Airport and bought her a ticket home to Los Angeles. Tina walked back out to the car, Wilder told her to give him a kiss on the cheek and that she was going to be famous as a result of being associated with him and should write a book. Tina later said that Wilder knew he was going to die and didn't want her to die too, so he let her go.

Tina then safely caught her flight, without raising the alarm that she had just been released by America's most wanted man, and went to see her boyfriend when she landed. Her friends then took Tina to a police station. Her face had been on every TV station for the past week, as the police knew she was a Wilder victim. But they certainly did not expect her to walk into a police station. They thought they were looking for another body. From Tina's perspective, her compliance may have developed into a bond with Wilder, borne of a need to survive. This is known as Stockholm syndrome, a psychological condition whereby a hostage begins to identify closely with their abductor, as well as with their agenda and demands, perhaps even appearing to be complicit in criminal acts. This may have led Wilder to like Tina, or maybe he just found having her around made abducting other women easier, as he could use Tina to make the other targets feel safer. The day after Wilder let Tina go, he was killed in a shootout with two state troopers in New Hampshire.

Possibly the most interesting thing about Christopher Wilder is what I, and others, believe may be his first crime, and one of Australia's most enduring mystery cold cases – the Wanda Beach murders. On 11 January 1965, best friends Marianne Schmidt and Christine Sharrock, both 15 years old, went to Wanda Beach, near Cronulla in Sydney, with four of Marianne's younger siblings. At around 1 pm the two older girls went off alone into the sand dunes, giggling, and there is evidence to suggest they were keeping a prearranged appointment with someone. From their behaviour, it seems logical that they had arranged to meet a boy or man. The younger children waited until around 5 o'clock, but when Marianne and Christine did not return, they left for home. At 8.30 pm the girls were reported missing by their families as they lived next door to each other.

The girls' bodies were found the next afternoon, partially buried in the sand. Both girls had been violently murdered. Marianne had likely been attacked first; her throat had been cut and she had been stabbed a number of times. From the scene, it appeared that Christine had tried to get away but had been grabbed from behind and had been incapacitated, before being dragged back to where Marianne lay. Christine's skull had been fractured, and she too had been stabbed multiple times. The girls' clothes had been cut, and there had been an attempt to rape them, as semen was found on the outside of their clothing (it's unclear if this sample remains available today for DNA testing).

This was a frenzied attack, with far more wounds caused than necessary for death. The perpetrator must have been prepared, as he had brought the knife with him to the scene, but there does not seem to be the level of skill evident with practised offenders. My criminological opinion is that the offender was young, possibly a teenager, or at least this was the individual's first offence of this type. The overkill, together with their inability to rape the young girls, suggests that the perpetrator found the experience overwhelmingly exciting. In turn, this indicates that he had fantasised about his crime for some time, perhaps years, and that he had got carried away in the moment.

This fits with the evidence provided by Wolfgang Schmidt, Marianne's 8-year-old brother who was at the beach that day. He described a young man who would become the primary suspect in Marianne and Christine's murders. He stated that he saw a teenage boy in the area three times, once with Marianne and Christine and twice alone. He appeared to have a fishing knife and a spear gun, or both.

Christopher Wilder became a suspect as he lived close to the girls in Sydney, was known to cruise the local beaches in his car, and two years previously had been found guilty of the rape. In addition, the composite image created by Wolfgang resembled Christopher Wilder, who would have been 19 at the time.

As part of the process of looking at Wilder as a suspect for the Wanda Beach murders, my colleague, Duncan McNab, and I arranged to have a photograph of Wilder age-regressed by a forensic medical artist, so that we could compare the eyewitness composite with Wilder at a similar age. We asked the artist to include a beachy hairstyle and sunblock on Wilder's nose, again to mirror the witness description of the teenager at Wanda Beach as closely as possible. Figure 11 shows two images (left is the original Wilder image taken during his arrest in 1982, and on the right is Wilder age-regressed to around 20).

In terms of comparing Milat and Wilder as offenders, both had developed MOs that allowed them to target their victim type – Milat sought out vulnerable travellers, and Wilder hunted pretty girls and

Figure 11: Christopher Wilder at 37 years of age (left); Wilder age-regressed to around 20 (right) (provided by FHID Pty Ltd, © 2018 Parabon NanoLabs, Inc. All rights reserved).

young women with his ruse to help them become models. They were both adaptable, skilled and practised hunters who lacked any ability to feel empathy for their victims. They fed off controlling others, and both used torture for sexual gratification. Perhaps most significantly, Milat and Wilder abducted pairs as well as single victims. So, although unusual, a dominant and confident enough offender will take more than one victim at a time, possibly as this adds to his sense of power.

IN CONCLUSION

Ivan Milat is Australia's most infamous serial predator. He is a psychopath. He has been found guilty of murdering seven vulnerable young people, and although he has not been charged with Peter Letcher's murder, there is little doubt he is the culprit. Milat is also a credible suspect in five other abductions and murders. It is likely that his criminal career began with violent assault before Margaret and Greta's abduction and rape in 1971, as this is not a classic first-time offence. To abduct two adult females, and to be so bold and well organised, speaks to experience, confidence. Had Milat murdered before this time is probably a question that will never be answered. What is clear is that he had a taste for violence and a sadistic enjoyment of causing suffering in others. From what we know of other offenders of this type, it is that once they start, they don't stop.

So, logic would, sadly, dictate, that there are more Milat victims yet to be discovered. Perhaps the area around Jenolan Caves would be a good place to start looking.

I asked Colin if, in his opinion, we would be able to locate more victims. He said, 'Much more detailed information and intelligence would need to be examined and processed to do this effectively. However, if successfully sourced, completing a geographic profiling evaluation could be undertaken. The necessary detail invariably only comes from within the investigative process, be it current or cold case'. So hope of finding any other victims exists, providing the families the answers they have been waiting so long for.

Importantly, Colin was also of the opinion that Milat acted alone, based on the fact that he disposed of his victims close together, supporting the psychological profile as well as Clive Small's assessment of the case.

I'm left convinced that Milat is a lone serial predator who would have kept offending until he was caught. I'm also sure that Milat is guilty of additional crimes not yet attributed to him.

In late May 2019 it was announced that now-74-year-old Milat had terminal cancer of the oesophagus and stomach. Police conducted death-bed interviews in an attempt to gain further information regarding any additional crimes that Milat may be responsible for. I also took the opportunity to write to Milat at Goulburn Correctional Centre, appealing for information, largely focused on those named as potential additional victims in this chapter, or anything else he wanted to confess. I am not naive enough to think that any response would be as a result of a crisis of conscience – Milat doesn't have one. Instead, I appealed to his ego, that any confession now would lead to one last moment in the spotlight, which his narcissistic personality constantly craves. At the time of writing, he was yet to respond.

FORENSIC SCIENCE EXPLAINED: FIREARMS AND BALLISTICS

Forensic science has many sub-specialties; one of these is forensic firearm examination, which focuses on the assessment of firearms and ballistics evidence. The study of firearms and ballistics is divided into three stages: internal, external and terminal. Internal relates to what happens in the gun in the very short period of time between the person pulling the trigger and the bullet leaving the muzzle. External covers the bullet's flight trajectory upon exiting the muzzle and hitting a final target, and terminal ballistics focuses on what happens when the bullet hits a target.

Forensic firearms and ballistics experts are used to link weapons with bullets and cartridges, as well as multiple scenes together when the weapon has been used in more than one crime. Firearms examiners also recover fingerprints and other trace evidence left on weapons, bullets and cartridges, and employ various techniques to recover serial numbers that have been erased.

Bullets can be traced to a specific weapon that fired them due to individuating features that are caused during the manufacture of the gun. One aspect of the process is 'rifling', which relates to the lands and grooves that are intentionally added to the firearm's barrel to make the bullet spin (to the left or right) for improved accuracy. The direction of rifling, as well as the number of lands and grooves, can be determined through studying the inside of the barrel. When a projectile, such as a bullet, spins down the barrel, the patterning of lands and grooves is imparted onto it. Firearm manufacturers use a number of methods to add the rifling to the barrels, and this, together with the direction and pattern of lands and grooves, makes the markings on each gun barrel unique, and all bullets fired from that weapon will exhibit the same rifling patterns.

A contemporary case that relied largely on ballistics evidence was that of Ivan Milat. Milat was deeply into guns, and items located at his houses and those of his associates during police raids linked him to all seven killings and helped secure seven life sentences.

However, the history of ballistics evidence being used in court goes back much further. One of the earliest cases relates to the murder in 1915 of Charles and Margaret Phelps, with a .22 calibre revolver. Charles Stielow, who owned a .22 calibre gun and was the Phelps's neighbour in New York, and his brother-in-law, Nelson Green, were convicted of the couple's murder and were subsequently sentenced to death by electrocution.

A ballistics 'expert' had been brought in to determine if Stielow's gun was the murder weapon. Unfortunately, the person selected had no training or experience in forensic ballistics and, without firing Stielow's gun, determined that the two bullets recovered from the victims were fired from the accused's gun. He testified at trial that no other gun could have made the markings on the bullets found at the crime scene. The defence sought advice from the firearms expert from the NYC Police Department, who conducted his own examination of the evidence and concluded that Stielow's gun had not been fired in three or four years, and that the rifling on bullets he fired through the accused's gun did not match that found on the crime scene bullets. Stielow's gun was not the murder weapon, and both Stielow and Green were exonerated. Not the most auspicious start to the application of forensic ballistics evidence, as two men were almost executed on the basis of flawed expert testimony, but they were ultimately saved by a real expert, and the use of bullets in criminal investigations was established.

Nowadays, many of the comparative processes are automated. For example, since the 1990s automated ballistics imaging and analysis systems have been developed, which have significantly augmented the ability of law enforcement agencies to identify linked investigations. In a similar way to fingerprint databases, these systems comprise computerised catalogues of stored digital images of cartridges and bullets, which are automatically compared when a new item is scanned into the system. This allows the details to be captured, analysed, matched, and correlated very quickly, locally, nationally and internationally.

SIX

AVENGING ANGELS: BRINGING DANIEL HOLDOM TO JUSTICE

In 2013 I found myself standing in Belanglo State Forest, looking at the site of a violent murder that had occurred in 2008. Strange, now, to think that a young woman had been killed only metres from where I stood. I found myself thinking 'Why here? Why did the killer choose this place?'

He remained uncaught, and I wanted to get inside his head, to figure him out, as it was my job to help raise awareness of the case by covering it for a true crime program as this was the best shot the police had to help catch a violent killer.

It was around 11 am, and I was about 8 kilometres into the forest, standing by one of the hundreds of fire trails that litter the area like a cobweb. Dappled sunlight filtered through the trees and it was warm for July. I was struck by the silence. No birds singing, no insects buzzing. There was literally no sound.

I was not alone – I was with a TV film crew – but the sense

of isolation was still intense. As was the strange, lurking foreboding that I felt just being there. My instinct was to get out of there as soon as possible, and I was relieved when we finished filming the segment for our true crime series and returned to civilisation and safety.

And starkly I was reminded that a young woman hadn't been so lucky. She had been brought to this disturbing place by a monster, who brutally killed her and left her here in the forest.

That place shouldn't be anyone's final memory, and disturbed as I was by the scene, I was more committed than ever to doing everything I could to help get the woman identified and her killer caught.

What I didn't know then was that I would have to wait another five years, and that this would turn into one of the most distressing cases I had been part of. This was not just the death of a young woman, but her little girl had also fallen prey to the same monster.

THE CASE

When two-year-old Khandalyce Pearce's remains were found in a suitcase in 2015, no one knew it would be the beginning of one of the most shocking and callous double murder investigations in modern Australia's history. The breakthrough came after two calls to Crime Stoppers provided crucial information that initially identified Khandalyce, and then in a twist no one saw coming, linked her identity with that of the 'Angel of Belanglo' – a cold case murder in NSW. In 2010 a young woman, dubbed 'Angel' because of a motif on a T-shirt associated with her skeleton, had been found in notorious Belanglo State Forest. She had been brutally murdered. DNA technology was used to link the two cases officially, and the nation – in fact the world – reeled as they learned that the two murder victims were mother and daughter.

The motive for these horrendous deaths: sex and money.

The perpetrator: Daniel Holdom, the mother's partner.

A number of points make this case stand out against others as deserving to be included in a book about cold cases. Ignore, if you can, the horror of a body being carelessly dumped by the highway in an old suitcase like trash, doubly horrific when it transpired that inside were the remains of a child. Also ignore the incredible twist that the deceased was the child of a young woman whose remains had been located in Belanglo State Forest almost five years earlier – a place forever linked with Australia's most notorious serial killer Ivan Milat. This case deserves to be discussed and the details shared because of the incredible police work that it took to get to the bottom of the who, why, when and how of this hideous crime, and that actually gave the family the answers they needed to begin grieving. Through sheer dogged hard work, the police gave the deceased back their names.

BACKGROUND

In 2013 I was working on a true crime program for Channel Ten entitled *Wanted*, the purpose of which was to gain information from the public around ongoing police investigations. My first case to review was that of a young woman who had been given the name Angel by the press, because her skeletal remains had been discovered with a size 10 T-shirt bearing the distinctive motif 'Angelic'. The police had the T-shirt motif recreated by an artist (figure 12), so that it could be publicised as part of the TV story when it aired.

The remains of Angel's body had been discovered totally by accident by some trail bike riders on 29 August 2010. A group of around 10 riders had been exploring the fire trails in the forest, when one of them, Jeff Stiffle, missed a bend and went off the track. He found himself in an open area of brush and saw what he thought was a human femur (thigh bone) next to a log. Jeff had a look around

Figure 12: NSW police drawing of the T-shirt found with 'Angel's' remains (used with permission by NSW police).

and found a tibia and fibula (the two long bones of the lower leg). He told his friends, but they all thought the remains belonged to a kangaroo or some other large animal, and that Jeff was just spooked because of the links to Milat and the seven murdered backpackers found in that forest. They decided to have some lunch, but Jeff couldn't get the idea out of his head that the bones could be human, so after lunch he insisted they go back. That's when they found a pelvis and realised that the bones were definitely human.

They called the police, and the remains were forensically recovered. A post-mortem examination revealed that multiple ribs on both sides of the body had been broken. The breaks were in a straight line, and the pathologist determined that the injuries had occurred peri-mortem (around the time of death), likely as a result of someone kneeling or stamping on Angel's torso. It is likely that Angel was lying down when she sustained these traumatic injuries, but it was not possible to tell if she had been lying on her back or her front. The pathologist also found that Angel died as a result of one or more applications of blunt force trauma, which occurs when a blunt object hits the body, or the body collides with something hard. Common causes of blunt force trauma include being hit with a fist, a bat or other hard object, as well as when hitting the ground in a fall from height. No other injuries were in evidence from the remains, but given they were fully skeletonised this is not surprising. It should also be noted that the laryngeal structures were not recoverable, which includes the soft tissue of the throat as well as the hyoid bone. This is important as the hyoid (which is in the middle of your neck at the front) is often broken during strangulation. If it is not recovered, it is not possible to determine if someone was strangled or suffocated to death.

It was estimated that the remains had been in the forest for between 6 months and 10 years; and by the time they were found, Milat had been in prison for 18 years, so the police knew he was not involved. This seems like a huge potential time span, but once remains have fully decomposed and all that's left are bones, the only way to estimate time since death is to look at the context of the scene. For example, have tree roots grown through the bones and, if so, can a forensic botanist estimate how long the bones and tree have been in contact?

EXPERT INSERT: TIME SINCE DEATH (TSD)

Estimating time since death is a crucial factor in any death investigation. However, it is a very difficult task with many variables affecting the estimation.

In recent deaths, the pathologist bases TSD conclusions on the temperature of the body as compared to the ambient temperature. In general terms, the greater the difference between the body and the surrounding air, the longer the person has been dead. In temperate climates, the body temperature is normally relatively stable for the first 30 minutes up to 3 hours after death. Between 4–12 hours the surface cools to ambient levels, but the core of the body may take 2 to 3 times that long to reach the environmental level. Temperature is considered the most reliable estimate of TSD for the first 24 hours after death. Once decomposition starts to accelerate, a number of different experts can help to narrow down the TSD window. These include anthropologists who look at tissue discoloration and loss, as well as forensic entomologists who study the activity of insects and their arthropod relatives that inhabit human remains.

It must be noted that there are many factors that can cause variations at every stage of analysis of the TSD interval. For example, if the environment in which the body is located is very cold, this will slow the onset of decomposition. Conversely, a very hot and humid ambient temperature will accelerate it, and exposure to strong sun can cause all of the organic components to expeditiously leach out of the bones very fast so that the person can appear to have died many years earlier than their actual date of death. There are also individual variations; for example, a very large person with significant body fat will lose heat more slowly as the fat creates an insulating effect, and what a person was wearing or has been wrapped in when they died may also increase or slow down decomposition. In addition, some prescription or illicit drugs may affect decomposition as well as entomo-logical activity, but as research on this is currently scarce (as few facilities study human decomposition), these factors are very difficult to quantify.

There is one research facility in Australia that does study TSD, and that is the recently opened Australian Facility for Taphonomic Experimental Research (AFTER). All types of death investigators – including police, anthropologists, forensic chemists, odontologists (who assess the head and neck, focusing on the teeth and jaws, looking for signs of trauma, disease or factors that may help identify the person being examined) – are working at the site in collaborative research teams, studying multiple cadavers to improve avail-able research data. This is an Australian first, as previously all of the information relating to human decomposition was based on research that has come out of the US. This is funda-mental research, as death information is context dependent, so it is essential we can collect our own data from cadavers that have decomposed in a local environment. The research that will come from AFTER will be invaluable in narrowing TSD intervals, helping the police to limit missing persons pools and identify unknown deceased persons.

It is likely that the bones that weren't recovered (which included small bones of the hands, feet and the hyoid bone) were taken by scavengers and have either been eaten or scattered across the forest. This is normal, and you would not expect to recover every single element if scavengers (such as foxes, wild pigs and birds) had access to the remains.

The police also sought the assistance of a forensic anthropologist to provide a biological profile, which includes a person's estimated age at death, estimated living stature, sex determination, and any information that may be available regarding ancestral origin. The purpose is to narrow the search of a missing persons list. In Angel's case this evaluation concluded that the deceased person was a Caucasian female, aged between 15–25 years at the time of her death, around 150–165 centimetres tall. These details were run against the missing persons database but didn't match anyone listed. The police were also able to obtain a full DNA profile, but this did not match any of the individuals on the national DNA database.

The only item of clothing found in association with the remains was the T-shirt, which the police were confident had been worn by the victim at the time of her death.

The police then turned to a facial reconstruction expert, Dr Susan Hayes, at the University of Wollongong. Susan specialises in human facial variation, identification and depiction in the forensic and archaeological sciences. You can find more information on Susan's research at https://www.researchgate.net/profile/Susan_Hayes.

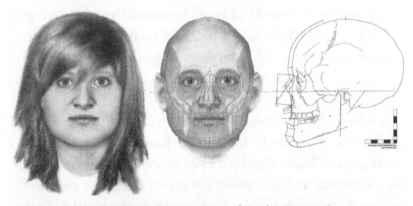

Figure 13: 2011 facial reconstruction of Karlie Pearce-Stevenson (used with permission from Dr Susan Hayes).

Susan recreated the face of the young woman from the skull, and added long blonde hair in three distinct lengths, as hair had been found with the remains, and this allowed Susan to make the resultant image as accurate as possible (figure 13). The facial reconstruction was heavily publicised, but whilst a number of tips were received by the police, none led to Angel being identified.

EXPERT INSERT: FACIAL RECONSTRUCTION

Facial reconstruction (also known as facial approximation) describes an estimation of a deceased person's facial appearance when all that remains are bones and teeth. The main reason for a reconstruction is to stimulate new leads from the general public in order to identify the person.

The materials and methods used to create a facial reconstruction are varied, and very much depend on whether the practitioner is an artist, a biological anthropologist, or a combination of the two. By far the most popular and enduring approach is either applying clay over a cast of the skull or drawing the face over a photographic print. A relatively recent development is the use of computer graphics to estimate the face, referencing a virtual skull. A major advantage of a virtual facial reconstruction is that it is literally methodologically transparent – nothing is hidden, nothing is obscured – and therefore the work can be constantly reviewed as it progresses and the results updated when new information becomes available. However, whether the face is sculpted, drawn or digitally rendered, all facial reconstructions require a high level of proficiency in the practical techniques of artistic depiction. It is no surprise, therefore, that most facial reconstructions are performed by forensic artists, and why many facial reconstruction recommendations are based on artistic principles.

Over the past decade, the science that informs a facial reconstruction has increased dramatically in both quantity and quality. This is largely due to the development of CT scans, which allow researchers to directly, and accurately, examine recurring relationships between the skull and its soft tissues. A lot of this research has involved putting popular facial reconstruction methods to the test and, sadly, nearly all of these, both 'scientific' and artistic, have failed. Some of these failures have been because most forensic handbooks include inaccurate reporting of published research findings (e.g. soft tissue depth angles, nasal tip projection), a lack of awareness of research findings from the anatomical sciences (e.g. size, placement and projection of the eyeball), and because artistic canons are predominantly based on ancient notions of idealised Greco-Roman beauty.

The good news is that recent scientific research includes the development of robust skull-soft tissue relationships to replace most of the failed facial reconstruction recommendations. As a result, and for the first time in well over a century, it is now possible to estimate a deceased person's facial appearance with scientific justification. This does not, however, mean that the resulting face will be exactly how the person appeared in life – a facial reconstruction is always going to be an estimation. Scientifically robust relationships are averages calculated from large numbers of people – and then tested to see how well they perform with equally large numbers of different people. A robust relationship is therefore a statistical average, and to be useful this statistical average needs to fit reasonably well within the range of most people. Although, by definition, most of us have pretty average facial features, it's how we slightly differ in the shapes and placements of our features that makes our faces unique. Average relationships cannot help but dilute our subtle individual differences, but this, I think, is preferable to no actual science at all.

Of course, there is still much more research to be done. Faces are complex patterns of interlocking features, and facial reconstruction's scientific journey has really only just begun. But it's an exciting journey, and with the promise of semi-automating aspects of the process it is possible that a more scientific approach will become much more widely accepted, expected and applied.

Dr Susan Hayes, facial anthropologist

The case went cold, until in 2013 the police asked if we could cover Angel's story on *Wanted*, to see if we could generate some intelligence that might lead to her being identified. I spoke to the original witnesses who found Angel's remains, we had a mock-up of the T-shirt created from the drawing provided by the NSWPF, and did a re-enactment of events with an actress in Belanglo.

It was as part of our investigation that I went to Belanglo in 2013 with the officer in charge of the investigation at the time, Detective Sergeant Tim Attwood. We had to drive about 8 kilometres from the main road, and as we drove in I remember saying to him that this was not the kind of place a young woman would come alone, or for fun. Belanglo is not a tourist destination. We didn't know how

Angel had got into the forest, but she hadn't walked in, and no car had been found near the body.

So someone had brought her here. But who and why? Was she, like Milat's victims, a backpacker, someone with a transient lifestyle whom no one would miss?

We had all the information we could need to identify Angel, surely? We had DNA, dental records, biographic information (sex, living stature, ancestral origin, approximate age at death); we even had a facial reconstruction and details of the colour and length of her hair when she died. But still we couldn't find out who she was.

Why? Because this is not the make-believe world of CSI, where cases are solved in a tidy TV hour. This is real life, where all the information in the world won't lead to an identification of a John or Jane Doe if the police don't have one of two things: 1) an ante-mortem (before death) sample from the victim, for example a DNA sample or a fingerprint, that leads to a hit against an existing database; or 2) a potential name (sometimes provided by a missing persons records search) as a starting point from which to source ante-mortem data to compare to the post-mortem (after death) information. Only the scientific comparison and matching of ante- and post-mortem data can result in a legal identification. Full stop. If you haven't got those things, an identification is impossible.

The TV program aired in 2013, and even though the police got various new leads as a result, Angel remained unidentified.

It looked like she might remain a Jane Doe forever.

And until the police could identify Angel, there was no chance they were going to be able to find out who killed her.

I remember feeling sad that a young woman could disappear for years, be brutally murdered and no one was looking for her. I moved on to work other cases but I never forgot about Angel of Belanglo.

THE CASE BROKE OPEN

Sometimes breaks in cases come from the most unexpected directions. And so it was with Angel.

On 14 July 2015 the daily news announced that the skeleton of a child had been found by a passing motorist in a suitcase on the side of the Karoonda Highway, around 1.5 kilometres west of Wynarka in South Australia. Various items of clothing were also found in the suitcase, as well as a blanket.

A post-mortem examination was conducted two days later. Because the remains of the child had been placed in the suitcase shortly after death, all of the bones were present. It was determined that the body belonged to a little girl, and a forensic odontologist estimated that her age had been between 1.2 and 4.8 years at the time of her death.

There were no obvious injuries, but as the remains were fully skeletonised, with no soft tissue remaining at all, it was difficult to determine cause and manner of death. Cause and manner of death are separate yet interlinked. Cause of death relates to the specific injury or disease that leads to death. Manner of death refers to how the injury or disease led to death. For example, someone could be stabbed and their carotid artery in their neck severed – the cause of death would be sharp force trauma, and the manner of death exsanguination (bled to death).

However, the killer had forced a ball of light blue and white disposable dishcloths into the child's mouth, and wrapped several layers of grey adhesive tape around her face and head, including covering her mouth and nose. The pathologist concluded that the child died as a result of the gag in her mouth and tape over her nose and mouth, and that the manner of death was suffocation.

Initially the police had no idea who the child was, as no toddlers matching her description had been reported missing. They knew they needed to enlist the assistance of the public, so they compiled media posters for public circulation. Fortuitously, some of the clothing items recovered from the suitcase in which the child's body had been found were unique, and these were pictured on the posters (figure 14).

The police were in luck. On 6 October, after over 1200 calls about the case to Crime Stoppers, one caller – number 1267 – identified the quilt as having been made by Colleen Povey, for her granddaughter, Khandalyce Pearce. The caller also recognised some of the clothing as belonging to Khandalyce, specifically a dress from the suitcase. Two days later caller 1271 gave details about Khandalyce's mother, as well as providing a photograph showing Khandalyce standing behind a stroller with the same dress found in the suitcase with her remains (figure 15).

Now the police had a name and a location for the child's birth and could use this information to confirm the remains were those of Khandalyce. They did this by accessing the child's hospital records, as Khandalyce had a DNA sample on file as a result of having been tested as part of the Newborn Metabolic Screening Programme, which checks all newborn babies for rare but potentially serious disorders such as phenylketonuria, cystic fibrosis, and congenital hypothyroidism. Between 48–72 hours after birth the baby has one of their heels pricked with a pin, and a blood sample is taken for testing. Often referred to as the Guthrie Test, this type of screening has been part of the routine care for all neonates for over 40 years.

Police were able to compare Khandalyce's DNA on record with that of the remains found in the suitcase. The test came back positive: the toddler in the suitcase was Khandalyce Pearce. She had been born on 19 June 2006 in Alice Springs in the Northern Territory, and was two and a half years old when she was murdered.

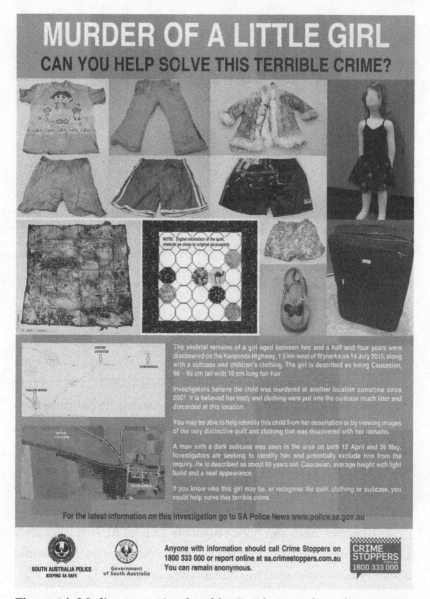

Figure 14: Media poster circulated by South Australia police in 2015 (used with permission of South Australia Police).

Figure 15: The photo provided by Crime Stoppers caller 1271 of Khandalyce (left), and the dress recovered from the suitcase containing Khandalyce's remains (right) (used with permission of South Australia Police).

The question now loomed, where was her mother, as the last time their family had heard from the pair they had been together. This time the police searched the unidentified deceased records, and because they now know that Khandalyce and her mother had already travelled from the Northern Territory to South Australia, they did not limit their search by state. They were looking for a young Caucasian woman's remains, around 160 centimetres tall, and 20 years of age.

A hit came back from New South Wales police: Angel of Belanglo fitted the profile.

In October 2015 the police formally linked the two cases after DNA testing confirmed that Angel, now known to be 20-year-old Karlie Pearce-Stevenson, was Khandalyce's mother.

THE QUESTIONS HAD ONLY JUST BEGUN

Although we knew the names of the two victims, the questions had only just begun. One of the big ones – how could a young mother and her child disappear for so long and no one be looking for them? To find that out, the police had to step back through Karlie and Khandalyce's lives, to see who might have a reason to want to murder them.

Post-mortems had revealed that both mother and daughter had died violent and unnatural deaths, but at this stage the police were no closer to finding out why the pair had been killed and by whom. More puzzling still, how and why did the two sets of remains end up 1200 kilometres apart, and Khandalyce's remain undiscovered for 7 years?

As the police dug through Karlie's life looking for answers, they learned that she had been falsely kept alive in the minds of family through calls and texts from Karlie's phone – for years after Karlie's death. Bank accounts had been accessed until at least 2012 in four states and territories across Australia. Could this really be a case of murder for money? If so, why kill Khandalyce? That question remained unanswered until they had a suspect, the last man to see them alive: Daniel James Holdom.

THE MAIN SUSPECT

Karlie and Khandalyce had last been seen alive in December 2008, at which time Karlie was in a relationship with Daniel Holdom. Karlie and Holdom had known each other in Alice Springs, having met earlier that year before becoming romantically involved in October 2008, even though Holdom was in a relationship with another woman at the time.

In September of that year, Holdom and a friend were involved in a serious car accident. Holdom was driving, and two of his friend's children were killed. The passenger had been left wheelchair bound after having her leg amputated. After the children's funerals, Karlie, Khandalyce and Holdom travelled to the ACT together. They spent time with Holdom's cousin Christine Lancaster, and her partner, Dereck Dover, in Charnwood, a suburb of Canberra.

Around this time, the passenger in the car messaged Holdom to tell him she was suing him over the accident, as she had increasing costs due to expenses from her rehabilitation.

On the evening of 14 December 2008, and into the early hours of the following morning, Karlie and Holdom had an argument, which resulted in them leaving the house in Charnwood in Karlie's car – a maroon 1996 Holden Commodore station wagon – around 2.30 am on the 15 December. Khandalyce remained behind, in the care of Lancaster and Dover.

Tracing Karlie after she left the house in Charnwood was essential, as this was the last time anyone other than Holdom was known to have seen her alive.

The police used mobile phone tower technology to track Holdom's phone, which pinged off towers from the ACT to Belanglo State Forest. The mobile phone data showed Holdom arrived at Sutton Forest (a small village about 10 kilometres from Belanglo, and the closest cell tower to the forest) just before 5 am on 15 December. This represents a drive of around 170 kilometres, which would have taken them about 1 hour and 50 minutes.

Holdom's phone kept pinging off the Sutton Forest tower until 12.16 pm that day. Police believe during this time, Holdom was murdering Karlie in the forest. Holdom also sexually assaulted Karlie; we know this, even though there was no evidence on the skeletal remains, as Holdom took photographs of the assault, which he kept. These photographs were later obtained by police and admitted into evidence against him.

Holdom then drove back to the ACT, getting back to Charnwood just before 2 pm. Again, his return trip was tracked using information from mobile phone towers. When he got back, Karlie wasn't with him, even though he was driving her car. Karlie's mobile phone was in the car and had done the same trip as Holdom, pinging off the same mobile phone towers.

Lancaster asked Holdom where Karlie was, and he said they had continued to argue, and he had dropped her at a bus stop. Lancaster was surprised by this, asking, 'How could she leave Khandles [their nickname for Khandalyce]?' Holdom explained by saying that sometimes Karlie did that, and they had agreed Holdom would take Khandalyce to her grandmother's house in South Australia.

Two days later, on 17 December, Holdom sold Karlie's car at a dealership in the ACT, trading it in for a white 1991 Holden Statesman.

Khandalyce is known to have stayed in Charnwood with Holdom and his cousin until the early hours of 19 December, when Holdom packed his and the child's possessions and left in the white Statesman, telling his relatives he was taking the child to her grandmother's. They drove west, through New South Wales, and down towards South Australia.

The child was now a liability, and the police investigation reveals that Holdom was planning on that drive south to kill her. The evidence for this comes from the fact that his credit card activity shows that he stopped at Woolworths in Wagga Wagga, in NSW, just before 9 am, where he bought garden sacks, silver duct tape, body wash and antibacterial wipes. These items matched those found with Khandalyce's remains when her body was discovered in 2015.

Holdom then drove on a further 100 kilometres and checked in to the Narrandera Midtown Motor Inn with one child, Khandalyce. Holdom's payment was registered through EFTPOS at 11.05 am. The police then used mobile phone tower technology to determine that he stayed in the vicinity of the motel for a further 2 hours and 30 minutes, until 1.20 pm on 19 December.

Clearly Holdom was not trying to hide. He had left credit card evidence of his purchases as well as his motel registration; he has signed the motel registration form (confirmed by a forensic hand-writing expert), and left a fingerprint on it. He even checked in with the child. Further, a towel found in the suitcase with Khandalyce's remains had the same batch number as ones supplied at the motel.

This was after he had bought the items he was later going to use to murder Khandalyce, and we have to assume that murder was his intention when he bought them – what else would a man who was ostensibly dropping a child at her grandmother's be doing buying items that appear focused on tidying up a mess?

The police concluded that Holdom murdered Khandalyce at or near Narrandera on 19 December 2008, and that manner of death was suffocation, resultant from the cloths forced into her mouth and the tape over her face.

It appears Holdom's motive was sexual, in that he was planning to or attempted to sexually assault the child at the time she was killed, although during the legal process the Crown was unable to establish how far the assault progressed due to the level of decom-position of Khandalyce's body when she was discovered.

Holdom then drove on to his friend's house in South Australia. He arrived alone: Khandalyce was never seen alive again.

HOW WE GOT HERE

As this story unfolded, I was again struck by the fact that a young woman with a child could disappear without anyone looking for them.

But it came out later that someone had looked.

On 4 September 2009, Colleen Povey reported her daughter and granddaughter missing. She had last seen the pair in October 2008, when they had left on an adventure to see Australia. Karlie was well known for being a fiery young woman, and the relationship between her and her family was often strained. So it wasn't all that strange that after she left communication was sporadic, but in September 2009 Karlie's family did become worried after several months of not hearing from her. This must have caused the murderer some concern, as he didn't want anyone looking for the mother and daughter. This would also indicate that the murderer was monitoring Karlie's social media pages, as he was aware a missing persons report had been filed and the family were actively reaching out to Karlie via Facebook, asking her to get in touch.

Phone records showed that Karlie had last called her mum on 13 December 2008 – two days before she was murdered. Colleen had tied to contact her in the months since, but calls and texts to her mobile went unanswered. Povey gave descriptions of Karlie and Khandalyce, as well as Karlie's car (the maroon Holdom Commodore) to police.

The police made enquiries, which soon led to Holdom. The NT police contacted him by phone, and he told them that Karlie had moved to Queensland and that he hadn't seen or heard from her since February 2009. He said he may have an alternative number for her and asked the police to call back later that day to get it. They tried but Holdom didn't answer their calls.

At this stage the police were simply investigating two missing persons, and had no reason to assume anything untoward had happened to them. They looked for what we would call 'proof of life', and when they checked Karlie's bank records, they found it. The police made contact with the Australian Central Credit Union, where Karlie held an account, and found that it was being accessed regularly, as recently as 7 September 2009 via an ATM in South Australia – the same date they made contact with Holdom. Colleen was informed that whilst the police now believed Karlie was alive, they would leave the missing persons report open until someone heard from her or there was a confirmed sighting.

A few days later, on 10 September 2009, 'Karlie' reached out to her mum and Colleen contacted the NT police to say that Karlie had contacted her, and whilst she didn't want to leave any information about where she was, she was okay. This contact was made by text from Karlie's phone, either by Holdom or someone associated with him, and mobile tower data showed that this text was sent from the area where Holdom was living at the time. Importantly, Holdom's phone was also pinging this tower at the same time, so Holdom was in the area too.

By this point, Karlie had been dead almost nine months.

TO CATCH A KILLER

After Holdom murdered Karlie and Khandalyce, he continued to engage in 'proof of life' activities, so no one suspected what had really happened. This included a lot more texts sent from Karlie's phone to friends and family.

This appears to have had two purposes for Holdom – the first was to convince them not to worry about the mother and daughter so they wouldn't call the police, and the second was to request money.

These texts didn't stop, and later police search warrants found a mobile phone with Karlie's number, which Holdom had been using between September 2009 and May 2011, over three years after her death.

But that wasn't all. Someone was accessing Karlie's bank account for years after her death, and across four different states. Corresponding with many of these withdrawals were withdrawals from Holdom's account. This information was circumstantial, but police did uncover evidence that directly linked Holdom to withdrawals from Karlie's accounts. In May 2011, $12,500 was deposited into Karlie's account from the Australian Taxation Office. A few days later, $5000 was transferred out of Karlie's account into the account of an acquaintance. A few days after that, a further $5000 was transferred into the same account. The acquaintance then withdrew $5000 and gave it to Holdom, on his instructions. Even more compelling, on 27 September 2011, Holdom started having his wages paid directly into Karlie's account; at this stage Karlie had been dead almost two years. Holdom also had access to Karlie's credit card, as in February 2012 he used it to buy an airline ticket from Canberra to Adelaide in his name.

In January 2009 there were a number of suspicious activities, including that the ride-share card account details for an acquaintance of Holdom's were charged to Karlie's. In June 2010 Karlie's card expired, but the account details had been updated to list Holdom's residential address as the cardholder's, so the new card was sent there.

Karlie's bank account was accessed over 1200 times between 2008–2012.

The evidence against Holdom was mounting but there was more to come.

In January 2013, a full four years since Karlie's murder, Holdom was stopped by police in Narara, NSW. His wallet was searched, and a card in Karlie's name was discovered. This was confiscated and destroyed by the police.

Holdom was also fraudulently accessing Karlie's Centrelink, Medicare and child support. We know this because in December 2010 an associate of Holdom's attended an interview with a social worker regarding Khandalyce's child support. The impostor provided a copy of the child's birth certificate at that interview. Khandalyce's birth certificate was found to be in Holdom's possession when the police executed a search warrant at a property associated with him in October 2015. After another search at a different property linked to the offender, police recovered a Medicare card in Karlie and Khandalyce's names.

In total, Holdom fraudulently acquired $71,771 from Karlie's accounts after her death.

THE NOOSE WAS TIGHTENING

If Holdom's acquaintance was involved in the fraud, it seems implausible that they did not know more. So what was their role in these gruesome crimes?

It appears they may not have known initially that Holdom had murdered Karlie, but in 2009 they must have had an inkling something was wrong when they found a number of Karlie's cards and Khandalyce's birth certificate in the boot of Holdom's car, the same car he had returned to South Australia in 2009, the white Holden Statesman. They thought Holdom was cheating on his girlfriend with Karlie, but he put them straight, telling them Karlie was 'gone . . . she's dead'.

Over the weeks and months that followed, Holdom shared awful details of Karlie's death, telling an acquaintance he'd sexually assaulted Karlie, crushed her trachea (windpipe) and left her dead body by a tree. He also confided that he had suffocated Khandalyce, admitting the sexual element to the crime.

In 2010, an SD memory card was found in Holdom's possession. There were a number of sensitive images of Karlie on the card, which appear to have been taken around the time of her death. One was a photograph Holdom had taken of Karlie in a forest (which it was later concluded was Belanglo). It showed the young woman lying on her back, wearing the 'Angelic' T-shirt. These photographs were taken at 11.23 am and 11.34 am on 15 December 2008. The surrounding bushland visible in the images matches the scene where Karlie's skeletonised remains were discovered in 2010.

Perhaps as disturbing, the same SD card also contained images not associated with Karlie's murder. One in particular showed an image of one of his then-girlfriend's deceased children taken at the scene of the fatal car accident. Holdom told a number of people, including a psychologist, that he took this photograph. Only a very sadistic mind would want to take and keep an image of a child's body after a fatal car accident for which they were responsible. It speaks to his total lack of empathy for his victims, which was also evidenced by his treatment of Karlie and Khandalyce.

Other images on the SD card were innocent, but clearly depict Holdom and close associates (including his then-girlfriend and her children), demonstrating the card was Holdom's.

The SD card was eventually given to police, who were able to establish that the photographs had been taken on a mobile phone.

Holdom also told other people that he'd murdered Karlie and her daughter. In 2012 he began an intimate relationship with another woman. In January 2013 that woman wrote in her diary that Holdom had confessed to her, saying he'd killed the mother and daughter in December 2008 and made everyone think they were alive. She appears to have not believed him, as she wrote: *Daniel Lied to me! Said he killed Karlie and Khandel but there* [sic] *still alive! Its all over Facebook . . .*

HOLDOM'S EVEN DARKER SIDE

The fraud committed against a vulnerable young woman and her daughter, both of whom had been violently murdered, was bad enough, and then there was the sexual violation of Karlie at the time of her death, some of which Holdom had captured on his phone as a memento.

But more horrendous details of Daniel Holdom's depravity were yet to come.

Also recovered during the police investigations was a notebook that contained a list of children, identified by their age. Against their age (and sometimes their first name) was a note such as 'rape' and 'forced'. This book belonged to Holdom; it was his handwriting and his fingerprints and DNA on it. 'Khandles' (the nickname for Khandalyce) was listed, as was her age of two years, with the word 'rape' next to it.

It wasn't the only notebook of this kind recovered. Another blue A4 pad containing details of child abuse fantasies was also located. This notebook predates the car accident that left his then-girlfriend wheelchair-bound.

The police found no evidence that Holdom had harmed any of the other children on the list, but considered this a fantasy list.

Daniel Holdom was not only a murderer but was also a child sex offender.

And he had form, with a significant violent criminal history dating back to the 1990s. When he was eventually charged for Karlie and Khandalyce's murders, he was already in prison serving four years on a separate offence – sexual intercourse with a child under the age of 10, which occurred in April 2013. In 2000 Holdom had been convicted of assaulting a woman the year before. He allegedly broke into her room one night and tried to suffocate her with a pillow, before he tried to strangle her. In a strikingly similar manner to his later murder of Khandalyce, Holdom tried to duct-tape the woman's mouth. In 2001 Holdom was convicted of breaching an apprehended violence order, after stalking another woman.

THE ARREST AND COURT CASE

Initially when interviewed as a suspect by police on 21 October 2015 in Cessnock, NSW, Holdom denied any knowledge of either Karlie's or Khandalyce's murders. He said the argument in Canberra that led to Karlie leaving Lancaster and Dover's house was over unpaid board Karlie owed to the couple, and that Karlie and Holdom had agreed to sell Karlie's car to pay his cousin off. Holdom also said that during her absence he had paid for Karlie to stay in a hotel in Canberra, to avoid the arguments at Lancaster's house.

Holdom then stated that he decided to get back with his ex-girlfriend, so he took Khandalyce to the motel, where he left her with Karlie, before leaving Canberra for Adelaide. He told the police he had had various contacts, via telephone and in person, with Karlie and Khandalyce since that time. He also claimed never to have been to Belanglo State Forest, and in fact didn't even know where it was. Of course, his phone records told a different story.

A few days later he backtracked, perhaps concerned that the police were fact-checking his statement and would soon be able to prove he was lying. So he beat them to the punch. On 28 October Holdom asked to give another statement, which was again electronically recorded and made under caution. He admitted that much of what he'd told them during his last interview was untrue, and that he had not seen the mother and daughter again after his cousin's partner, Dover, dropped them at a bus station. He then tried to slide blame onto Dover, saying that he had disposed of Karlie's car on his own. He admitted committing identity and financial fraud, using Karlie's bank card, but again tried to blame Dover, saying to Dover 'I don't know what you've done, don't care, just whatever', clearly insinuating that Dover had killed Karlie and her daughter. He also said that Dover had sent him Karlie's card when he was living in Queensland, and asked him to use it to make the police think she was up there.

He then offered to go Crown's witness against Dover.

Holdom may not be the smartest criminal on the block, but he was clearly aware enough to know that he needed to try to deflect some of the police attention that would be coming his way. Obviously the police didn't fall for this transparent web of lies and arrested Holdom on the spot for Karlie's murder.

Initially the media speculated as to why he was not being charged simultaneously with Khandalyce's murder. But from a policing perspective this made complete sense. They had strong evidence against Holdom for Karlie's death but were still collating information about Khandalyce. In a multiple death scenario, it is better to charge a suspect on a strong case and add more charges later, rather than try to raise charges too soon and fail because of lack of evidence.

It took the police almost seven more weeks before they had enough grounds to charge Holdom with Khandalyce's murder too, but on 15 December 2015, Holdom was arrested at Parramatta Police Station, NSW.

It was seven years to the day that Holdom murdered Karlie.

Bail was refused and the case was adjourned until January, then it was adjourned again until March 2016 to allow the Crown sufficient time to collect all of the evidence against Holdom. At his 2017 committal hearing Holdom decided to represent himself, at which time he was remanded for both murders.

On 31 July 2018, one week before the trial began against him for two counts of murder, Holdom changed his plea from innocent to guilty. As a result, the families did not have to sit through a long and painful court case. They did, however, have to endure the arraignment hearing in late September 2018, where the awful details of Holdom's crimes against the mother and daughter were outlined. Even as someone who has seen the worst things people can do to each other, I was sickened when I heard what Holdom had done.

Holdom offered little. When the details were read before the court, he simply sat, head down. Avoiding eye contact.

But Holdom wanted his say, and in a move reminiscent of the attention-seeking Ivan Milat, he wrote letters to the outside world from his cell at Goulburn Correctional Centre, detailing the abuse he suffered as a child, his illicit drug use, and attempted suicide after the accident that killed two of his friend's children and left her in a wheelchair. Much of this abuse and hardship was later detailed in court, and although there were inconsistencies in Holdom's story to different people, it does appear he suffered abuse and neglect as a child.

The defence suggested Holdom was suffering from a depressive illness, a probable undiagnosed personality disorder and a substance abuse disorder. They also contended that there was a causal link between Holdom's upbringing, his substance abuse problems and his offending history.

Whilst of course I sympathise with any child who is the victim of maltreatment, nothing excuses what Holdom did to Karlie and Khandalyce. And, we have to remember, Holdom took photographs at the scene of the car accident he claimed traumatised him so badly – photographs of a dead child. He kept those images. Also, Holdom took photos, likely as mementoes, at Karlie's murder scene, and he murdered a defenceless two-year-old girl. Does his bad childhood mitigate any of that? I will let you make up your own mind.

Far from having no one who cared about them, the family's deep love for Karlie and Khandalyce was clearly evidenced in court, as highlighted in their victim impact statements. The purpose of these statements is to allow the victims' family members to express the effects the crime has had on them, once an offender has been convicted and is to be sentenced. These statements empower victims by giving them a voice in the criminal justice process, and they can be deeply affecting. Like many victims' loved ones, Karlie and Khandalyce's family had one overriding question for the offender, poignantly yet simply stated by Bruce Pearce, Karlie's father and Khandalyce's grandfather, 'The one question I want you to answer for me is a simple one – why?'

At the conclusion of proceedings, Mark Tedeschi, the Crown's prosecutor, asked for two life sentences to be imposed when the court reconvened for sentencing.

On 9 November 2018 Holdom was back in the Supreme Court of New South Wales in Sydney for sentencing, and I was there. I'd followed this case since 2013.

I wanted to look this man in the eye myself, to see if he was what I expected: the cold, calculating psychopath. I've met them before, and they can be all bravado and charm on the outside, but deep down they are driven by a need to dominate, control and (for violent offenders) hurt other people. This comes from a deep-seated insecurity they could never admit, not even to themselves. Men like Holdom and Milat before him never recognise the harm they do because they simply don't care; it's all about them and their needs. In Holdom's case he needed money and access to a toddler to fulfil a sexual fantasy. The trauma he caused to his victims and their families is meaningless to him, so I was not expecting him to show any remorse. If he had, it would have been contrived, a façade, designed to help himself by convincing the judge he was truly sorry and therefore did not deserve the most severe sentence possible.

Holdom appeared in person, so I was able to witness his reaction when he was sentenced. He appeared nervous, anxious and frustrated. But his lack of remorse was also on show – immediately the proceedings started, Holdom's solicitor told the judge that his client wanted to withdraw his guilty plea for Khandalyce's murder, and that he no longer agreed with some of the points as given in the 'agreed list of facts' (points the defence and prosecution concur on). No solid reason was given for this change, and the judge, Justice Hulme, rejected the submission, saying that the remorse Holdom had claimed to feel for his crimes appeared to have been rescinded by his attempt to change his plea.

Many of the details of Karlie and Khandalyce's murders were read again in court by Justice Hulme, who described Holdom's crimes as 'despicable' and of 'very great heinousness'.

This time Holdom did not sit passively by. Whenever his crimes against Khandalyce were mentioned, he shook his head. I am not naive enough to think that Holdom felt anything, hearing these details. I suspect he knew that crimes against children are looked upon very badly by other inmates, and that he would have a long, long time in prison to watch his back.

Karlie and Khandalyce's family were at the sentencing hearing too. Justice Hulme extended his most sincere condolences for what they had suffered. The family conducted themselves with dignity throughout, staying quiet until Justice Hulme read out the sentences: two counts of life. No minimum parole was set, and Holdom will spend the rest of his life in prison.

At that point one of the Pearce family simply looked at Holdom and said, 'Enjoy'.

CASE CLOSED, BUT QUESTIONS REMAIN

Why Belanglo? That's an interesting question.

In September 2008, just when Holdom and Karlie were beginning their two-month relationship, before he murdered her in December of that year, Ivan Milat was back in the headlines. This time because he had, yet again, made a written submission to the NSW Supreme Court arguing that his 1996 conviction for the murder of the seven backpackers was unsound. This was the third occasion in which Milat had asked for an inquiry into his convictions.

There are a number of similarities between Milat and Holdom. Both planned their attacks and took (or purchased on the way) the items they would need to carry them out. However, although I would describe Holdom as an organised offender, he wasn't as clever – or at least as rat cunning – as Milat, as he didn't plan or execute his crimes particularly well. Regardless, he got away with double murder for seven years, and it was only due to luck in Karlie's case that her body was found.

Milat was more advanced in his MO and was arguably a more overtly dominant offender, in that he liked taking adult couples for the buzz it gave him to control them. They both tortured their victims, although Holdom was sexually attracted to children, whereas Milat showed no signs of being a paedophile. And, importantly, both kept trophies of their kills – Milat the backpackers' belongings, and Holdom the photographs he took of Karlie in the forest.

Both lacked any empathy for their victims, a sign of psychopathy, and whilst neither Holdom or Milat have ever been officially diagnosed, there is a significant chance that both would rate highly on the psychopathy scale.

Holdom had a particular reason for driving the 170 kilometres from the ACT to Belanglo. It isn't a known anchor point for him, and no witness has ever linked him with the forest for any other reason. Did he see the similarities between himself and Milat too; was he even inspired by Milat to emulate his kill site after seeing Milat in the news again in September 2008? Is that why he chose Belanglo? Or did Holdom mistakenly believe that if Karlie's remains were ever discovered, the police would assume she was another Milat victim?

If so, he was wrong.

This case was solved through investigative excellence, forensic intelligence gathering, scientific advancement and the one piece of the puzzle that, if missing, can see all other efforts come to nothing – the public's help. Without Crime Stoppers callers 1267 and 1271 the police might never have discovered the identities of Karlie and Khandalyce. That piece of intelligence led to them pulling the thread that unravelled the whole case.

Colleen Povey died of cancer in 2012, believing her daughter and granddaughter were alive and well and travelling Australia. Perhaps, given the awful nature of their deaths, it's a blessing she never learned the truth.

As with many offenders like Holdom, I am left with a nagging doubt. Not over his guilt – there is overwhelming evidence of his culpability.

Holdom is not unique – he is a serial, violent offender, who fantasises about sexually abusing children. We know he had already assaulted a woman in 1999. He also has a conviction for stalking in 2001, and went on to offend against an eight-year-old girl in 2013. For a man who gets his kicks from harming others, what was he doing between 2001 and 2008 when he killed Karlie and Khandalyce? And why did he wait five years before striking again after killing them? My concern is that he didn't stop and there are more victims yet to be found or identified. My sense is that we will be hearing more from Daniel Holdom.

FORENSIC SCIENCE EXPLAINED: STABLE ISOTOPE ANALYSIS

Forensic science has a plethora of techniques that can be used to help solve a crime or identify an unknown deceased person. This includes the science of stable isotope analysis.

Atoms of one element share a common number of protons but may vary as a result of having a different number of neutrons present in their nuclei; as a result they have a different atomic mass. This is true of all but 12 elements on the periodic table. Unlike radioisotopes, stable isotopes do not decay over time.

Using isotope ratio mass spectrometry, experts in stable isotope profiling (SIP) are able to measure the abundance of stable isotopes of certain chemical elements in organic and inorganic compounds, creating what is known as an 'isotopic signature' – in essence an isotopic fingerprint. The natural abundance of these isotopic signatures results in ratio values that are specific to an area, which illustrates when compounds originate from different geographical locations. Think of it as a heat map, with all of the ratios of the stable isotopes varying by region.

There are a number of ways that stable isotope analysis can be used. For example, the country of origin of illicit drugs can be determined, due to our understanding of isotopic variation of organic plants. The profiles of seized shipments of illegal drugs can be used to assess patterns of illicit drug production and trade globally.

The isotopes we consume – in water, meat and vegetables – become incorporated into the hard and soft tissues of our body (hair, nails, dental enamel, and bones), and therefore the SIP of human tissue contains important information regarding a person's geographical life history and diet. For example, analysing the SIP of these tissues can provide information as to whether someone is predominantly a meat eater or consumes more fish, and the geographical origin of their food and water. This technique has been widely used in archaeology to investigate trends in human diet as well as movement from place to place.

Let's take the element hydrogen as an example. The body's main source of hydrogen is water; either it has been drunk or consumed as part of foodstuffs such as vegetables. We know that human head hair grows at around 1.25 centimetres per month, and we can show that the hydrogen profile found in that hair will closely resemble the hydrogen profile in the water the person has drunk. Drinking water is derived from rainfall, which varies in its SIP according to geographical location. As a result, if hair is cut into 1.25-centimetre sections, each section will illustrate where the person was geographically when that hair was growing.

SIP can be used to help determine diet and geo-location of an individual in a forensic context. In 2005 the dismembered body of a middle-aged African man was found in the Royal Canal in Dublin, Republic of Ireland. The body had been stabbed 21 times, 6 of which would have been fatal. Intelligence led the police to believe the victim may have been West African. A search of missing persons reports yielded no leads, and the police were unable to identify the victim. A team of SIP experts were provided with samples of pubic hair, toenails and a portion of bone from the centre of the femur (thigh bone), as each tissue type would tell the experts about the man's diet and pattern of movement. The analysis revealed that the victim had immigrated to the Republic of Ireland three to nine years before death, prior to which he had lived in a hot climate near the equator, such as the Horn of Africa. This information allowed detectives to undertake further local investigations and eventually to identify a child believed to have been fathered by the man. A DNA comparison between the victim and the child proved a familial link, and this was sufficient to prove the victim's identity – he was a 39-year-old Farah Swaleh Noor, who had originated from Kenya (in the Horn of Africa) and had relocated to Ireland in 1998, seven years prior to his death. The victim was the live-in boyfriend of the mother of two sisters, Linda and Charlotte Mulhall who killed him after an argument.

Whilst SIP cannot be used to identify an individual in the same way that a fingerprint or a DNA sample can, an understanding of a person's diet and movements can help investigators know where to target searches and reduce person of interest lists – in other words, SIP is an excellent intelligence-gathering tool. I am not aware that SIP has ever been used in Australia to help identify a person, although there certainly is scope to utilise this scientific method. For example, had Karlie Pearce-Stevenson's SIP been analysed from her hair and a portion of her femur, an SIP analyst with knowledge of human tissue development would have been able to establish that she originated from the Darwin area and to determine elements of her movement across the country. This would have helped narrow down where to undertake any further investigations.

SEVEN

WILLIAM TYRRELL -
THE BOY IN THE
SPIDERMAN SUIT

I've seen many cases where children have been abducted or hurt. As disturbing as this can be, I think that if you're trying to figure out the likely perpetrator, you need to stand where they stood, to see the environment through their eyes. Where a predator hunts and the victims they choose tell us an awful lot about them: when + where + how = who.

When it came to the kidnapping of three-year-old William Tyrrell, the scene was incredibly important. I'd seen the abduction on the news, but that did not give me a true sense of the place where William was last seen in 2014. So I decided to take the drive north from Sydney, to stand on the road where the offender must have stood to access the garden where William disappeared.

What struck me as I pulled up outside the house was how quiet it was here. The house plots were large and the gardens well tended. The house I was interested in sat on a slope, with a long curved driveway to the front door. There were large trees and bushland, sprawling lawns, and it was very lush. The ideal playground for a child.

Safe. That was the word that struck me. It looked so safe.

Turning from the house, I looked up and down the road. There were woods all around and it was easy to see how a child could get lost here, wander off and be blinded by all the trees. But I didn't believe that was what had happened. William was taken.

The street was a dead end as the road at the top is a dirt track and passable only by four-wheel drives, so there was very little passing traffic. In the half-hour I was there I saw only one car; it felt like the driver was local because she slowed down to look at me, clearly wondering what I was doing here. This quiet location was not like any random abduction site I'd been to. When predators hunt indiscriminate, vulnerable victims, they are being opportunistic. For that to work, there needs to *be* opportunity. Multiple potential victims. They watch, they wait, they groom. That just wasn't the case here.

I already knew the 'when', and now I had a clear feeling of the 'where'. I also thought I knew the 'how'. All we needed was the 'who'. I say all, but that's often that hardest part of the puzzle to find.

I also knew that to try to understand who took William I was going to have to forget everything I'd seen on the news, all the theories that have swirled around his abduction. But because it didn't appear random, that meant the answers to this puzzle existed. We just needed to look in the right places.

THE CASE

Every 15 minutes someone goes missing in Australia. The majority are located safe and well within the first few days of disappearing; however, around 1600 people per year remain unaccounted for, for at least three months. A few, like the three Beaumont siblings, have been missing for decades. Some of these missing persons remain anonymous, their lives and disappearances never making a dent in the public consciousness. But occasionally one stands out. William Tyrrell is one of those standouts. In 2014 his happy little face was on every television in the country. The situation was every parent's nightmare – the three-year-old had vanished whilst playing metres from his carers in his family's back garden.

Just like the Beaumonts over five decades earlier, William disappeared without a trace. And also just like the Beaumonts, interest in William's story has endured. There are few people who wouldn't recognise William in his Spiderman suit, the epitome of innocence and delight, smiling at the camera (figure 16).

Figure 16: Widely publicised photograph of William taken minutes before he disappeared.

What happened to the cheeky little boy? How did he disappear?

Although we can't say for sure, there are a finite number of possibilities, some more likely than others. In this chapter we will look at the various scenarios the police will have considered to explain William's disappearance, including who may have taken him and why, and we will contemplate why some cases strike a chord with such a huge number of people.

Parallels will be drawn with other infamous missing child cases, such as three-year-old British girl Madeleine McCann who disappeared from the family's holiday apartment in Portugal in 2007 while her parents ate dinner nearby, and 21-month-old Ben Needham, who vanished as he played outside his grandparents' home on the Greek island of Kos in 1991.

One of the reasons these names are so familiar is because they are children, and people are particularly chilled when kids go missing never to be heard of again. But there are missing children who are overlooked, whose stories you probably don't know. Faces you don't recognise. Or have forgotten. And I will ask you a challenging question – why don't their cases resonate with us as a community in the same way?

WHAT HAPPENED TO WILLIAM?

This story starts with William's birth on 26 June 2011. William is the second oldest of four siblings, with an older sister and two younger brothers.

The biological parents' (whose names are subject to a suppression order) relationship was troubled with domestic violence and allegedly both drug and alcohol abuse, and William's older sister was initially taken into foster care, followed later by nine-month-old William. Fortunately, social services were able to place both siblings into the same family.

On 12 September 2014, William was playing hide-and-seek with his older sister in the backyard of his foster grandmother's house on the New South Wales mid-north coast. The family had driven from Sydney the day before to visit William's foster grandmother.

Although the garden the kids were playing in was big and sprawling, the adults weren't far away, sitting on the verandah watching the children. Somewhere between 10.25–10.30 am William's foster mum went inside to make a cup of tea. As she went inside she could hear William 'roaring' playfully at his sister like a tiger, while running around the side of the house.

When she came back outside she found his sister but couldn't see William and it was too quiet.

She began to search the garden and was joined a short time later when William's foster dad returned to the house. He began knocking on neighbours' doors, wondering if William had wandered into someone else's house or garden to hide as part of the game with his sister, but there was no trace of the toddler.

By 10.56 am the family were frantic and called the police. His foster mother knew straightaway what had happened, saying in an interview to Channel 9's *60 Minutes* (her identity was suppressed) 'Right at the beginning, I was saying someone has taken William. It was absolutely screaming at me'.

The police response was swift, as it always is when a child goes missing today, with the first officers arriving at the house within 10 minutes of the emergency call. The search that day was extensive, both on land and from the air, and it went right on into the night. At this stage there were over 200 police, State Emergency Services members and volunteers from the Rural Fire Service on scene. The search was complicated by the fact that there was so much forested area to cover, as well as numerous creeks and other natural features where a small child could get lost. Neighbours and locals also joined the hunt for William, but all was in vain.

Although the teams were initially looking for a child that may have got lost by accident, specialist police were immediately notified. Human scent detection dogs did pick up his scent, but only within the boundaries of the backyard. It soon became clear that William could not have simply wandered off, as some trace of him would have been found.

As any investigator will tell you, the first 48 hours are critical in any major investigation, and decisions about how best to proceed have to be made based on the evidence available. In William's case, within 24 hours the family, police and other searchers had to accept that William had been abducted: he must have been carried away, otherwise the dogs would have been able to track him.

This changed the focus of the search, as they were no longer looking for a little boy who had wandered off; they had to start looking for the person or persons who had taken him. What route had they taken from the house, what car had they been driving, how had they chosen William?

The window of opportunity had been very small, from when his foster mum last saw him as she went to make tea, to her coming back outside and seeing he was gone. Maybe five minutes, tops.

Sadly 24 hours stretched into 48, and then into a week, and the police were no closer to finding the little boy.

A week after William vanished, the police told the family there was nothing else the family could do, and that they could go home to Sydney. The distraught foster parents had to pack all William's belongings, his clothes and toys, and take them away.

The one thing they didn't have was William.

Within four days of William being taken Strike Force Rosann was established by State Crime Command to investigate what police now firmly believed was a case of child abduction.

This strike force was assisted by hundreds of police officers from across the state.

Within the first year of William's disappearance, the strike force had collated over 5000 documents and over 1400 information reports from the public, and over 1000 people had been interviewed. This was an extraordinarily large police investigation, but at the time of the first anniversary, the police did not have one primary person of interest, but rather a number of people they were looking at.

By 2016, over 11,000 pieces of information and 628 exhibits had been collected and checked by officers from Strike Force Rosann, including 2800 reports that had been made to Crime Stoppers, 196 reports directly to the strike force, and over 1078 possible sightings of William. Investigators had also canvassed 450 addresses and interviewed 690 persons of interest. The strike force had also been boosted by a second contingent of staff, called Strike Force Rosann 2, which included expert officers from the Sex Crimes and Fraud Squad and the Armed Hold Up Squad (the remit of which are to provide specialist support to Police Area Commands across NSW), as well as police from local area commands across the state.

LIKELY SCENARIOS TO EXPLAIN WHO TOOK WILLIAM

The scene of William's disappearance tells us a lot about the likely kidnapper. William was snatched from a dead-end street, so the only people who would have been there were either locals or had another specific reason for being there. It's not the sort of place you just find yourself accidentally.

No one besides the foster parents and grandmother knew of the visit, and they had only arrived the day before.

William had to have been taken in a vehicle, and it would have been risky to carry a child any distance. Strangers would have stood out, and even parking a car for too long in such a close-knit community would have gained unwanted attention.

This is evidenced by the fact that a number of cars were seen in the area the morning William vanished, including a grey sedan and a white station wagon, which were seen parked opposite the foster grandmother's house; William's foster mum noticed them at 7.30 am and again at 9.30 am, but they were gone by 10:30 am (the time William vanished). The police haven't been able to discover why the cars were on the street and view their presence with suspicion, as the house blocks are big and the drives for the houses spaced quite a long way apart. If people are visiting a house, they park on the ample drives, so what were these two cars doing parked opposite the house, with their windows down, that morning?

William's foster mother saw another car driving out of the road at around 10.30 am, describing the car as older, green or teal in colour, with alloys and non-tinted windows. One man was in the car alone, whom she described as in his late 50s, Caucasian with a 'weathered' look, sandy-red hair cut short and no facial hair. She has tried to do a facial composite with a police sketch artist, but the software was not working at capacity, and another attempt will be made – as she can still clearly see his face in her mind's eye.

None of these cars or their drivers has been identified.

The police checked hundreds of persons of interest, from family members to people who had visited the house, to those in the local community (including 20 known sex offenders living in the area), as well as people who had been named in tip-offs to Crime Stoppers. They needed to know whether this was a familial abduction, an acquaintance kidnapping, or a stranger abduction.

FAMILIAL ABDUCTION

Familial abductions account for around 50% of all disappearances. This normally occurs as a result of a custody dispute and women are more likely to commit this type of abduction than men, with children under six the most common victims.

This case was complicated by the fact that William was in state care at the time he was taken, and obviously the police had to look very closely at both the biological and foster families, given the data available on likely offenders in child abduction cases. The most common type of familial abduction is parental non-custodial, and in this situation the child is unlikely to be harmed intentionally. The foster parents were cleared of any involvement early on, as there was no reason for either of them to take and hide the toddler as they were a stable family unit.

The biological family were also investigated and cleared.

Back in western Sydney the day William was taken, William's biological mother was out shopping for baby clothes as she was eight months pregnant. She had just got home when the police arrived at her house, looking for William. The biological father was also there, having taken the day off work. They searched the house and found a little boy playing in the back garden. They thought it was William, but it wasn't, it was his younger brother.

The police interest in the Tyrrells continued, with officers visiting his biological mother almost daily. This is not unusual; the police were simply working with what the research tells us – because William was in foster care, the biological family were statistically likely to be strong suspects in his abduction.

ACQUAINTANCE ABDUCTIONS

Acquaintance child abduction accounts for around a quarter of all cases of child kidnapping. Juvenile perpetrators are the most likely to commit this crime, and the victims are often older, commonly teenagers. Included in this category are children kidnapped by extended family and those people who have met the child in a superficial manner, for example neighbours. It's possible William was taken by an acquaintance, but if so, it would have been random and unplanned, as no one except the immediate foster family knew that William would be at the house at that time, unless they had happened to see the child since he arrived the day before. We can discount that any of the neighbours took William as all houses and gardens were searched thoroughly within the first 24 hours, and remember, the police were on scene within 10 minutes of receiving the 000 call from William's foster mother, so it would have been impossible for a neighbour to snatch him, hide him, and then sneak away with so many people around looking for him.

He could potentially have been taken by someone he met elsewhere, or extended family, but there is simply no evidence to support this.

STRANGER ABDUCTIONS

Around 25% of all offenders in child abduction cases are strangers, so it is a relatively rare occurrence, regardless of what the media tells us about 'stranger danger'. Sometimes children are lured away and sometimes they are snatched. The vast majority of children are found alive, but around 20% are killed, usually within three hours of being kidnapped.

Early on in the investigation the police suspected that William might have been abducted by a paedophile ring operating in the area. The police soon discounted this possibility, but did look closely at one man who had previously visited the foster grand-mother's home. This person fully co-operated with the police; there was no evidence of William when police searched his house in 2015 and there is no evidence to suggest he had any prior knowledge of the family's arrival. There is therefore no reason to conclude he was aware of William's presence at the house that day or that he had any involvement in William's disappearance.

Another person of interest was Tony Jones, who was sentenced to 3 years in prison for the aggravated indecent assault of an 11-year-old girl, and who was living in the area. Jones was interviewed by the police on a number of occasions, and a car he had access to was forensically examined. The car matched the description of a white station wagon William's foster mother saw parked across the street from their house the day William vanished. Jones was also linked to Paul Bickford, another man living in the area who received a suspended prison sentence for the indecent assault of an underage person. Bickford was also investigated by detectives from Strike Force Rosann. Both men deny any involvement with William's disappearance. Neither Jones nor Bickford has been charged, and there is therefore no reason to conclude that either has anything to do with William's disappearance.

THE POLICE'S HYPOTHESIS

In 2015, a year after William went missing, Detective Chief Inspector Gary Jubelin went public with his theory as to what had happened. Jubelin discounted the idea that someone just happened to be on the quiet road, saw William close to the house and ran up the front drive to grab him. Looking at the house from the street, it's very open, and with other houses having clear sight of the front garden and the street. It would take a very brazen predator to take that kind of risk, and if he had snatched William close to the house and tried to carry a struggling, probably crying child back to a car, someone would likely have heard something. But they didn't.

Instead, DCI Jubelin suggested that William, who at home in Sydney had developed the habit of coming down the drive to meet his foster dad when he knew he'd be back soon, had done the same thing at his foster grandmother's house and was waiting near the road and a stranger opportunistically grabbed him and forced him into a waiting car. He stated that whoever was on the street that day was there for a reason.

THE POLICE WON'T STOP LOOKING FOR WILLIAM

On 12 September 2016, the NSW Police Commissioner Andrew Scipione and DCI Jubelin were joined by Premier Mike Baird to announce that the reward for information relating to William's recovery, alive or dead, had been increased to $1 million. This is a unique situation, in that this reward does not require that anyone be arrested, charged or convicted of William's abduction, and it is the highest reward ever offered in a missing persons case in NSW.

As at the date of publication, suppression orders are in place in relation to the identities of various people, though some believe earlier suppression orders had the effect of hindering the investigation, as it meant no family member could talk to the press and appeal for William's return.

In the case of Madeleine McCann's abduction, the family used the press to great effect to keep the search going; in fact it is because of their media campaign that we all know Madeleine's name today. William didn't have that kind of advocacy, but in his case it didn't matter, as we all recognise the boy in the Spiderman suit anyway. The public got behind the search, so I don't think the suppression orders harmed the investigation.

In 2017, facial anthropologist Dr Susan Hayes (whom you met in chapter six) produced a computer-based facial likeness of William, age progressed to show what he would look like as a six-year-old (figure 17).

Figure 17: Age progression of William Tyrrell (2017), incorporating known facial changes in boys (three years to six years) and data taken from a facial database (used with permission from Dr Susan Hayes).

This was the perfect time, developmentally, to perform an age progression on William, as a result of the changing dentition that significantly alters the face shape. At two and a half to three years old, William would have had all 20 of his baby (or deciduous) teeth (except perhaps his second molars), but he would also have had some of his adult teeth developing in his upper and lower jaws, ready to push out and replace his baby teeth at the right time. By the time he would be six years old, his adult teeth would be much more advanced in their development, and therefore larger, and his lower central incisors and first molars top and bottom would be pushing through his gums moving into their final adult positions. As the permanent teeth grow in the jaws, the face broadens, to accommodate the larger dentition, and the shape of the jaw changes significantly as a result.

EXPERT INSERT: FACIAL PROGRESSION

Facial progression (also known as age progression) is the process by which a person's face is made to look older by a given number of years, and is most often undertaken in missing persons cases. The aim of the age-progressed face is to estimate how a missing child or adult might appear today, and thereby stimulate leads as to their current whereabouts from the general public.

Facial progressions are based on photographs and can be either drawing-based or computer-graphic manipulations of individual features, with digital approaches being able to include some level of computer automation (a process that warps the facial features in accordance with relevant facial databases). Ideally, whatever approach is taken, a facial progression involves applying research findings from the most relevant and reliable studies – but there are practical, biological and environmental factors that will always ensure the results are very approximate.

Firstly, there is the quality, time and clarity of the photographs on which the progression is based. The perfect baseline photograph is well lit, full face, expressionless and taken at eye level (not from above, which is often the case with children), and the date the photograph was taken is known. This is because research into facial ageing is mostly linear measurements taken at specific ages with the head in a standard anatomical orientation.

Secondly, are there photographs of older siblings, parents, aunts/uncles and/or grandparents, and are these also of good baseline quality? Studies of heritability indicate which particular facial features are more likely to be shared between, say, mothers and sons (which includes the spaces between features as well as the features themselves), and relevant features can be age progressed to follow the growth patterns of the relevant biological relative.

However, for understandable reasons, such ideal baseline photographs are often not available.

Biological complications mean that human facial ageing is not consistent in the growth rate, feature or timing, and the sexes generally differ in how their faces age. This is very obvious in children, but not many realise that research consistently shows that our skulls and teeth, not just our soft tissues, continue growing throughout our lives. Individual adult skull bones grow at different rates, and in different directions, and there are also age-related losses as well as gains in the tissues. So, while adult facial ageing is more selective and less dramatic than in children and teenagers, there are still spurts and slowdowns that impact on the placement and shape of every single facial feature.

An additional complication is that our facial features are highly adaptable to, and influenced by, environmental factors. What foods you currently eat, how you prepare these foods, where you currently live, what you do there, your health and access to medical treatment, your current level of poverty, and your normal behaviours, will all be expressed to some degree in your face. And naturally all of these factors are confounded by the fact that ageing is not the same for everyone – which is why your biological age may appear older or younger than your age in calendar years. There are a number of cross-sectional studies of facial ageing (averages from groups of similar age, sex and environments), and these can be selected and applied to age

progress facial features. Unfortunately, there are fewer longi-
tudinal studies of facial ageing, so the most useful research for
an age progression – how individual people age through their
lifespan – is not as well known.

Related to facial progression is its less well-known coun-
terpart, age regression. This also (ideally) follows reliable
research into facial ageing, but results in a person made
younger by a given number of years. The usefulness of this
process is to indicate whether a person is more or less likely
to be of interest regarding a past event. For example, how
likely is it that this adult man was the child depicted in this
photograph, or how similar is this age-regressed woman to
the adolescent in this CCTV still?

Dr Susan Hayes, facial anthropologist

You can see from Susan's age progression that whilst she has
clearly shown the age progressed image of William on the right as
still having his deciduous teeth, his lower face has elongated and
taken on more mature proportions. William would have turned
eight on 26 June 2019, and all four permanent incisors would have
erupted, so he would start to look a lot less babyish as those central
deciduous teeth are lost.

The next suitable age for a progression is after puberty, as the
hormonal changes that boys go through between the ages of 12
and 16 years mean their faces take on a much more obviously adult
form, with the hit of testosterone that comes with boy's maturation.

If William has not been found by the time he's 14, a second age
progression could be done to estimate what he may look like as an
older boy, as by this time he will have all his adult teeth, except his
third molars, and his face will be taking on adult proportions.

240

IN 2018, THE SEARCH CONTINUED

On 12 June 2018 the police announced they would be doing a detailed, large-scale forensic search of three square kilometres of bushland that would last four weeks and would be run by search experts from the Public Order and Riot Squad of the New South Wales Police Force. This specifically trained team regularly undertake searches for missing or deceased persons, canvass crime scenes, and engage in disaster victim identification, therefore they are ideally placed to perform searches where maximum evidentiary recovery is essential, such as in a missing child case.

This was different to the original search back in 2014 when William was taken, as then the police and searchers were looking for a little boy possibly lost or injured, not evidence that could help identify his abductor. Midway through the search the team suddenly moved to another, smaller area of bushland outside the original search zone.

The police investigated this new area for two days.

DCI Jubelin said in a televised press conference that there is 'a person who knows why investigators are searching the area' and that 'they will no doubt be feeling pressure from the intensity of the investigation'.

During both searches the police were looking for any sign of William, any scrap of clothing, or items that looked out of place. But remember, this was almost four years after he disappeared, so many items – even if they had been forensically relevant – may have moved or been lost over the passage of time. Add to this the detritus that you would expect to be present, and which had nothing to do with William's abduction, and the huge task facing the police becomes clear.

DCI Jubelin said the purpose of the evidence collection was 'to prove that beyond reasonable doubt, William's disappearance was the result of human intervention and not misadventure'. This would be equally important in a coronial or criminal investigation, should anyone ever be charged with William's abduction. DCI Jubelin also said, aimed very pointedly at people they clearly believe know what happened to William, 'I suggest you come to us before we come to you'.

During the search William's biological grandmother made a public statement that the police were wasting their time and that William wasn't there. She also said the search was opening old wounds, and that she and her son, William's biological father, believed William was dead.

The searches in 2018 failed to find William, but as the police said, that wasn't the only purpose. Apart from finding evidence for the legal process, it was clear that they also wanted the offenders and those who know what happened to the toddler to be on notice.

That the net is closing.

In the meantime, the legal process continues, and on the fourth anniversary of William's disappearance – 12 September 2018 – detectives announced that they were handing the investigation to Deputy State Coroner Harriet Grahame. This does not mean the police accept that William is dead: rather, it is standard procedure in a case such as this.

The 'coronial inquest into the disappearance and suspected death of William Tyrrell' (official title) began in late March 2019 at the new Coroner's Court at Lidcombe, before Deputy State Coroner Grahame who was present at the search for William in July 2018.

Gerard Craddock, the senior counsel assisting the coroner, opened the proceedings with a summary statement and said that it was not clear that William had been abducted by a stranger, nor that William is dead; however, given the formal name of the inquest, it is probable that the coroner will conclude William is deceased when the inquest concludes in August 2019.

Following Craddock's opening statement, the first week of the inquiry focused on setting the scene as to why William was there on that day – why he was in care, and who knew about the foster family's decision to visit the foster grandmother. The inquiry will resume in August 2019, at which time persons of interest in the investigation will give evidence; this will include a new POI that has not been publicly named. It is hoped that the coronial inquiry will be an opportunity to test the police's evidence, and advance the search for William.

Finding William remains a priority for the New South Wales Police Force, and the criminal investigation – one of the state's most intensive in recent memory – is running parallel with the coronial inquiry. The police have made clear that they will continue to look for William as a missing person, and they consider that he is alive until they have evidence to the contrary.

OTHER WELL-KNOWN CHILD ABDUCTION CASES
MADELEINE McCANN

Madeleine McCann is a name synonymous with mystery and intrigue, and everybody has theories as to what happened to her. Everyone knows the story. On 3 May 2007, British toddler Madeleine, then three-years-old, was snatched from a bedroom in a holiday apartment in Portugal, whilst her parents ate dinner about 80 metres walk away. She was on holiday with her parents, Gerry and Kate, and her two-year-old twin siblings, as well as other families with children. All the children of the group had been put to bed before the adults ate, including the three McCann kids, and the parents were taking it in turn to check on the children sleeping in various apartments.

Around 10 pm it was Kate McCann's turn to check, and when she went into her own apartment, she found that Madeleine was gone. About the same time, a witness later reported seeing a man carrying a child wearing pyjamas towards the ocean.

A search was immediately initiated, but Madeleine, like William, had vanished.

The rumours soon started, and over the next few weeks the Portuguese police began to believe that the child had been accidentally killed by one or other parent and that her body had been covertly disposed of before they raised the alarm. This became an allegation, and in September 2007 the parents became formal suspects in Madeleine's disappearance. They remained suspects until 2008, when the Portuguese Attorney General archived the investigation due to a lack of evidence. It was later proven that the McCanns had nothing to do with their daughter's disappearance.

Gerry and Kate McCann didn't give up looking for Madeleine, and they hired a private investigator until Scotland Yard established Operation Grange in 2011. This came about after a personal appeal by the McCanns, after which then Prime Minister David Cameron asked the Metropolitan Police Force to 'bring their expertise' to the inquiry. Astonishing really to think that one set of parents could make such a request, then a prime minister act on it and such huge resources be put aside for one missing person investigation. Operation Grange was scaled back in 2015, but the case remains live, with significant ongoing public interest.

Government funding for this investigation is reviewed every six months. As of October 2018, around AUD $21 million has been spent investigating this case and a request for an additional $270,000 was being considered to continue the investigation.

This may be the most widely reported and investigated missing child case in history.

Why are people so interested in the disappearance of one little girl?

The answer to that lies in Gerry and Kate McCann's media strategy. From the earliest days of the search, they clearly knew that the best chance they had of finding their child was to keep her at the centre of public attention, which meant courting the media. They were very heavily criticised for this by some, but without the constant photos of Madeleine on the front page of newspapers and magazines, she was soon going to be forgotten, and with that their chances of finding her would plummet.

To give you an idea of just how much of an impact this case had in the UK, in 2013, *Crimewatch* (a true crime program equivalent to Australia's *Wanted*) ran an update on the case and released an e-fit of the man seen carrying a child in pyjamas around 10 pm the night Madeleine was taken. The program received 1000 calls, an astonishing result over 6 years after the event.

What struck me as I watched was the fact that *Crimewatch* had run this follow-up appeal at all; it is not something they generally do, focusing instead on more recent crimes the police need public assistance with. I wondered how many other children had gone missing in 2007 that weren't having millions of dollars spent on their case and weren't having specially dedicated programs broadcast.

BEN NEEDHAM

The story of Ben Needham, a 21-month-old British boy, is another that most people know, and is a case that is somewhat similar to William's disappearance. Ben vanished at around 2.30 pm on 24 July 1991 whilst playing outside a derelict farmhouse he was visiting with his grandmother. His grandfather was renovating the farmhouse on the Greek island of Kos, where he lived. The family raised the alarm and called the local police, but literally no trace of Ben could be found.

One lead looked promising: a number of eyewitnesses told police that a boy matching Ben's description was seen at the local airport the day Ben vanished, but this boy has not been found.

The police established Operation Ben to discover what happened to the toddler. Unlike William, the police don't believe Ben was abducted, but instead think he may have been the subject of an accident, crushed by a digger during construction on the farmhouse. They think his body was hidden to cover the accident. It's impossible to ask the digger driver, Konstantinos Barkas, as he died of stomach cancer in 2015.

In 2016, almost 25 years after he vanished, the police took a team of officers and search experts to Kos to look for Ben's body. The dig lasted for weeks and focused around the farmhouse where Ben was last seen. At around this time an anonymous man came forward to police, after a local appeal for information. The witness said he knew of a second site the digger driver, Barkas, had used, about 750 metres from the primary site of interest. The dig at site two resulted in a toy car being found. This car was known to have belonged to Ben and he had been playing with it the day he disappeared. This is only the second piece of evidence definitely linked to Ben – the first was a scrap of sandal found in 2012 at the site where Konstantinos Barkas was operating a digger. These items were taken back to the UK and tested, but the expert could only establish that there were chemical markers suggestive of blood decomposition on the sandal. That is not the same thing as blood being present, it just means that someone was bleeding and came into contact with the items. The next stage is for a forensic biologist, a DNA expert, to test the samples. However, even today, with techniques that have advanced since 2016, these traces of blood are too small to currently analyse to confirm the blood is Ben's. The UK police hold Ben's DNA on file in case this ever becomes a possibility.

There is also the chance Ben was taken and is still alive. This hope has been fuelled several times, as young men, believing they may be Ben, have come forward, only to be ruled out following DNA analysis.

This offers some hope in William's case, however, as if he has been taken, he was so young at the time that he may be living elsewhere and not know who he really is. If he ever suspects and comes forward, it would be a simple matter to confirm or refute his identity through a familial DNA match to his biological parents.

A genetic genealogy search might prove useful in finding biological relatives, or he may himself be found if he ever uploads his DNA to a public database, via a process known as 'genetic genealogy' (see the expert insert below), a technique used to great effect in adoption cases but now being applied to forensic searches too.

Ben's disappearance is one of the longest running missing person cases in the UK's history. The search for him continues.

EXPERT INSERT: GENETIC GENEALOGY

Genetic genealogy (GG) is the combination of genetic analysis with traditional historical and genealogical research. For forensic investigations, it can be used to identify remains by tying the DNA to a family with a missing person, or to point to the likely identity of an offender.

By comparing a DNA sample to a database of DNA from volunteer participants, it is possible to determine whether there are any relatives of the DNA sample in the database and how closely related they are. This information can then be cross-referenced with other data sources used in traditional genealogical research, such as census records, vital records, obituaries and newspaper archives.

GG is not only a powerful *identification* technique but also an *intelligence* technique that can generate leads on unknown subjects and help the police narrow down a suspect list to a region, a family or even an individual. Identity can then be confirmed using traditional DNA analysis.

Genetic genealogy uses autosomal DNA (atDNA) single nucleotide polymorphisms (SNPs) to determine how closely related two individuals are. Unlike other genetic markers, such as mitochondrial DNA or Y chromosome DNA, atDNA is inherited from all ancestral lines and passed on by both males and females, and thus can be used to compare any two individuals, regardless of how they are related.

The standard atDNA metric used by genetic genealogists is the amount of DNA that two people are likely to have inherited from a recent common ancestor. This can be estimated by looking for long stretches of identical DNA, as these are unlikely to be shared by unrelated people. Therefore only segments above a certain length are counted. The length of these shared segments is measured in centimorgans (cM), a measure of genetic distance, and the total number of cM shared across all chromosomes can be used to determine approximately how closely related two people are. Consumer DNA testing companies employ thresholds between 5 cM and 7 cM to identify relatives; however, a significant number of these segments may not be identical by descent. Segment sizes of 20 cM are highly likely to represent a genealogically relevant relationship. At the time of writing, using a public genetic genealogy database GEDMatch, DNA from an unknown person can be compared to roughly 1.25 million people to see whether any of them are related. However, it will be significantly larger by the time this book goes to press, as the database receives about 1000 new uploads per day.

DNA database results serve as clues on which traditional genealogy methods can build, starting with constructing the matches' family trees using a wide variety of information sources. During the tree-building process, the genetic genealogist searches for common ancestors who appear across multiple family trees of the matches. Ideally, marriages between the descendants of the identified common ancestors are discovered. Descendancy research is employed to search for descendants below the intersection of these common ancestors who were born at a time that is consistent with the subject's estimated age range. The goal of this search is to narrow down the possible individuals to a family group, a set of cousins or siblings, or even an individual.

The amount of information available can vary widely. In some cases, genealogists have been able to produce names and contact information for the person of interest. In other cases, they have only been able to produce a small region in a US state or specific population group from which the family of the POI originated. However, when this happens, continuous monitoring for future matches can be arranged.

These techniques have primarily been used to discover the biological family history of adopted individuals, but they apply equally as well to forensic applications. Genetic genealogy has been used to identify victims' remains, as well as suspects, in a number of high-profile cases.

In 2018, over 30 suspects in criminal cases were identified in the US through genetic genealogy, leading to many arrests, including in the high-profile Golden State Killer and April Tinsley cases.

CeCe Moore, genetic genealogist

BUT HAVE YOU EVER HEARD OF THESE MISSING CHILDREN?

If you go the Australian Federal Police's missing persons pages, you will find endless images of people considered long-term missing. Some names, like the Beaumont siblings, you will recognise, but others you won't. Most of the faces you see are adults, but some are children. And of course when a child goes missing, it usually causes significant public interest and concern. But not always.

Why do some stories resonate and others don't?

Darren Shannon was just 11 months old when he was last seen on 9 June 1973 at his grandparents' house near Adelaide, South Australia. Initially his disappearance was not a mystery – he was taken from the house by his father, John Shannon, on an access visit. However, at around 9.15 pm, just over two hours after leaving the grandparents' house, the car John was driving was involved in a head-on collision with another vehicle. John was killed and his body found in the car. The scene was searched thoroughly, but little Darren was missing and he has not been seen again. The entry on the Crime Stoppers SA website lists Darren as 'missing, presumed murdered'. The police believe that at some point before the accident,

Darren was either killed by his father and his body disposed of at an unknown location, or he was given to a friend or relative to raise in secret: a classic case of non-custodial parental abduction. But these remain theories, as no evidence has been made publicly available.

Darren vanished in June 1973, just two months before Joanne Ratcliffe and Kirste Gordon – two more names you are likely to know – were abducted from the Adelaide Oval. Have you ever heard of him? I hadn't until I started researching this chapter, and his disappearance is certainly not considered one of Australia's enduring mysteries, in the same way the Adelaide Oval disappearances are.

Another child I imagine most people have not heard of is Rahma El-Dennaoui. Rahma was 19 months old when she was allegedly taken from her bed on the morning of 10 November 2005, from the family's home in Lurnea, a western Sydney suburb. One of eight siblings, Rahma was between two of her sisters in a double bed under the bedroom window when she was last seen. At 8.30 am, when her parents checked on the kids, they found Rahma was missing. They searched the house, but when they couldn't find her they called the police. A hole was found in the flyscreen across the window, large enough for Rahma to have climbed or been lifted through. Some sources suggest the flyscreen had been cut. No one remembered how long the hole had been there. Strike Force Kilt was established to try to find Rahma, with the police concluding the little girl was kidnapped, but despite a $250,000 reward and extensive police investigations, including the police questioning known sex offenders in the area, no trace of Rahma was ever found.

In 2010 the police stated that they thought Rahma had been abducted and taken abroad, although they did not say what led them to this conclusion. A coronial inquest held in 2013 failed to provide any clear answers as to what had happened to Rahma, and indicated that there was 'no conclusive evidence' the family had staged her kidnapping. However, Deputy NSW Coroner Sharon Freund also said that the family's behaviour in the weeks after Rahma's disappearance was 'puzzling . . . In particular, the joking and laughing by Rahma's parents with third parties about the kidnapping and the splitting of the reward money, the specific references to avoiding talking about the inquest on the telephone and actually talking in code'. In 2015, the police confirmed they had new information, suggesting that they might learn at last what had happened to Rahma, but in 2019 her whereabouts are still unknown.

A number of journalists have likened Rahma's case to that of Madeleine McCann, but I bet most people would not know Rahma's little face if they saw it.

When I started writing this book, I wanted to bring something new to each chapter. I didn't want to simply rewrite about cases you all know, and I wanted to show that cold cases are not over, not forgotten. And it was really important for me that the focus not simply be on the offenders. I wanted the victims to be centre stage, as these are their stories, their lives, their deaths.

There is no doubt William Tyrrell's disappearance is heartbreaking, for his family and for the community where he lived and where he vanished. The whole country grieves with them. What is also sad to me are the forgotten children, the stories we don't know, the families we don't grieve with. What makes one face, one case, stick in our minds more than another? I don't know the answer to that question, but this has been a chance to remember some of the forgotten, as every missing child deserves to be found.

And someone knows what happened to William, or suspects they know who might have taken him. If that's you, and you're reading this now, don't hesitate – call Crime Stoppers (1300 333 000) and get William home.

FORENSIC SCIENCE EXPLAINED: DNA DATABASES

Today, everyone is familiar with the concept of DNA databases – they are used to store genetic information for a diverse range of reasons, from researching genetic diseases to solving crimes and identifying deceased persons.

In Australia, the Criminal Intelligence Commission provides police and forensic scientists across all states and territories with access to the National Criminal Investigation DNA Database (NCIDD), which is a powerful investigative tool. The database is available 24 hours a day, 7 days a week, and has been operational since 2001. Over the last 17 years, over 1.2 million DNA profiles have been added. These range from samples collected at crime scenes, to samples taken from suspects and offenders, as well as profiles of unknown deceased persons and those obtained from items belonging to missing persons.

These databases are used in a number of ways. Firstly, a crime scene sample can be added to the database to see if a match can be made to a known person. This is often referred to as a 'cold hit'. In addition, multiple crimes can be linked through DNA samples taken at multiple scenes, even when no offender is identified. Another essential aspect of DNA

searches occurs when an unknown deceased person is identified when their DNA is matched to a sample on the database,
either through an item belonging to the person (such as their
toothbrush) or through a familial match.

An extension of the identification of unidentified remains
is the use of DNA matching in disaster victim identification
(DVI), which occurs in situations where there are mass fatalities.
The Bali nightclub bombings in 2002 killed 202 people in two
venues, including 88 Australians, and injured a further 209. In
this incident, which was a terrorist attack, the Australian Federal
Police's function within the DVI team was to collect forensic
material from the crime scenes, suspects, unknown deceased
persons, as well as from personal items and blood relatives of
the missing persons. The identification process occurred in
four steps: an assessment of physical characteristics such as sex,
eye colour, height; an examination of unnatural markings such
as tattoos and scars; evaluation of dental records; and DNA
analysis. However, due to the nature of the incident, many of
the victims were highly fragmented, and it has been estimated
that 70% were identified through DNA analysis, primarily
undertaken at the AFP's lab in Canberra. Instead of using the
NCIDD, a specific DVI DNA database was established, and
43 matches were achieved through this database, with a further
67 being obtained through a kinship database provided by
Queensland Health.

When a match is achieved between two samples of
DNA, this is a very powerful indicator that the two originated from the same person, with the likelihood of two
people sharing the same DNA profile being one in a billion.

Sometimes, however, an offender's DNA may not be in the
database, and police use other mechanisms to identify violent

offenders. One method they can employ is DNA screening, where the police will collect volunteer DNA samples from all the people in a discrete locality who fit a general description. This allows the police to exclude people from their inquiries, as well as being a tactic to flush out suspects – those who refuse to provide a sample.

A very early example of mass DNA screening helped catch a man who had raped and beaten an elderly woman in her home on New Year's Day in 1991. Rita Knight (91) lived in Wee Waa, northern New South Wales, and it appeared she was the victim of a robbery gone wrong. After 14 months the police were no closer to catching the attacker and the case had gone cold. In April 2000, for the first time in Australian history, the police announced they planned to undertake a mass DNA screening. All men between the ages of 18 and 45 years living in the Wee Waa area were asked to volunteer to have a cheek swab (known as a buccal swab) taken. Civil rights groups raised privacy concerns; however, ultimately 470 of the 500 males provided samples that would be tested against DNA left at the crime scene. Among these men was 44-year-old farm labourer Stephen James Boney. Ten days later, before all of the hundreds of samples had been processed, Boney walked into Wee Waa police station and confessed to the crime, acknowledging the inevitability that the police were going to identify him from his DNA sample.

The process of mass screening was clearly successful and established DNA as a key tool for investigators. It also supported the need for large DNA databases to store DNA profiles to help solve serious crimes more quickly, as well as linking multiple crimes across jurisdictions, and identifying long-term deceased persons.

PULLING THE
THREADS TOGETHER

One of the key things I have noticed writing this book is that the offenders are clearly of a 'type'. They are cold, calculating, violent individuals, without empathy for those they prey on. These are the ones who are truly born bad.

Consider Harry Phipps, the possible killer of the Beaumont children. Outwardly Phipps was a charming, charismatic, successful man, but beneath that façade lurked a brutal child sex offender and possible murderer. Phipps was highly intelligent and cunning, an organised offender who took calculated risks to fulfil his sexual fantasies. The question remains as to whether he evaded detection for the abduction and murder of the Beaumont siblings for over half a century. Triple murderer Ashley Coulston was a narcissist with a love for danger. He was another organised offender, who took his kill bag with him when he hunted.

Although Mr Cruel has never been identified, his modus operandi shares some things in common with Phipps and Coulston, in that he planned crimes that were based on his sexual fantasies, and people are either an asset to them, something they can use and take advantage of, or you are in their way. Both are dangerous positions to be in.

Ivan Milat is Australia's most notorious serial killer. He is a violent, serial predator who still seeks attention from prison and enjoys his notoriety. He has never admitted to any of his crimes and has expressed no empathy for the victims. Similarly Daniel Holdom, who savagely assaulted and murdered young mum Karlie Pearce-Stevenson and her two-year-old daughter, Khandalyce, showed no empathy for his victims or the pain their family feels.

All these men are the monsters that walk among us. They thrive on power and the euphoria they feel when they dominate and hurt others. I've met men like this, violent, predatory psychopaths, throughout my career, in one form or another – in different skins, as I think of it – but in one way they are all the same. Push them out of their comfort zone and they forget themselves and drop the mask. Then you can see what lurks beneath. Their eyes can turn almost black, their muscles tense, as if, like a wolf, they are about to spring. Then, because I have only ever encountered them in the company of others, they temper their urges, get control of themselves, and the mask is replaced. Hiding the predator within.

These were all men.

I didn't intentionally select cases where men are the offenders, but it's clear that the majority of serious, serial violent offenders are men. So here, at the end, I'm left wondering why the cold, calculating predators tend to be men; why women – perfectly capable of extreme and premeditated violence – are less likely to become predatory sex offenders and killers, seeking power and dominance over others.

COLD CASE INVESTIGATIONS

One of the main reasons I wanted to write this book was so people would realise that just because a case is cold does not mean that it won't be solved. I can illustrate just how 'alive' the cases covered in this book are with a simple summary of what happened in 2018 and 2019, when I was writing it.

The Beaumont siblings, Jane, Arnna, and Grant, were abducted and probably murdered over 50 years ago, yet in 2018 I was involved in a reinvestigation of their case which led to a (sadly unsuccessful) forensic dig looking for their remains. This new search made headlines worldwide and proves that the Beaumont children may be gone but they are not forgotten, and that the police and community are still committed to finding out what happened to them. Also in 2018, Ivan Milat's name came up again, linked to an alleged attempted abduction in the 1980s of a British man backpacking in Australia, and Daniel Holdom was arrested and pleaded guilty to murdering Karlie Pearce-Stevenson and her daughter, Khandalyce, in 2008 in what was one of the highest profile murder cases of recent times.

2018 saw a new search undertaken for William Tyrrell. The coronial inquiry into his disappearance began in early 2019 (it was unconcluded at the time of writing).

Out of the cases we've looked at, some decades old, four were still making headlines in 2018 and 2019, and many are still being actively investigated.

The police never give up trying to bring justice to the victims, and to see those guilty of heinous crimes held accountable. They are the true heroes. Remembering the victims' stories is an important part of keeping them in the public consciousness, and we are all hoping justice will be done and one day these cold cases will be solved.

And please, if you have any information about any of the cases covered in this book, contact Crime Stoppers (1300 333 000 or www.crimestoppers.com.au) and let the police bring justice to the victims and their families.

EXPERT BIOGRAPHIES

TIM DORAN – FRICTION RIDGES

Tim Doran is an Assistant Chief of Police in Colorado and a retired Federal Bureau of Investigation Special Agent. While assigned to the Evidence Response Team Unit at the FBI Laboratory, he authored the FBI Evidence Collection Manual and worked with educators and law enforcement crime scene investigation teams worldwide to develop these protocols. Educated at the United States Military Academy at West Point, Tim chose a career in law enforcement, which has spanned 28 years.

DR SUSAN HAYES – FACIAL RECONSTRUCTION AND FACIAL PROGRESSION

Dr Susan Hayes is an applied researcher in evidence-based facial approximation at the University of Wollongong, who works with the skeletal remains of modern humans to approximate their facial appearance. Susan's research focus has been predominantly within an archaeological context, however she collaborated with the Sydney Homicide Squad of the NSW Police Force when they were investigating the unidentified remains found in Belanglo State Forest that were later identified as Karlie Pearce-Stevenson, as well as providing an age progression of William Tyrrell, the three-year-old boy who went missing in 2014. For more information on Susan's research go to https://www.researchgate.net/profile/Susan_Hayes

COLIN JOHNSON – GEOGRAPHICAL PROFILING

Colin Johnson is an internationally accredited and operational geographic profiler and was the first ever European Fellow of his discipline. He holds a master's degree in psychology. A police officer in the UK for 30 years, principally as a detective, he specialised in investigating major crime, including murder, stranger rape and abduction. He became one of the first officers selected for the National Crime Faculty, UK. This pioneering team was set up to provide, on request, specialists to support enquiries across the UK following police failings in the Yorkshire Ripper case. Working as a geographic profiler, he continued this support role, most recently with the Serious and Organised Crime Agency (UK) and the National Crime Agency (UK).

CECE MOORE – GENETIC GENEALOGY

CeCe Moore is a genetic genealogist and founder of DNA Detectives (https://thednadetectives.com), a group that aims to solve mysteries and reunite families. CeCe undertakes forensic GG casework with Parabon NanoLabs, Inc., a US-based company that develops advanced DNA technologies with pharmaceutical and forensic applications. For more information on Parabon NanoLabs, Inc.'s, forensic work go to https://snapshot.parabon-nanolabs.com.

TIM WATSON-MUNRO – CRIMINAL PROFILING AND FORENSIC PSYCHOLOGY

Tim Watson-Munro is a criminal psychologist. He spent his formative years in Sydney and San Francisco. Educated at Sydney University, Tim rose to prominence as a pioneering prison psychologist at Parramatta Gaol. During the 1980s and 1990s he gave expert evidence in some of the country's most notorious court cases, including mass murderer Julian Knight who shot and killed seven people, injuring a further 19 in 1987 in Clifton Hill, Victoria, in a crime that became known as the Hoddle Street Massacre. He has written several books, most recently *A Shrink in the Clink* (Pan Macmillan, 2018).

DR IAN MOFFAT – GEOPHYSICAL TECHNIQUES

Dr Ian Moffat is a scientist specialising in the application of geological techniques (particularly geophysics, geochemistry, geomatics, and geoarchaeology) to archaeological research questions. He has contributed to a wide range of academic and consultancy projects within Australia and internationally including locating and mapping features such as historic and Indigenous graves, hearths, buried pottery, middens, shipwrecks, lost anchors, and tracing migrations with isotope geochemistry and reconstructing palaeoenvironments using sedimentological techniques. For more information on Ian's work go to https://www.flinders.edu.au/people/ian.moffat.

ACKNOWLEDGEMENTS

There are many people I need to acknowledge for their invaluable contributions to the production of this book. Firstly, my friend, agent, and warrior woman Lauren Miller, who is always willing to go into battle for me – or with me – as needed. My good friend and colleague Duncan McNab has my gratitude for patiently answering all of my many crime-related questions (his fault for being the crime guru) as well as for being my co-conspirator on so many great projects. I would also like to thank Dr Joel McGregor for being a sounding board for my good, and often bad, ideas, and for always being (brutally) honest in his feedback. My gratitude also goes to my friend Tim Doran, who was always willing to answer policing questions, and offering whatever insight or advice he could.

Thanks to Bill Hayes for allowing me to listen to the interviews he conducted with Haydn Phipps, as well as for the support all of the way through the Beaumont investigation and beyond. I hope one day our work will help bring some closure to the case. I would also like to acknowledge the production team at Channel 9's *Murder, Lies & Alibis*, including Mark Llewellyn and Duncan McNab, for providing information for the Wanda Beach/Wilder chapter and for the opportunity to work with them on a number of fascinating investigations. Long may it continue.

My thanks to everyone at Pan Macmillan including Angus Fontaine who offered so much great advice to improve my writing, pushing me well out of my comfort zone, as well as the rest of the team; Ingrid Ohlsson, Danielle Walker, Julia Stiles and Hannah Membrey, who were all fantastic to work with.

A number of people made expert contributions to this book; these include: Dr Ian Moffat for his contributions regarding geophysical search techniques; Colin Johnson for his insights into geographic profiling; Tim Watson-Munro for his expert insights into criminal psychology; Chris O'Connor provided his policing insights into the Mr Cruel case; Clive Small who made invaluable contributions to the Milat chapter; Duncan McNab for providing information on Chris Wilder; Thom Shaw at Parabon NanoLabs, Inc. for creating the age regression of Chris Wilder; Dr Susan Hayes for her knowledge of facial reconstruction and age progression; Dr CeCe Moore for providing her expertise with regards to genetic genealogy; Dr Rachel Berry for her expertise on stable isotope profiling; and Tim Doran for his expert contribution regarding forensic friction fridge identification.

I would like to recommend three books that relate to cases covered in this book: Alan Whiticker and Stuart Mullins's *The Satin Man* (New Holland Publishers, 2013) on Harry Phipps; Clive Small and Tom Gilling's *Milat: Inside Australia's biggest manhunt. A detective's story* (Allen & Unwin, 2014), and Duncan McNab's *The Snapshot Killer* (Hachette, 2019) about Chris Wilder.